Through the Year
with Zwingli and Bullinger:
A Devotional

What Are They Saying About This Volume?

Patiently and skillfully compiled by Dr. Jim West, this booklet is the first ever attempt to have a collection of prayers and short texts of Huldrych Zwingli and Heinrich Bullinger as a tool to assist and deepen the prayer life in private and public worship throughout the whole year. It is a unique resource for unwrapping the riches of their teaching in simple, yet profound sentences. Nonetheless, at the end of the day, they are records of how the gospel has been rooted in the lives of the two reformers and as such provide to some extent models of how Christians can find words for their own prayers. The more that happens, the more the designed purpose of the booklet will be fulfilled.

—**Emidio Campi**, *professor emeritus of Church History and former director of the Institute of Swiss Reformation Studies, University of Zurich.*

§

Reformed Spirituality is not an exercise in godly enthusiasm nor reserved for religious virtuosi. It is a Christ centered life, starting with a simple prayer every morning. We are thankful to Jim West for reminding us what the Fathers of Reformed Protantism, Ulrich Zwingli and Heinrich Bullinger meant by "worshipping God in Spirit and Truth".

—**Peter Opitz**, *Professor für Kirchen und Dogmengeschichte von der Reformationszeit bis zur Gegenwart, University of Zurich*

Jim West (ThD) is Professor of Biblical Studies at the Quartz Hill School of Theology, Adjunct Professor of Old Testament at Ming Hua Theological College, and Pastor of Petros Baptist Church, Petros, Tennessee. He has written a Commentary on the Bible, several works of theology and Church History, and numerous articles on both the Bible and Theology. Additionally, he serves as Associate Editor for the Scandinavian Journal of the Old Testament *and for the* Copenhagen International Seminar.

Through the Year
with Zwingli and Bullinger:
A Devotional

By Jim West

Quartz Hill Publishing House
Publishing arm of Quartz Hill School of Theology
Quartz Hill, California

ISBN: 978-1-329-56029-1

Quartz Hill Publishing House
43543 51st Street West · Quartz Hill, CA 93536
www.theology.edu
info@theology.edu

Preface

Huldrych Zwingli and Heinrich Bullinger were two of the leading Reformers of the 16ᵗʰ Century. They are not as well or widely known as Martin Luther and John Calvin, but they had much to say to their contemporaries and they continue to have much to say today.

In the pages which follow extended selections from Zwingli's and Bullinger's works will serve as guides to devotional thoughts and each will be followed by a brief prayer.

The texts selected were chosen because of their power and spirit. They offer readers an opportunity to, metaphorically, sit with Zwingli and Bullinger at their desks and listen to them as they turn our attention towards God. But readers will also be, slowly and carefully it is hoped, introduced to the theology of Switzerland's greatest Reformers. Step by step and day by day users of this volume will not simply be pointed to devotional thoughts, but to theological education.

This book, then, has a dual purpose: to offer spiritual guidance and to offer theological instruction.

The texts are also linguistically modified only when necessary, and for the sake of clarity alone, by the present editor.[1] I have deemed it important to allow something of

---

[1] All citations from Zwingli and Bullinger are excerpted from the following volumes:

Zwingli, Huldreich. *The Latin Works of Huldreich Zwingli*. Edited by Clarence Nevin Heller. Vol. 3. Philadelphia: Heidelberg Press, 1929.

Zwingli, Huldreich. *The Latin Works of Huldreich Zwingli*. Edited by William John Hinke. Vol. 2. Philadelphia: Heidelberg Press, 1922.

Zwingli, Huldreich. *The Latin Works and The Correspondence of Huldreich*

the dated flavor of their words to remain, just as long as their thought remains clear, precisely so that readers may experience something different than the normal language of Christian discourse today.

My most heartfelt thanks are extended to Quartz Hill Publishing House for bringing this book to the public; my editor R.P. Nettelhorst for his careful work, and to Peter Opitz and Emidio Campi for their unwavering encouragement and support for this project as well as for their kind remarks about it.

This devotional is dedicated to the memories of Zwingli and Bullinger. These two Christian leaders left a bigger impression on the history of Christianity than they are given credit for and their spirituality is not only second to none, it is imminently instructive. My hope is that we will all draw closer to God as we walk along with Zwingli and Bullinger and listen to their words as they direct us heavenward.

Zwingli: Together with Selections from His German Works. Edited by Samuel Macauley Jackson. Translated by Henry Preble, Walter Lichtenstein, and Lawrence A. McLouth. Vol. 1. New York; London: G. P. Putnam's Sons; Knickerbocker Press, 1912.

Zwingli, Ulrich. *The Christian Education of Youth.* Translated by Alcide Reichenbach. Collegeville, PA: Thompson Brothers, 1899.

Bullinger, Henry. *The Decades of Henry Bullinger: The Third Decade.* Edited by Thomas Harding. Cambridge: Cambridge University Press, 1850.

Bullinger, Henry. *The Decades of Henry Bullinger: The Fourth Decade.* Edited by Thomas Harding. Cambridge: Cambridge University Press, 1851.

Bullinger, Henry. *The Decades of Henry Bullinger: The First and Second Decades.* Edited by Thomas Harding. Cambridge: Cambridge University Press, 1849.

Bullinger, Henry. *The Decades of Henry Bullinger: The Fifth Decade.* Edited by Thomas Harding. Cambridge: Cambridge University Press, 1852.

January 1[2]

First of all, let me say that, although man can in no wise draw his own heart to faith in the only true God, even if one could surpass in power of speech the celebrated and eloquent Pericles, but only our heavenly Father who draws us to Himself can do these things; then faith comes, according to the apostle Paul, by hearing, in so far as such hearing is the hearing of the Word of God. Do not understand, however, that the preaching of the mere spoken Word can accomplish so much, unless the Spirit within attracts and speaks. For this reason, must faith be implanted in the heart of a man with pure and sacred words coming, as it were, from God himself. The speaker should, at the same time, also pray to Him who alone can work faith, to the end that He may enlighten by his Spirit, the one who is being instructed in the Word of God. From this the man will learn that the providence of God provides all things, orders all things, upholds all things; for, of two sparrows bought for a farthing, one does not fall to the ground without the providence of God, who has numbered the very hairs of our heads. His care and watchfulness surely do not diminish when the object for which God cares is small or insignificant.

Prayer: Merciful Father in Heaven, help us this day, as we begin this new Year, to realize that your providential hand guides us in ways we do not and cannot know. Then, we can trust and believe that that hand will never lead us either astray nor leave us unattended. In your Son's name, Amen.

---

[2] This and following excerpts are from "How One ought to Bring Up and Instruct Youth in Good Manners and Christian Discipline; A Few Short Precepts," by Ulrich Zwingli.

January 2

When we are attacked by disease, therefore, whether it be of the soul or of the body, we are taught to pray to God alone for the true remedy. When the enemy oppresses us and with envy and hatred makes our burden heavy, we are to flee to Him alone. When we desire knowledge or skill or wisdom, we know that we are to ask these things of God. Even wife and children are to be asked of Him. When riches and honor are bestowed upon us more freely than upon others, we ought to pray to God that our hearts may not grow faint and that we be not led astray. What more need I say? If our minds be so informed as I said before, we shall feel that all things are to be sought from God. We shall also regard it an offense against God to ask of Him favors which should not be bestowed upon us; Yes, we shall be ashamed to desire or to possess anything unbecoming to us in the sight of God; on the contrary, we will strive only after those things which are enduring and will further our salvation.

Prayer: Dear Father, today I ask that you teach me to patiently ask for what you will and gratefully receive from your hand what you send. Moreover, I also beg that you grant me the wisdom to refuse to complain or quibble if my requests receive a 'No' from you. Remind me that your no is really yes, for something better. In your Son's name, Amen.

January 3

The innocence, purity, and righteousness of Christ, which He offered up for our guilt and condemnation, deliver us from sin, guilt, and suffering; and we are reckoned worthy of the favor of God, for the reason that Christ, who was absolutely free from all sinful inclination, was able to satisfy fully the justice of God. Although He is so high and holy, namely, very God, He nevertheless is our Savior. From this it follows that his righteousness and innocence, which are wanting in us, are also imputed to us; for God made Him to us wisdom, righteousness, sanctification and redemption. So we now have access to God through Christ, because He is our Savior and a pledge of the grace of God to us. He is our surety, our bondsman, our mediator, our advocate, and our intercessor; Yes, He is a perfect Savior to us. This truth accounts for the fact that those who are born again through the Gospel do not sin; for he that is born of God does not commit sin. Whoever believes in the Gospel is born of God. So, then, do those not sin who are born again through the Gospel. To explain more fully, it will suffice to say that their sins are not reckoned to them to death and damnation, because Christ has paid the debt and has washed away their sins, by having become a precious ransom through his death on the cross.

Prayer: Heavenly Father, my sins are a constant source of pain to me and their remembrance a daily reminder of my failures. Please, this day, remind me of your kind forgiveness and let its truth fill my life in every crevice. Especially where and when the enemy attacks. In you Son's name, Amen.

January 4

Such assured confidence in Christ, however, does not make men lazy, does not make them negligent nor careless; but on the contrary, it awakens us, urges us on, and makes us active in doing good and living righteous lives, since such assured confidence cannot come from man. How could it be that the human mind, which is given almost wholly to impressions from without, would lean entirely, and in all hopefulness and confidence, upon a thing which is invisible and which can in no wise be perceived by the senses? From this it is to be understood that this faith and assured confidence in Christ must come from God only. Now, where God works, you need not fear that the cause will not prosper or that good deeds will not follow. Now he who has well learned the mysteries of the Gospel and rightly understands them will endeavor to live a righteous life; therefore the Gospel should be taught most diligently and, as much as may be, in all its purity. We should also very early teach the young how to practice those things which please God most, those,—in fact, which He continually is to us, namely, truth, justice, mercy, faithfulness, and righteousness.

Prayer: Dear Lord, how easy it is for me to forget that I do not belong to myself, but to you and to others. Help me, then, to be submissive to you and heed you and hear you and follow you unwaveringly this day. I can do nothing about yesterday and tomorrow is then to be, but I need your help to live today so as to be pleasing to you and of service to others. In your Son's name, Amen.

January 5

He will learn from Christ when to speak and when to be silent, each in its own time. He will be ashamed to speak, in his early life, of those things which belong only to the conversation of men, when he learns that Christ did not begin to speak in public till he was thirty Years old; therefore long after he had given proof of his mission, before the doctors in his twelfth Year. Hence, rather than to put himself forward when he is very young, the man will early seek to understand great things that are pleasing to God. I do not mean that they shall be silent five Years, as Pythagoras commanded his pupils; but I would restrain them from being too eager and hasty to speak, and unless it be to speak about useful or necessary matters, they should not speak at all. If a man is learning the art of expression from his teacher and if the latter has any defect or any disagreeableness in his speech, the man should not imitate these unpleasant things in his teacher's speech. This hint is by no means to be regarded as being of little account; for we learn from the writings of the ancients that some imitated their masters not only in errors of speech, but also in the awkward movements of the body.

Prayer: Lord help me, when I'm more interested in speaking than in listening, to repent and become more interested in hearing than in speaking. In your Son's name, Amen.

January 6

These things he should regulate in such a manner that they serve the cause of truth instead of flattering his hearers; for how can a Christian heart endure the lascivious manners of some persons? I have no other object in view, when I want a man to refine his manners, than that every one may be led thereby to free himself from external rudeness or unbecoming manners; because these are not uncertain signs of uncouthness or coarseness of character. Let every man flee from intemperance as he would from a poison; for, in addition to the fact that it makes furious the body, which is of itself inclined to vehemence, it brings on premature old age; because the body becomes disordered from the beginning. From this it follows that, if the intemperate man becomes old at all and believes that he will find rest in his latter days, he will be deceived and will find nothing but disease. For it can not be that he who has habituated himself to revel in wine does not, in the end, suffer from dangerous diseases. I refer to epilepsy, paralysis, dropsy, leprosy, and the like. So, then, if you desire to be old a long time, become old [wise] early.

Prayer: As I journey through life, heavenly Father, help me master myself and take control of my urges—not bowing to them at their first whimperings, but using everything in life only insofar as it is proper and helpful. Keep me from excesses of all kinds. In your Son's name, Amen.

January 7

Nothing seems to me to be more foolish than to seek honor and praise, by wearing costly clothing. Those who put on strange or new clothing every day thereby show how fickle, or at least how effeminate and childish they are. Such persons do not belong to Christ. While they thus clothe themselves in rare attire, they let the poor suffer from cold and hunger. For this reason a Christian should beware of foolishness and extravagance in dress, as well as of any other evil. Why need I forbid a Christian man to love money and worldly honor, since these evils are also condemned among the heathen? No one who will serve covetousness will become a Christian, for this vice has not only ruined individual characters, but also well fortified cities and powerful kingdoms. Covetousness will overthrow any government that comes under its sway. When this vice has taken possession of the mind, no good influence can affect it. Covetousness is a deadly poison and then, sad to say, it has spread and has become very powerful among us. Only through Christ can we destroy this vice within ourselves, and we can do it if we very diligently and unceasingly follow Him; for what did He oppose more than this root of all evil?

Prayer: Lord of heaven, remind me this day that the greatest evidence of my faith is a life lived in self-control and godliness. Keep me from extravagance and the quest for wealth or fame. Guard my heart and my spirit from falling victim to the world's belief that only through things can I find happiness and through dominating others can I find joy. Amen.

January 8

Every young man should, from early youth, strive after steadiness, faithfulness, truth, faith, righteousness, and piety; and he should diligently practice these things. With these he can serve, with fruitful results, the cause of Christianity, society around him, and his country; for he will be useful to the body politic as well as to the individual citizen. Those are weak-minded persons who are concerned only about living a quiet life. They are not so godlike as those who, to their own detriment, diligently serve all men. One who is a Christian will look upon the fortune or misfortune of others as if either one had happened to himself. If another person is fortunate, the Christian will rejoice as if good fortune had befallen himself; on the other hand, he will be sad when misfortune falls to the lot of another. The Christian will regard a community as a household, Yes, as one body in which all members enjoy pleasure or suffer pain. Such members will so assist one another that what happens to one will be regarded as happening to all. For this reason the Christian will rejoice with them that rejoice and weep with them that weep. Any event in the life of another he will regard as occurring in his own life; for, as Seneca says, what happens to one person may happen to any other person.

Prayer: Holy Father, help me this day refrain from selfishness and self-centeredness. I am normally inclined to be concerned only for my interests, so I ask your aid to think more of others than I do of myself. In your Son's name, Amen.

January 9

A Christian youth should not so manifest joy or sadness as the common custom is, however; that is to say, he should not become proud and vain in prosperity, nor should he become impatient and finally despair in adversity. Inasmuch as a Christian will not be able to pass through life without these and other temptations and trials, he will, if he be wise, so deliberately and discreetly control them that he will at no time and in no place deviate from that which is becoming and right. He will thus be as glad when others are prosperous, as when he is prosperous; but he will not give way to despair when reverses come. In other words, he will endure all things calmly and with moderation. Where persons assemble in social gatherings, every youth attending them should see to it that he go away morally benefited; so that he may not, as Socrates complains, always come home morally worse than he was before. He should therefore be watchful and diligent to follow the example of those who conduct themselves honorably and uprightly on social occasions; but, on the other hand, when he observes persons behaving themselves unbecomingly or shamefully, let him beware of imitating them. When a neighbor is in trouble, we should at once visit him. In such cases it is, indeed, becoming for us to be first to go to his rescue and last to leave him. We should exert ourselves manfully in his behalf, by investigating the harm done, by doing something to remove hindrances, and by rendering any other assistance or giving advice.

Prayer: Most gracious Lord, help me to become day by day more holy, and a better member of my community thereby. In your Son's name, Amen.

January 10

If, at any time, we cannot accept and bear injustice or insults heaped upon us, because it seems to us too much to be endured, we should bring the matter before the magistrate or any other proper government officer. To return a reproachful remark for an insult or to abuse again, when we are abused, is nothing else than to become like him whom we thus treat. All our walk and conversation should be such that those with whom we live will be benefited thereby. If it be necessary at any time to reprove or punish any one, let it be done so pleasantly, so thoughtfully, so skillfully, and with such judgment that we shall be enabled to drive away the evil, and shall win back the person and draw him more closely to ourselves. We ought to be so diligent and firm in standing by the truth, that we not only weigh our own words but also the words of all other persons, in such a manner that no deception, no lie can be concealed therein. A candid mind should never be more displeased with itself than it is, when it finds itself giving utterance to a lie, even under oppression and therefore unwillingly; and I need not say that a youth should be not a little frightened and ashamed, were he to observe that he willfully gives utterance to light, untruthful language, whether such language be imitated from other persons or whether it be his own invention.

Prayer: Lord, in my leisure and in my lifestyle please help me to be subject to your will. Let even my play, which you give as gracious gift, glorify you in that I exhibit the highest ethical standards and purity. In your Son's name, Amen.

January 11

What more shall I say? Let every youth diligently see to it that he drinks from the clear and pure fountain of life, which is the Lord Jesus Christ. He who does this will be shown by Christ how to live, how to speak, and how to act. He will no more regard himself above exercising piety and doing right; he will never despair. He will grow in grace daily; nevertheless he will observe that he often fails and falters. In this way he will make rapid progress, but he will still count himself among the most unworthy. He will do good to all men and will revile no one; for thus did Christ set an example. Hence, he will be perfect who undertakes diligently to follow Christ only. It will be necessary, however, for you to go to work vigorously and to strain every nerve. This will help you very much to drive away indolence, the mother of all vice; for many persons, having formed habits of laziness, in early youth, soon become so shamefully indolent that they loiter about, as if they purposely wanted to be devourers of other persons' goods, or even cess-pools of all vices. You, on the other hand, devote the spring-time of your life to that which is good and useful, because time passes rapidly and better opportunities seldom present themselves in later Years. No time of life is more promising for doing good than youth. Not the man who can only talk much about God is a Christian, but he who labors faithfully with God to do great and holy things; therefore, my pious and noble youth, continue to lift up and adorn your noble family, your handsome person, and your patrimony—all advantages that you enjoy—with these true ornaments.

Prayer: Heavenly Father, teach me to love you sufficiently to obey you fully. In your Son's name, Amen.

January 12[3]

The word prayer is very largely taken among writers, and in daily use. At this present we use it after the same manner that David the prophet used it, saying: "Hear my prayer, O God; and let my cry come to you." For prayer is an humble and earnest laying forth of a faithful mind, whereby we either ask good things at God's hands, or else give him thanks for those things which we have received. And of prayer chiefly there are two parts; invocation or asking, and thanksgiving. By petition we lay open to God the requests and desires of our heart; beseeching him to give us good things, and that he will turn from us evil things, as may be to his glory and good pleasure, and according to our necessity. In invocation or petition we comprehend obsecration, which is a more vehement prayer; and also intercession, whereby we commend other men's matters to the Lord.   For we offer prayers to the Lord our God, not only for ourselves, but also for our brethren, and for their manifold necessities; for them that are distressed with perils; for those that be sick; for them which suffer persecution, or are in a manner oppressed with other calamities and afflictions.

Prayer: Gracious Lord, I can only pray when you teach me to do so. Give me the grace to know how to pray and what to pray and when to pray, so that I can intercede properly for those in special need of your presence. In your Son's name, Amen.

---

[3] This and following excerpts are drawn from Heinrich Bullinger's *Sermon of the form and manner how to pray to god; that is, of the calling on the name of the lord: where also the lord's prayer is expounded; and also singing, thanksgiving, and the force of prayer, is entreated.*

January 13

K inds of prayers are these. There is a private prayer of every faithful man; and there is also a public prayer of the whole church. Private prayer is made to God by every faithful man, in what place soever, either in the house or without doors, in the closet of his heart and temple of his own body: for St Peter went up into the uppermost part of the house and prayed; St Paul says, "I will therefore that the men pray everywhere, lifting up pure hands;" and Christ our Lord himself very often departed even out of the temple into the mount to pray. And in the gospel he says: "When you prayest, enter into your chamber; and when you hast shut your door, pray to your Father which is in secret." Public prayer is that which is used of the church, which is made to God in the holy assembly, according to the accustomed order of every church. Men by nature are slow and slack in the study of religion, and therefore we have need of a sharp spur; and the charge and office of stirring up, and provoking, is committed to the pastors of churches.

Prayer: Heavenly Father, when I engage in prayer, either public or private, please lead me to consider all those you would have me consider and not just the few who I call friends and family. And when I grow lax in prayer, I ask that you goad me to return to it so that I can serve you faithfully and properly. In your Son's name, Amen.

January 14

Behold, the Lord himself is in the midst of the assemblies of saints; and where the Lord is, there is both plenty and the treasure of all good things. And therefore experience itself which we have of matters teaches, that the supplications of the church are effectual; for the Lord hears the prayers of the church, and delivers from evil those whose safety the church commends to him. We have oftentimes had experience, that they which were in extreme danger have found very present help, even at the same instant wherein the congregation has offered their prayers to the Lord. Moreover, the example moves very many, otherwise hard-hearted and barbarous; for they see the devout godliness of the holy congregation, and the fervency of the faithful in assemblies, and are thereby moved; so that entering into themselves, they acknowledged that they are miserable, and desire to be partakers of this fellowship, according to the saying of St Paul: "If therefore, when the whole church is come together in one, and all speak strange tongues there come in they that are unlearned, or they which believe not; will they not say, that you are out of your wits? But if all prophesy, and there come in one which believeth not, or one unlearned, he is rebuked of all men, and is judged of all. And so are the secrets of his heart made manifest; and so he will fall down on his face, and worship God, and say plainly, that God is in you indeed."

Prayer: Teach me, in prayer and worship, to find what you have to offer me and help me neglect neither worship nor prayer, understanding, as I do, that without both I will be sorely distressed.

January 15

I saiah had spoken to Hezekiah out of the mouth of the Lord, "You shalt die, and not live:" but when the king poured forth his prayers, even from the bottom of his heart to the Lord, God changed his sentence that he had pronounced. For the Lord himself says in Jeremiah: "I will speak suddenly against a nation or a kingdom, for to pluck it up, and to root it out, and to destroy it: but if this nation, against whom I have pronounced, turn from their wickedness, I will repent of the plague that I thought to bring upon them," etc. Wherefore the prayers of the faithful are effectual, staying the wrathful judgments of God, Yes, and taking them clean away. For whereas they object again that prayer is a declaration of things which we require of the Lord; and that God foreknows all things; therefore that these things are unprofitably and superfluously declared to him, which he already knows; and so for that cause that prayer is unprofitable: it is confuted of Christ our Lord himself, who, when he had plainly said, "Your heavenly Father knows what things you have need of, before you ask of him;" then nevertheless, adding a form of prayer, he teaches us to pray. In another place he commands us and stirs us up to pray often: "Watch and pray," says he, "lest you enter into temptation." And Paul says: "Rejoice always; pray continually." In every place there are many precepts of this kind.

Prayer: Lord, teach me to pray like the prophets and apostles prayed so that I might, like them, be inundated with your power and fortitude. Amen.

January 16

Neither do we declare our matters to him as to one that knows them not; but we utter them to him that understands the desires of our heart, and do humble ourselves at the feet of his majesty. We ask that of him which we know we want; but then of him certainly to be received, who is the author of all goodness; for we believe his sure and infallible promises.   In the meantime prayers are not superfluous, for that the Lord would assuredly give that which we asked. The Lord promised the delivery of his people, whereof the godly doubted nothing at all: then with incessant supplications they prayed to the Lord, crying, "Deliver us, O Lord our God;" neither did they think they labored in vain. To the anabaptists, pretending absolute pureness, and therefore, being pure, neither can nor ought to pray, "Forgive us our debts," since there remain no debts, the most holy evangelist and apostle John answers and says: "If we say we have no sin, we deceive ourselves, and the truth is not in us. If we acknowledge our sins, he is faithful and just to forgive ns our sins, and to cleanse us from all unrighteousness. If we say that we have not sinned, we make him a liar, and his word is not in us." For as long as we live in this world, there remain remnants of sin to be washed away every moment by the grace of Christ.

Prayer: Merciful Father, help me never fall into the false belief that I am perfect or have arrived at perfection. And help me to remember as well that just as I am imperfect, so too are all others and that, therefore, I should be patient with them as they are, and as you are, with me. In your Son's name, Amen

January 17

Therefore we say, that the prayers of the faithful are not only profitable and effectual, but also necessary to men. For we are men, defiled with sin, destitute and void of all goodness. "Every good giving, and every perfect gift is from above, and cometh down from the Father of lights." He commands us to pray, and offers to them that pray very large promises. Wherefore our fathers were both very often exercised, and very fervent, in prayer; by their example teaching us that prayers are necessary. The scripture also diligently and at large relates, how great things by their prayers in very weighty affairs and dangers, Yes, in matters most necessary, they obtained of our most true and most bountiful Lord and God. Again, how much the faithful prayers of Moses, David, Jehosaphat, Hezekiah, and other valiant men, prevailed in wars, in famines, in sickness, and in other exceeding great dangers, it were long to recite. These examples prove that prayer is both always necessary to men, and very effectual. For we plainly see that God is moved with the prayers of his faithful; for he is good and merciful, he loves us, he took flesh, that he might be touched with feeling of our infirmities, lest we should be dismayoud at him: he is true and faithful, performing those things faithfully which he promises. What? does he not freely, liberally, and bountifully call all men to himself, offering himself wholly to them that call upon him in faith?

Prayer: Father this day I ask you to teach me to pray in faith and fearlessness—reminding me every moment that I too am obligated to hear and assist my fellows as often and as patiently as I can. In your Son's name, Amen.

January 18

Again: "Though you make many prayers, then will I hear nothing at all, seeing your hands are full of blood." So again in Solomon Wisdom cries, testifying that she will not hear them that call on her, because they would not first hear her giving them warning in time. All these things in a manner are gathered from the person of them that pray: from the thing itself which they pray for, that which follows is derived. St James said: "You ask and receive not, because you ask amiss, even to consume it upon your lusts." For the Lord also, answering two even of his chosen disciples which required the highest rooms in the kingdom of Christ, said: "You know not what you ask." Furthermore, holy men when they ask holy and necessary things, or at the least not unjust or evil, which nevertheless they receive not of the Lord; they forthwith think, that God is a God of judgment and justice, and therefore that he will not immediately deliver out of afflictions: then desire they deliverance with continual prayers.

Prayer: Merciful Lord, teach me to pray in such a way that I exercise true faith in you, evidenced by my willingness to wait for your answer and accept it whether it is yes or no. Help me to truly believe. Help, too, my unbelief. In your Son's name, Amen.

January 19

Furthermore, the Lord deferred to perform that which is asked, yes, and at times seems altogether to neglect our prayers: but he does that by prolonging to try his, that he may make their faith the more fervent, and his gifts also more acceptable; which are so much the more joyfully received, by how much they are looked for by an ardent desire. In this temptation let that saying of the prophet comfort us: "Can a woman forget her child, and not have compassion on the son of her own womb? Though they should forget, then will not I forget you." For the church had said: "God has forsaken me, and my Lord has forgotten me." Let us now consider what manner of prayer that should be which he that calls on God use. That question cannot be better resolved than by weighing the circumstances. First therefore let us consider, Who must be called upon of them that pray. None but the one and only God. For three things are required of him which is prayed to: first, that he hear the prayers of all the men in the whole world; that he pierce and exactly know their hearts; yes, that he know more rightly and better all the desires of men than men themselves can utter them: secondly, that he be present everywhere, and have power over all things in heaven, in earth, and in hell; which has in his power all the ways and all the means to help: thirdly, that his will is exceedingly good and ready prepared; that that which he can, he may also be willing to do.

Prayer—Dearest Lord, help me direct my prayers to you and to you alone, never glancing sideways at any other created thing, trusting only you and your merciful goodness. Keep me from every semblance of idolatry. In your Son's name, Amen.

January 20

B ut these properties are found in God only. For God only searches the reins and the hearts: he only sees and hears all things: he only knows more perfectly those things which are within and without man, than man himself: he only is present in all places: he only is almighty: he only is wise: the will of God only embrace man with most perfect goodness, and is always ready, and only procureth faithfully that which is profitable for man: therefore ought God only to be called upon. But who can attribute these properties, were it to the most chosen souls in heaven, without blasphemy and sacrilege? Therefore the souls in heaven, living with God, are not to be called upon; especially since the scripture in plain words testifies, that "Abraham and Jacob know us not;" and commands us to call on God, and forbids to communicate those things which are God's to creatures.

Prayer: Heavenly Lord I ask that you help me this day to be willing to live under your all seeing gaze without shrinking in fear, knowing that you love me and know all things of me and never abandon me. Give me the courage of your familiarity. Amen

January 21

The scripture, that only rule of truth, sets forth to us one mediator, intercessor, patron, and advocate, by whom we may come to God, and by whom we may present our prayers to the Lord. All the prayers of all men are unpleasant and abominable, which are not made by Jesus Christ. Neither does true faith teach us to forge and imagine another advocate for Christ, or some other with Christ, in the sight of God; nor ourselves alone without our advocate Christ to rush into the presence of God the Father. Here true Christians are separated from Jews, from Turks, Yes, and papists also. For they, despising the Son of God, call upon the Father only, without the mediation of Christ Jesus. But the voice of God, by the gospel and his apostles, pronounces against them. In the gospel we read the Lord said: "The Father has committed all judgment to the Son, because that all men should honor the Son, even as they honor the Father. He that honors not the Son, the same honors not the Father which has sent him." And again: "I am the way, and the truth, and the life. No man cometh to the Father, but by me."

Prayer: Merciful God, give me the strength to share the truth of your claim that your son alone is the way to you in a world of many ways and many claims. Amen.

January 22

I have told you, who is to be prayed to or called upon of the godly worshippers of God; and by whom: to wit, God alone, by the only Son of God, our Lord Jesus Christ. Let us now see, what should stir up man to call upon God. Surely, the Spirit of our God principally; for prayer is rightly counted among the gifts of grace: for neither could we earnestly nor heartily call upon our God, unless we be stirred up and provoked thereto by the Spirit of God. For albeit the commandment of God will us to pray, and present necessity and danger drive us, and the example of other allure us to pray; then all these things would do nothing, unless the Spirit enforce our minds to his will, and guide and keep us in prayer. Therefore, though there be many causes concurring which move men to prayer, then the chief original of prayer is the Holy Ghost; to whose motion and government, in the entrance of all prayers, whosoever pray with any fruit do beg with an holy preface. To this pertain these words of the holy apostle: "The Spirit also," says he, "helps our infirmities; for we know not what to pray as we ought; but the Spirit itself makes requests for us with sighs which cannot be expressed. But he which searches the hearts knows what is the meaning of the Spirit; for he makes requests for the saints according to the will of God."

Prayer: Gracious Lord, let me be this day and each day sensitive and open to your Holy Spirit's moving and urgings, so that I might this day be drawn nearer to your love and peace. In your Son's name. Amen.

January 23

But let us consider, with what abilities he must be furnished, which cometh of purpose to pray to God. First, it is necessary that he lay aside all opinion of his own worthiness and righteousness; that he acknowledge himself to be a sinner, and to stand in need of all good things; and so let him yield himself to the mere mercy of God, desiring of the same to be filled with all things that are good. For that great prophet of God, Daniel, says: "We do not present our prayers before you in our own righteousness, but in your manifold mercies." Also you read the like prayers offered to God, Psalm 79; for the people of the Lord cry: "Help us, O Lord of our salvation, for the glory of your name: deliver us, and be merciful to our sins, for your name's sake. Remember not our sins of old; make haste, and let your mercy deliver us." In the new Testament, the Pharisee in Luke, trusting in his own righteousness, is put by, and cast off from the Lord; but the publican, freely confessing his sins and craving mercy of God, is heard and justified. For unless we acknowledge our nakedness, weakness, and poverty, who, I pray you, will pray to God? "For not they that be strong, but they that be sick, have need of the physician." And the Lord in the gospel says: "Ask, and you shall receive; knock, and it shall be opened to you; seek, and you shall find."

Prayer: Without your help, Heavenly Father, I am incapable of the patience to ask and seek and knock as I should. Grant me the first so that I can perform the rest. Amen.

January 24

He therefore that is commanded to ask, that he may receive, has not as then that he asks; he that knocks, by knocking signifies that he stands without doors; and he which seeks, has lost that which then he seeks for. We therefore, being shut out from the joys of paradise, by prayer do seek and ask for that which we have lost and have not. Therefore, whereas David and Hezekiah and other saints of God in prayer do allege their own righteousness, for which they seem worthily to require to be heard; truly they regard not their own worthiness, but rather the truth of God. He has promised, that he will hear them that worship him; therefore the godly say: Behold, we are your worshippers; therefore it is meet you should not neglect us, but deliver us. In the meanwhile, in other places they speak in such sort of their righteousness, that we cannot doubt that in their prayers they made mention of their righteousness with a certain measure and limitation. "Enter not into judgment with your servant," says David; "for in your sight shall no man living be justified," etc.

Prayer: My righteousness comes only and alone from you, Father. I ask then, that you keep me in your presence and power and permit me to always be one who worships you. Both alone and more importantly, in and among and with the community of faith. Amen.

January 25

Furthermore, and that which is the chief of all; it is needful that they which pray must have a true and fervent faith. Let the doctrine of faith, therefore, in the matter of prayer, show us light as the morning-star; and with an assured hope to obtain of God the thing which is asked, let him that prays make his petition. "Let him ask in faith," says St James, "nothing wavering: for he that wavers is like a wave of the sea, tossed of the wind, and carried with violence. Neither let that man think that he shall receive anything of the Lord." And Paul also says: "How shall they call upon him, on whom they have not believed?" I have spoken of faith in the fourth sermon of the first decade. But to the end that faith may increase in just measure, and flourish and continue stable; we must labor in the promises and examples from every place gathered together. We will recite a few. In the book of Psalms we read: "Offer to God thanksgiving, and pay your vows to the most Highest." And: "Call upon me in the day of trouble, and I will deliver you, and you shalt glorify me." Again: "The Lord is nigh to all that call upon him, to all such as call upon him in truth (or faithfully).

Prayer: Lord, I really do believe. But I really need you to help my unbelief. I am in the same condition as all who have come before me. And in the same condition as all who will come after me. I believe. Mostly. Pity us, Father. In your Son's name, Amen.

January 26

But since faith is not a vain imagination, but an effectual power, working by the Holy Ghost all kind of good works, (though they neither trust to these, neither think in consideration of them to be heard;) then nevertheless such sinners as are faithful do not impudently, and without repentance, trust to their own wits, dealing only in words with the Lord; but they join a holy life with prayers. For Solomon says: "He that turns his ear from hearing the law, his prayer shall be abominable." And the Lord says in Isaiah: "Though you make many prayers, then will I hear nothing at all, seeing your hands are full of blood." Of such impenitent persons we understand that in the gospel: "God hears not sinners." But that more is; the saints shall obtain nothing, if they continue prayer for such; for Jeremiah, praying earnestly for his people otherwise being obstinately wicked, hears: "You shalt not pray for this people; you shalt neither give thanks nor bid prayer for them; make you no intercession for them; for in no wise will I hear you. Seest you not what they do in the cities of Judah? The children gather sticks, the fathers kindle the fire, the women knead the dough to make cakes for the queen of heaven. They pour out drink-offerings to strange gods, to provoke me to wrath."

Prayer: Lord, please, let me never grow so hard of heart that I cannot and will not seek you or move so far from you that you hand me over to myself. Amen.

January 27

Moreover, whosoever desires to have his prayers to be acceptable to God, let him lift up his mind from earthly things to heavenly things. Touching that thing the blessed martyr of Christ, Cyprian, eloquently and holily entreating, says: "When we stand occupied in prayer, we must with our whole heart watch, and be diligent in prayer. Let all worldly and fleshly thoughts depart; neither let the mind think upon anything else at that time than only that which it prays. Let your breast be shut against the adversary, and let it be open to God only; neither let it suffer the enemy of God to enter into it in the time of prayer. For he oftentimes steals upon us, and enters in; and, subtly deceiving us, turns away our prayers from God, that we may have one thing in our heart, and another thing in our mouth. But not the sound of the voice, but the mind and sense, ought to pray to God with an unfeigned affection."

Prayer: Father, without your aid my prayers will become pretense and my spirit will grow cold and indifferent. Spare me this misery, Holy Father, by sending me the constant fire of your good Spirit. In Christ's name, Amen.

January 28

B ut that the mind of him that prays may be lifted up from earthly things to heavenly things, that is chiefly the work of the spirit of true faith, the steadfastness of hope, and the fervent love of God; if also we have in remembrance the dreadful majesty of God, before whose eyes we stand praying. Him all the creatures in heaven and earth do worship and reverence; and thousands of angels serve him. Let us think with ourselves, how profitable and necessary things we ask of God, without which we cannot be happy. Let us, moreover, remove from us all those things, which either detain and keep us in this world, or pull us back to earthly things; of which sort are these, slothfulness, covetousness, and surfeiting, and, to be short, all other sins like to these: and contrariwise, let us apply ourselves to watchfulness, soberness, gentleness, and liberality. Surely the scripture almost everywhere encourages to prayer fasting and mercy; for these virtues make us more cheerful and ready to pray through faith. Daniel says: "I turned my face to the Lord God, and sought him by prayer and supplication, with fasting, sackcloth, and ashes." Neither unlike to this do Jonah and Joel teach. Yes, in the gospel and writings of the apostles we everywhere hear: "Watch; be fervent in prayer; be sober." For, the belly being full, either no prayers at all, or else fat and unwieldy prayers, are made.

Prayer: When my strength leaves me give me strength to be prayerful. Thank you. Thank you. In Jesus' name, Amen.

January 29

A nd surely God requires of us fervent prayer; but it cannot choose but be cold, which is not inflamed with charity. Therefore they that be cruel, and unwilling to forgive their brethren their trespasses, and do still retain hatred toward their brethren, cannot pray before God, who says: "And when you stand praying, forgive, if you have ought against any man; that your Father also which is in heaven may forgive you your trespasses." And again: "If you forgive men their trespasses, your heavenly Father shall also forgive you: but if you forgive not men their trespasses, no more shall your heavenly Father forgive you your trespasses." And in another place he says: "Therefore if you bring your gift to the altar, and there remember that your brother has ought against you, leave there your gift before the altar, and go your way; first be reconciled to your brother, and then come and offer your gift:" for otherwise all your gifts shall not be acceptable to God. Let us therefore willingly forgive, and let as love and do good to our neighbors; so our prayers shall pierce the heavens.

Prayer: This and every day, Father, remind me that there are things I must do. And things I must not do. In order to be your faithful servant. So that, as your servant in good standing I might approach you boldly and without fear of rejection. Help me remain faithful. Amen.

January 30

Agreeable to this is, that we pray not only with the mouth or voice, but with the mind and inward affection of the heart, and with the spirit and fervency. There was no voice heard of Moses, neither of Hannah, the mother of Samuel, when they prayed; but most earnestly in spirit they cried to God: who also heard, and led him safely with all the people of Israel through the Red sea, out of the most bloody hands of the Egyptians; and her which afore was barren he made fruitful. And contrariwise we read that the Lord in the gospel out of Isaiah alleged these words against the Pharisees: "This people draweth nigh to me with their mouth, and honors me with their lips, howbeit their heart is far from me: but in vain do they worship me, teaching doctrines precepts of men." Therefore aptly said Paul: "I will pray with the spirit, and will pray with the understanding also;" where he calls the lively breath and voice of man "spirit." By these heavenly testimonies their prayers are condemned, who, with a marvelous rolling and swiftness of the tongue, in a short space babble many words, and those maimed and curtailed, uttering words without sense; for their mind in the meanwhile is otherwise occupied.

Prayer: Oh most holy Father, keep me from the grasping of hypocrisy this day, this moment, every moment. In Christ's name, Amen.

January 31

No other desire is there felt of them, unless happily this seem a desire, in that they pant and blow, hasting to make an end of praying. Among which kind of men monks and priests are chief, who pray for money and for their hire; that is, sell a thing of nought for a great price to the mad people. Not that prayers are vain of themselves, but because, being used after that manner, they become vain. Of these men the Lord pronounces in the gospel: "Woe be to you, scribes and Pharisees, hypocrites; for you devour widows' houses, and that under a pretence of long prayer; therefore you shall receive the greater damnation." I know what those sophists do here bring forth and allege for the defense of prayers said for reward or stipend; but in few words I give them this knot to loose. These men, that pray in this sort, either have faith and charity, or else they have not: if they have, they pray without reward, for charity's sake; if they have not, their prayers are of no effect: and therefore with a false show they deceive the ignorant people, paying their money for lawful prayers, whereas they requite them with unlawful; and if they were lawful, then were they neither to be sold or bought.

Prayer: The first month of the year is done, gracious Lord. My sins are greater now than when the year began and for that I am truly sorry and repent with bitter tears. Move in my heart, and make the new month a month of authentic love for you and those you send my way. Amen.

February 1

This is also required of him that prays; that he desire not things unworthy for God to grant, nor require those things that are contrary to the laws of God. For St John the apostle says, "If we ask anything according to his will, he hears us:" therefore when we ask things unworthy for God to grant, he hears us not Moreover, always and in all our prayers our will and our desires ought to be obedient to God and his will. Therefore let no man go about wickedly to tie God to certain circumstances; let no man prescribe to God at what time, in what place, or after what manner, he shall bring to pass anything that he will do. God, who is only wise, knows when it is time to help. He is also both faithful and omnipotent, and able indeed to do greater things than either we can ask or understand; which thing we also read that Paul has said. Therefore, not without cause is that most honest widow, Judith, very angry with Hosea the priest, because he appointed a set number of days to God; which being ended, he should deliver, or otherwise they would give up the city.

Prayer: Lord, never allow me to slacken my hands from the tasks you have assigned me. Help me, by your grace, to maintain your purpose in my every breath. Amen.

February 2

And now also long continuance is very needful in prayers. "Ask," says the Lord in the gospel, "and it shall be given you; seek, and you shall find; knock, and it shall be opened to you." And by this heaping together of words, he often remembereth us of continuance in prayer. "Ask," says he, earnestly and constantly, as they do which require things whereof they stand in need; "seek," as they are wont, that search for things that are hidden and precious; "knock," as they are wont, who with earnest desire covet to come in to their friend. For all these sayings do not only signify a desire, but also a continual study to obtain things required. In the gospel according to St Luke, the Lord put forth a parable tending "to this end, that we ought always to pray, and never to be wearied." For Paul also says: "Rejoice always; pray continually; in all things give thanks." Then let no man think, that by these words of the Lord and the apostle the error of the heretics Psallini, or Euchitæ, is confirmed. They did nothing else but pray. The Lord commands to pray always; that is to say, as often as we conveniently may, at all times and in all places, to be of an upright heart toward God in all things, which should always wait for good things at God's hand, and give him thanks for benefits received; which should also continually ask favor of him.

Prayer: Father let joy fill my heart in such a way that my life becomes itself a prayer to you. In the name of Your Son, Amen.

February 3

Such an endeavor is commended to us in Hannah, the daughter of Phanuel, of whom Luke makes mention, that she "departed not from the temple, but night and day served the Lord with fastings and prayers." Not that she did nothing else, having no regard to her body, nor did at any time eat, drink, or sleep; but because that was her continual and chief business. For at this day, speaking after the same manner, we say that the husbandman does labor without ceasing, and the student read night and day; when as then all men understand, that by this kind of speech is signified a continual and exceeding great diligence in work and reading. The woman of Syrophonecian, in Matt. chapter 15 shows to us a notable example of unwearied continuance in prayer or invocation. But if so be God seem to neglect us, or to defer our requests longer than is meet, let us always remember what the prophet has said: "Then a little while, and he that shall come will come, and will not tarry;" and, "The just shall live by faith," etc.

Prayer: Loving Lord, grant me this day the wisdom to have the patience to persevere in prayer and communion with you and your Son through your Spirit so that I might experience the glory of your fellowship without the hindrance and interference of sin. Amen.

February 4

Here it shall be very easy to show the time of prayer, whereof inquiry is made; to wit, when we ought to pray. We ought therefore privately to pray always; for continually while we live there is divers and manifold matter offered to us to pray. Pray therefore as oft as the Spirit moves you, and as often as necessity itself or matter provokes you to pray. Then let nothing here be of constraint; let all things proceed from a willing and free spirit. But public prayers are restrained to time; for there are set and fore-appointed hours to pray. Set hours are those certain times received of the church, wherein in the morning or evening the whole congregation assembles together, to hear the word of God, to pray, and to receive the sacraments. That the ancient churches, which were in times past, did not meet together in an holy assembly all at one time and the selfsame hours, Socrates in his history beareth witness; and in this diversity there is no danger. Let it be left to the discretion of the churches to come together to the service of God, when it shall seem most necessary, comely, meet, and profitable to themselves.

Prayer: This moment, Father, this hour, this day, this is the time you've given me for prayer. Let me spend it uninterrupted by the thoughts and plans of the day. Let me be, truly, here, in this moment, in your throne room. Amen.

February 5

Moreover, fore-appointed hours of prayer are those which are set or forewarned for a certain time by the church for present necessity's sake. In dangerous times, and in weighty affairs, the holy apostles appointed prayers and fastings; which thing also at this day is lawful, without superstition, and with just moderation. And that this is a most ancient ordinance, it appears out of these words of the prophet Joel: "Blow the trumpet in Zion, sanctify a fast, call a solemn assembly, gather the people together," etc. Does not the apostle command man and wife privately to separate themselves for a time, and to abstain from their lawful delights, that prayer in necessity may be the more fervent?

Prayer: Father today teach me that there is nothing in life more important than you—and time with you in your presence in worship. Help me recall that truth especially when my mind and heart wander away from you during our moments each day. Instruct my spirit to prefer your presence. Amen.

February 6

A nd now also it will not be hard to judge of the place of prayer; for as at all times privately, so also in all places, I have said in the beginning of this sermon, that holy men may pray. For the true prayer of holy men is not tied to any place, neither is it judged better in one place than in another; for the goodness or worthiness of the prayer is not esteemed by the place, but by the mind of him that prays. For the Lord in the gospel says: "The hour will come, and now is, when the true worshippers shall worship the Father in spirit and in truth, etc." But they are in no wise to be passed over in this place, who are persuaded that the godly may pray in no other place but at home in their chamber; to the confirmation whereof they wrest these words of our Savior: "But you, when you prayest, enter into your chamber; and when you hast shut your door, pray to your Father, which is in secret; and your Father, which sees in secret, shall reward you openly." But these words have an *antithesis*, or contrary sentence, to that which goeth afore. For there went before: "And when you prayest, you shalt not be as the hypocrites are; for they love to stand praying in the synagogues, and in the corners of the streets, that they may be seen of men." Against this immediately he opposeth: "But you, when you prayest, enter into your chamber."

Prayer: Father this is what I ask of you: that you lead me into the quiet place where you and I can commune alone. If I cannot find you there, help me to wait. In your Son's name.

February 7

A nd as in reproving the abuse of prayer, he did not properly condemn the place, but rather spake figuratively after this manner, The Pharisees, with their prayers which they make in the streets, do hunt after praise and commendation of the people; so on the contrary part, making mention of a chamber, he meant not that the place of itself makes the prayer either better or worse; but he taught by a figurative speech, that we ought to pray with an upright mind, and most free from hunting after the praise of men. For he that prays with a mind not troubled with affections, having regard only to God, he prays in his chamber, whether he pray in the church or in the street. For otherwise, the Lord prayed with his disciples in the temple, in the city, in the field, and wheresoever occasion was offered. Also it followeth: "And the Father, which sees you in secret, shall reward you openly;" that is to say, the Father, who alloweth the mind that is not proud, but humble and free from ambition, will reward you openly. But public prayers are used in the church or assembly of saints; which if any man despise, saying that prayer ought not to be tied to any place, I cannot think him worthy the name of a Christian, since he shamefully abuseth christian liberty. Finally, of assemblies I have spoken before: we will peradventure speak more in the last sermon of this decade.

Prayer: Father when I pray in public on behalf of the community of faith, help me to voice the concerns of all and not just those things which burden my heart. Help me speak for all and not just for myself. Amen.

February 8

B ut let all riot, all pride, all immoderate trimming of the body, be far from them that shall come into the church of Christ to pray. He should seem filthily to have scorned the godly magistrate, whosoever he were, that, in coming to crave pardon for his fault, would lay aside his mourning weeds; and, putting on white apparel, proudly appear before the assembly of grave and godly senators. Such a one might be judged worthy, not only to be denied of his request, but also to be cast into prison. And who will deny, that they more shamefully mock God, who, coming into the church to ask pardon, being oppressed with the burden of their sins, and then in that place to be so far off from being humble, that they rather appear before the presence of God and his saints having their bodies so attired, as they thereby both provoke the wrath of God anew against them, and do grievously offend the most godly that are in the church? Wherefore Paul at large teacheth, that modesty, comely and humble behavior, is to be used in the church. The place is to be seen in the 11 chapter of the first epistle to the Corinthians.

Heavenly Lord, more than anything I desire that I not mock you by pretending to pray. Make my prayer genuine or help me keep silent. Amen.

February 9

S ome foolishly imagine, that prayer is made either better or worse by the gesture of our bodies. Therefore let them hear St Augustine, Lib. ii. *ad Simplicianum, Quæst.* 4, saying: "It skilleth not, after what sort our bodies be placed, so that the mind, being present with God, do bring her purpose to pass. For we both pray standing, as it is written, 'The publican stood afar off;' and kneeling, as we read in the Acts of the Apostles; and sitting, as did David and Elias. And unless he might pray lying, it should not have been written in the Psalms, 'Every night wash I my bed.' For when any man seeks to pray, he placeth the members of his body after such a manner as it shall seem most meet to him for the time to stir up his devotion. But when prayer is not sought, but an appetite or desire to prayer is offered; when anything cometh on the sudden into our mind, whereby we are devoutly moved to pray with sighs that cannot be uttered; after what manner soever it findeth a man, doubtless, prayer is not to be deferred, until we have sought in what place we may sit, or where we may stand or kneel down."

Lord as I meet with you today I thank you that how I am here is not important at all. It is that I am here, and more, that you are here, that matters most of all. Do not allow me to think that folded hands are a pious act if my heart is far away. Amen.

February 10

Tertullian, making mention of the behavior of the Christians of his time when they prayed, in his Apology against the Gentiles, says: "We Christians are all of us evermore praying for all men, looking up into heaven, with our hands spread abroad, because we are harmless; we are bare-headed, because we are not ashamed; to be short, we need none to put us in remembrance, because we pray from the heart." Where, notwithstanding, we must chiefly have in our remembrance the doctrine of our Savior in the gospel, saying: "When you prayest, you shalt not be as the hypocrites are; for they love to pray standing in the synagogues and in the corners of the streets, that they may be seen of men. Verily, I say to you, they have their reward." For above all things we must beware, that we neither pray privately nor publicly to this end, neither then fashion the gesture of our body, to get the vain praise of the people, that we may seem to be renowned and accounted holy before men: it sufficeth that we please God, and be allowed by his judgment.

Hypocrisy, Father. Help me flee it! Amen.

February 11

In the discourse of prayer, no man will say that it is the smallest thing, to know what you ought to pray, what thing you should ask of God, or for whom you should pray. Here are to be considered the persons and things. Persons are either public or private. Public persons are bishops, teachers, magistrates, and all set in authority. For these men the writings of the prophets, evangelists, and apostles, give commandment to pray. Paul more than once requires intercessions to be made by the church to the Lord for him, that he might be delivered from disordered and fro ward men; and that he might freely preach the gospel, as it became him to preach it. The same Paul commands us to pray for all those that be set in authority, "that we may lead a quiet and peaceable life in all godliness and honesty." Private persons are our parents, wife, children, kinsfolk, allies, neighbors, citizens, friends, enemies, sick persons, captives, such as are afflicted, and, to be short, all that are nigh about us, whose health and safety nature and Christian charity willeth by prayers to commend to God; and whereof there are also testimonies and examples in the scripture.

Prayer: Lord help me overcome my inclination to pray only for those I like and help me to pray for those I do not. Amen.

February 12

B ut the things we should pray for are those good things that are to be desired; whereof some are heavenly, spiritual, or eternal; and other earthly, corporal, or temporal. Moreover, some things verily are common, other some again are private: those things that are common pertain to the whole church and commonwealth; neither belong they to a few, as do private things. And spiritual things are chiefly reckoned to be these; faith, hope, charity, perseverance, and that whole company of all manner virtues, the profit and safety of the church, forgiveness of sins, and life everlasting. Among the which not unfitly are reckoned the gifts of understanding, the liberal sciences, well ordered schools, faithful teachers, godly magistrates, and upright laws. Corporal things are, a peaceable commonwealth, strong and valiant armies for war, health, strength, and comeliness of body, abundance or sufficient wealth, the safe prosperity of wife and children, the protection and defence of friends and citizens, peace, a good name, and other things which are of this kind. But no man is ignorant, that we ought to have a greater care of spiritual things than corporal things, and principally to desire heavenly things.

Lord there are always many things to pray about. When I forget, open my eyes to everything that's going on around me and help me to bring to your sight and heart those things which need your help. Then I will surely never run out of things for which to pray. Amen.

February 13

A nd in corporal things there is also a choice to be used; that the profit of the commonwealth be preferred before our own private gain. For the commonwealth continuing in safety, the citizens may also be safe; and so long as schools and universities, or places of learning, be maintained, there is hope that the commonwealth shall never be destitute of wise and upright governors. There are also in temporal goods some better than other some: those things that are best, therefore, the saints or godly men do chiefly require of the Lord; and nevertheless those which are of less value they understand to come from him, and therefore they ask them also of the Lord. They that are but meanly exercised in the scriptures affirm, that it is not lawful in prayer to ask corporal goods of the Lord; but they are confuted by many examples of the scripture. For not only the patriarchs and prophets, but also the apostles of Christ, asked temporal goods of the Lord; as defence against their enemies, a good report, and other things necessary for the body. Which thing we shall learn anon by the form of prayer which the Lord himself has taught us, diligently showing us what we should ask.

Father today please remind me that I am free to bring all my concerns to you. All of them. None are too small. Thank you. Amen.

February 14

This also cometh in question, In what tongue prayer must be made? They that affirm that privately and publicly we must pray in Latin, seem in my judgment to be out of their wits, unless they speak of such as are skilful in the Latin tongue. For since we must pray, not only with mouth and voice, but also with heart and mind; how, I pray you, shall he pray with heart and mind, who useth a language he understands not? Indeed, he uttereth godly words, but he knows not what he says. For it cometh all to one reckoning, to pray never a whit or not at all, and to babble out words which are not understood. Let every nation therefore pray in that language, which it understands best and most familiarly. And no less madness is it in public assemblies to use a strange language: which thing also has been the root of the greatest evils in the church. Whatsoever the priests that were ordained of God, and the prophets which were sent from him, spake or rehearsed to the people of old time in the church, they did not speak or recite them in the Chaldean, Indian, or Persian, but in the Hebrew tongue, that is, in their vulgar and mother-tongue. They wrote also books in their vulgar tongue. Christ our Lord, together with his apostles, used the vulgar tongue. He furnished the apostles with the gift of tongues, that they might speak to every nation; and forsomuch as in that age the Greek tongue of all other was most plentiful and common, the apostles wrote not in the Hebrew tongue, but in the vulgar Greek tongue.

Prayer: Father, please, send love into my heart through your Son by your Spirit. Please. Amen.

February 15

Truly, it is appropriate that those things that are done in the public church for the holy assemblies' sake, should be understood of all men; for otherwise in vain should so many men be assembled together. Whereby it is clearer than the daylight, that they, that have brought in strange tongues into the church of God, have troubled all things, have quenched the ferventness of men's minds, Yes, and have banished out of the church both prayer itself and the use of prayer, and all the fruit and profit that should come of things done in the church. And truly, the Roman and Latin prince has brought this Latin abomination into the church of God. He crieth out, that it is wickedly done, if Germany, England, France, Poland, and Hungary, do use, both in prayer and other kind of service in the church, not the Roman or Latin tongue, but Dutch or German speech, English, French, Polish, or the Hungarian language. St Paul, once handling this controversy, says in plain words: "If I pray in a strange tongue, my spirit or voice prays, but my understanding is without fruit.

Heavenly Father, today is your day. Speak to me this day and I will apply myself to listening. And then I will speak of you to those who need to hear of you. Amen.

February 16

W hat is it then? I will pray with the spirit, but I will pray with the understanding also. I will sing with the spirit, but I will sing with the understanding also. Else, when you blessest with the spirit, how shall he that occupieth the room of the unlearned say Amen at your giving of thanks, seeing he knows not what you sayest? You verily givest thanks well, but the other is not edified. I thank my God, I speak languages more than yon all: then had I rather in the church to speak five words with mine understanding, that I might also instruct others, than ten thousand words in a strange tongue." And truly, this very place does Justinian the emperor cite *In Novell. Const.* 123, where he straitly commands bishops and ministers, not secretly, but with a loud voice which might be heard of the people, to recite the holy oblation and prayers used in holy baptism, to the intent, that thereby the minds of the hearers might be stirred up with greater devotion to set forth the praises of God.

Send, dear Father, your Spirit this day into my thirsting soul. I desire to live fully the promises I made at my baptism. To die to self, to bury the old life and to rise to a new way of living. I cannot, as you know, do it on my own no matter how hard I try. In your Son's name, Amen.

February 17

F urthermore, that our ancient predecessors had certain and appointed hours, wherein they prayed both privately in their houses and publicly in assemblies, all the holy scripture witnesseth in many places. David more than once in his Psalms says, that he will go to the Lord in the morning and evening. Daniel prayed to the Lord at three several hours or times of the day. Again, David says: "Seven times in a day do I praise you;" but by seven times he understands many times. For so elsewhere we read written: "I will smite you for your sins seven times;" and again: "The just man falleth seven times, and riseth up again;" and also: "If your brother sin seven times in a day, and turn seven times in a day to you," etc. Seven times therefore in divers places, as also in this of David, is put for many times. And Christ our Lord has tied the private prayers of the faithful (as we have also told you before) neither to place, nor then to time: he has not taken away public prayers; for he is the Lord, not of confusion, but of order: but his disciples, when they were in the land of Jury, did themselves also observe the accustomed hours of praying which that nation kept, at liberty, not of necessity, and specially for the assembly's sake.

Prayer: Father help me be as regular in prayer and as faithful in keeping my appointments with you as I am with others. Amen.

February 18

For Peter and John go up into the temple at the ninth hour of prayer. In the day of Pentecost all the saints with one accord were gathered together, and received the Holy Ghost, at the third hour of the day. And it is also read, that Peter privately went up into the upper part of the house about the sixth hour. The temple being destroyed, and the Jews scattered abroad, the churches gathered out of the gentiles did not observe like hours of gatherings together, or of assemblies; but at their own liberty, as to every church it seemed most meet and convenient. Of which diversity truly the ecclesiastical history also makes mention; then for the most part there were hours in the morning and evening used for assemblies. St Jerome, in his epitaph upon Paula, expounding not the rite or order of the universal church, what it should do in holy assemblies, but what the companies of solitary virgins are wont to do of their own accord, says: "In the morning, at three, six, and nine of the clock, at evening, at midnight, they did sing the Psalter by order.

Prayer: The ancient Church, Father, appointed regular times of prayer. They were wiser than we in so many ways and their habit of prayer puts me to shame. Help me to pray, dear Lord. Help me to be wise and spend more time with you. Amen.

February 19

Wherefore, when the Lord forbad much babbling or vain lip-labor in prayer, he did not simply tie the prayer of the faithful to a few and short sum of words: but he forbids us, after the manner of ethnics, to pour out many words without wit, reason, meaning, and understanding; and so finally to think, that we shall be heard for our much babbling sake, and often repeating of prayers; as at this day they do falsely think, which say a certain number of prayers, which they call Rosaries of prayers. For the Lord addeth: "They think they shall be heard for their much babbling sake." St Augustine makes difference between babbling much, and praying much. "To babble much," says he, "is in praying to make many superfluous words in a necessary matter. But to pray much, is to call to him whom we pray to with a long and godly stirring up of the heart. For this business, for the most part, is accomplished more with sighings than with speakings." And anon: "It is not wicked and fruitless, when we have leisure, to pray the longer; for it is written of our Lord himself, that he spent the whole night in prayer, and prayed a long time.

Prayer: Father remind me daily that it isn't the form of prayer that matters but the intent. Help me be intentional and thoughtful when I lift my voice to you. Amen.

February 20

"Wherein what did he else, but give us an example?" Thus far he. And if it be a hard matter for any man to pray long and continually, he may break off his prayer: howbeit he must to it again, and oftentimes renew the same afresh; for such short speaking in prayer is praiseworthy. And, that we may make an end of this place; let no man think, that in praying he declareth our affairs to God as not knowing them: let no man think, that he is heard for his setting forth, and even for his laborsome and exact setting forth, and that oftentimes repeated, and with most earnest outcries instilled or poured into the ears of God: let no man think, that his prayer must stand upon a certain number; that is to say, that *Paternosters* must be numbered up to our God as not having a good memory, and to a Lord ill to be trusted, upon corals and beads, put together upon a lace, serving (as it were) to make a reckoning or accompt.

Prayer: Lord, I have no words this day. Fill my heart. I have nothing to bring. Nothing I can say. I am downcast and filled with shame. Help, Oh Lord. Help. Amen.

February 21

A nd because I have said, which all godly men also throughout the whole world confess, that a most perfect platform of praying is delivered to us in the Lord's Prayer by our Lord Jesus Christ himself; it remaineth, that we cite word for word that most holy form of praying, orderly made with most divine words even by the month of the Lord, as Matthew the apostle has left it recorded to us; and then to expound the same as briefly and plainly as may be, to the intent that every one may the better understand what he prays, and feel a more effectual working inwardly. Of that most heavenly prayer this is the form: O our Father, which art in heaven; hallowed be your name. Your kingdom come. Your will be done, as well in earth, as it is in heaven. Give us this day our daily bread. And forgive us our trespasses, as we forgive them that trespass against us. And lead us not into temptation, but deliver us from evil. Amen. This most holy prayer of our Lord Jesus Christ, our Savior, our doctor or teacher, and highest priest, delivered to the catholic church to be a catholic form or rule to pray to God, is wont to be divided into a little preface, and six petitions. Some reckon seven. Some say, that the three former petitions serve chiefly to the spreading abroad of God's glory; the three latter concern the care of ourselves, and ask those things that are needful for us. But they seem in manner all to contain both.

Prayer: Father, as your Son taught his disciples to pray, teach me to pray. To really pray, and not just say words. Thank you. Amen.

February 22

The little preface is this: "O our Father, which art in heaven." By this we call upon God; and, dedicating ourselves to him, we commit ourselves wholly to his protection and mercy. And every word has his high mysteries; for our Lord would have us rather pray with understanding than with words. These therefore do admonish us, and suffice to be thought upon. But the mind, being instructed with the Holy Ghost, which I told you is needful before all things to them that pray, and being lifted up to the beholding of God and of heavenly things, does devoutly and ardently meditate these things. And truly the word, "Father," putteth us in mind of many things together. For first, it teacheth us, that all our prayers ought to be offered to none other than to him, which is a father; that is to say, that only God is to be called upon, and not another for him, or another with him. For our God and Father is one, the fulness and sufficiency of all good things, in whom only the faithful are acquieted and do rest, and without whom they seek nothing that is truly good. And verily this prayer can be offered to no creature. For to which of the angels, or the saints, canst you say without sacrilege: "O our Father, which art in heaven?" etc.

Prayer: Father, how I long to pray as Jesus prayed. If only I could pray so fervently that it looked to outsiders as though I were bleeding. If only I could pray so as to touch the hem of your garment. Give me that kind of prayer life. Amen.

February 23

F urthermore this word Father teaches us, through whom we should call upon this Father; not by the mediation or by the mouths of saints, but by Jesus Christ our Lord; through whom only we are made the sons of God, who were otherwise by birth and by nature the children of wrath. Who, I pray you, durst come forth before the presence of the most high and everlasting God, and call him "Father," and himself "son," unless the Father in his beloved and natural Son had adopted us the sons of grace? Therefore, when we say, "Father," we speak from the mouth of the Son, who has taught us so to pray, and by whom we be promoted into this dignity; that it needeth nothing at all to add the name of Christ, and to say, We pray you, O heavenly Father, for Christ's sake; since in the first word, "Father," we comprehend the whole mystery of the Son of God and our redemption. For insomuch as he is our Father, we are his sons, and that by the merit of Christ: therefore we call upon the Father, and so call him through Christ; that I may not now repeat, that we pray so from the mouth of Christ. Moreover, this sweet and favorable word, "Father," disburdens us clean of all distrust of heart; for we call him "Father," not so much in consideration of his creating of all things, as for his singular and fatherly goodwill toward us.

Prayer: Lord how can I thank you enough for your fatherly kindness and goodness and provision? Were I able to thank you through eternity the well of gratitude would never run dry. Help me, then, to live that gratitude and not merely claim it. Amen.

February 24

Hitherto appertain the testimonies of the prophets, especially that of David: "The Lord is full of compassion and mercy, slow to anger, and of great kindness. He will not alway chide, neither keep his anger for ever. He has not dealt with us after our sins, nor rewarded us according to our iniquities. For as high as the heaven is above the earth, so great is his mercy toward them that fear him. As far as the east is from the west, so far has he removed our sins from us. As a father has compassion on his children, so has the Lord compassion on them that fear him. For he knows whereof we be made, he remembereth that we are hat dust." A very excellent example of this thing is to be seen in the gospel after St Luke; where the loving father is painted out with wonderful affections receiving into favor again that prodigal son and waster of his wealth. Hereto is added this word "Our;" which putteth us in mind of two things. For first, it is a small matter to acknowledge God to be the God and Father of all, or to be the God and Father of others, unless we also believe that he is, our Father; unless we dedicate and yield ourselves wholly into his faith and protection, as of our Father, who wisheth well to us, loveth us, has a care over us, at no time and place neglecteth us.

Prayer: Come, Lord Jesus!

February 25

For unless we do so believe, neither with faith nor with the love of God is our prayer commended, and therefore not a whit acceptable to God. But that that best and greatest God is our God, we do understand as well by his manifold benefits, as also especially by the mystery of our redemption through Christ: of which thing we have spoken elsewhere. Furthermore, since he bad us pray, "Our Father," and not "My Father;" straightway, upon the very beginning, he requires love of us. For his will is, that we should not only have care of our own salvation, but of the salvation of all other men. For we are all the members of one body; whereupon each several one prays not severally for themselves, but every one for the safety of all the members and also the whole body. Touching that matter I spake before, when I entreated of the manner of praying to God.

Prayer: When I pray keep me praying for others and not only for myself. Remind me of all my brothers and sisters in Christ and keep me from being self centered. In your Son's name. Amen.

February 26

There is by and by added, "Which art in heaven;" not that God is shut up in heaven as in a prison. Solomon, the happiest and wisest king of all, confuting that error long agone, said: "If the heavens of heavens are not able to contain you, how much less this house!" To which words I think that may be annexed, which Stephen alleged in the Acts of the Apostles out of Isaiah concerning the same thing. He is therefore said to be in heaven, because his divine majesty, and power, and glory, shineth most of all in the heavens: for in the whole course of nature there is nothing more glorious, nothing more beautiful, than the heavens. Moreover, the Father exhibiteth and giveth himself to us to be enjoyed in the heavens. Heaven is the country common to us all, where we believe that God and our Father does dwell, and where we worship God and our Father; albeit we believe that he is in every place, and always present with all. For as heaven compasseth and covereth all things, and is everywhere distant from the earth by even spaces; so the presence of his Majesty also does fail us in no place. We have heaven everywhere in our sight; we are everywhere in the sight of God. But beside this, by mention made of heaven we are pat in mind of our duty, and our wretchedness.

Prayer: Lord, remind me to be dutiful and bring into your presence through prayer every situation and circumstance life proffers. In this way, help me be drawn to others through your love for them. And me. Amen.

February 27

It is our duty, to be lifted up in our minds, by praying, into heaven, and to forget earthly things; and more to be delighted with that heavenly Father and country than with this earthly prison and exile: it is our wretchedness, that being banished out of that country for our sins, and wandering in this earth, we are subject to divers calamities; and therefore, being constrained by necessity, we never cease crying to the Father. But first of all, saying, "Which art in heaven," we make a difference between the Father whom we call upon, saying, "our," and our earthly father; attributing almightiness to him. He surely, that is called upon and ought to hear, must know all, see all, and hear all; Yes, and more too, will and be able to do all. Therefore to his good-will to us-ward, which in these words, "Our Father," we have expressed, we do now join knowledge of all things, and power to do all things, adding, "Which art in heaven." By these words the faith of them that pray is stirred up and confirmed.

Prayer: Merciful God, help me to forget what needs to be forgotten and remember what needs to be remembered. Forgetting wrongs done to me in particular and remembering kindnesses. Amen.

February 28

Now there do follow in order six petitions. The first is, "Hallowed be your name." We have called God our Father, and ourselves his sons. But it is the part of sons to honor or glorify their father; and therefore immediately upon the beginning we desire, that the name of the Lord God, and our Father, might be sanctified or hallowed. That truly is holy and undefiled always in itself; neither is it made any whit the better or the worse by us. Whereupon we pray, that that which is and remaineth holy in itself should be acknowledged of us to be such, and always sanctified of us.

A name is the definition of anything whatsoever; and names are invented to make a difference of one thing from another, whereby they might be known among themselves. But God is infinite and immeasurable; moreover, he is one: therefore he has not a name whereby to be defined; he needeth not a name whereby to be discerned from other gods. Therefore those names, that are attributed to him in the scriptures, are attributed for our infirmity; to the end that by some reason and comparison we might understand some things that are spoken of him that is immeasurable and infinite. Therefore the name of God, in very deed, is God himself, with all his majesty and glory.

Prayer: Teach me to speak your name only with the greatest reverence and seriousness. Give me the wisdom I need so desperately in order to know when to speak and when to be silent. Teach me the economy of words. Amen.

March 1

To "sanctify," or "hallow," otherwise signifies, to separate things from a profane to an holy use. In this place it signifies to magnify, to praise, and to glorify. We desire therefore, that God himself, who of his own nature is a good, holy, and for ever blessed, gentle, bountiful, and a merciful, Father, might as he is in himself be acknowledged and magnified of all us; that all nations, leaving their error and heresies, might consecrate themselves in truth to this one only Father and God; that all things which defile the name of the Lord, of which sort are wicked deceits or practices, ungodliness, epicurism, an unclean life, and especially corrupt and antichristian doctrine, may be taken away; that, being enlightened, we might sanctify or hallow the name of the Lord.

Prayer: Father empower me to sanctify you in everything that I say and do and think. For your kingdom's sake. Amen.

March 2

Wherefore in this petition we desire the Holy Ghost, the very only author itself of all true sanctification; we pray for true faith in God by Christ throughout the whole world; we pray for holy thoughts and a pure life, wherewith we might glorify the name of the Lord; which is done, while every one doeth his own duty; while Satan, the author of all uncleanness, is cast out; while corrupt doctrine is taken away, and deceit ceaseth; while the filthiness of the world is banished. This petition the most excellent king and prophet David sets forth in these words: "God be merciful to us, and bless us, show us the light of his countenance, and be merciful to us; that your way may be known upon earth, your saving health among all nations. Let the people praise you, O God; Yes, let all the people praise you:" and as followeth in the threescore and seventh psalm. To this belongeth the whole prayer of our Savior, described by St John in the 17 chapter of his gospel.

Prayer: Merciful Lord, in all of life and in all my deeds and words, thoughts and acts, comings and goings, I, we, all, need your blessing and protection. Without you we are nothing at all and without you life is chaos and our world chaotic. Grant us that which we need most. Yourself. Amen.

March 3

T he second petition is, "Your kingdom come;" for the name of God and our Father cannot be sanctified or hallowed unless he reign in us. There is one kingdom of God, another of the Devil. Furthermore, one kingdom of God is said to be of glory, and another rightly of grace. The kingdom of glory is not of this world, but of another world. The kingdom of grace is the kingdom of Christ in this world; wherein Christ reigneth by the Holy Spirit in his faithful ones, which of their own accord submit themselves to him to be governed, saying and doing those things which beautify and beseem Christians. The Devil also reigneth in the children of unbelief, which yield themselves to him to be governed according to his ungodliness and wickedness; doing those things which are not only delightful to the flesh, but which turn to the reproach of God's majesty; whom after this life, by the just judgment of God, the Devil, the king of the ungodly, catcheth to hell, into the kingdom of death and judgment, there continually to burn. Moreover, the earthly kingdom, which princes of this world govern, is called either the kingdom of God, or the kingdom of the Devil, even as it shall fashion and frame itself to one of the twain. All these things we do knit up in few words, because we have more plentifully entreated of them in another place.

Prayer: Father keep me a faithful citizen of your kingdom and an enemy of Satan's. In Christ's name, Amen.

March 4

Wherefore we pray in this second petition, that Christ might reign and live in us, and we in him; that the kingdom of Christ might be spread abroad, and enlarged, and prevail through the whole world; that doctors or teachers, and ecclesiastical magistrates, finally, that princes also, Yes, and schools too, and whosoever may further the kingdom of Christ, being anointed and watered with his graces, may flourish, overcome, and triumph. Furthermore, we pray that the kingdom of the Devil and antichrist may be broken and vanquished, lest it hurt and annoy the saints; that with the kingdom of the Devil all ungodliness may be dashed and trodden under foot: to be short, that all the weapons and armour of antichristianism may be broken into shivers, and come to nought. Lastly, we pray in this second petition, that, after we have sailed out of the tempestuous gulf of this world, we might be received and gathered to Christ and all the saints, into the everlasting kingdom of glory. For as we desire the kingdom of God to come to us, and God to reign in us; so we pray to come or to be received into his kingdom, and to live forever with him most holily.

Prayer: A holy life is the only life which will satisfy me, Father, so please, make me holy. Amen.

March 5

The third petition is: "Your will be done, as well in earth as it is in heaven." God reigneth not in us, unless we be obedient to him; therefore after his kingdom, we desire the grace of perfect obedience. For we desire not that God do what he will; for continually God's will is done, albeit we never pray for it, and though we wrestle and strive against it with all our might. For the prophet says: "Our God is in heaven; he has done whatsoever pleased him in heaven and in earth." We ask, therefore, that what he will, the same he may make us both to will and to do. For his will is always good; but our will, through the corruption of sin, is evil.

Prayer: My sins are so odious to me, when I remember what your grace has provided and what your Son suffered. Forgive my rebellion and help me each day, but particularly this day, to be a true Child of Heaven rather than citizen of this world. Amen.

March 6

Therefore we pray him to be present with us with his grace, that our will may be regenerated and framed to the good will of God, that of its own accord it yield itself to the Holy Ghost to be framed; that his grace will that which he inspireth; that he finish in us that which he has well begun; give us, moreover, strength and patience hereto; that, as well in prosperity as in adversity, we may acknowledge the will of God, lest we will anything of ourselves, and swell and be puffed up in prosperity, in adversity also faint and perish; but that we may apply ourselves in all things, and through all things, to be governed by his will; to wit, after this manner to submit our will to his will: furthermore, if we ask anything contrary to his will, that he would not grant it, but rather pardon our foolishness, and weaken our will, which is not good for us; to instruct and teach us in his good will, to the end we may doubt nothing that this is always to be followed, that this is always good, and that this worketh all things for our commodity and benefit.

Prayer: Father when I do enter your presence lead me to pray without pretense or selfish motives. Help me to utter each word I speak in sincerity and with the full awareness that it is your will I'm seeking, and not my own. In your Son's name, Amen.

March 7

I n this point the faithful feel a very great battle in themselves; Paul witnessing and saying: "The flesh lusteth against the Spirit, and the Spirit against the flesh. And these two are at mutual enmity between themselves, that what things you would that you cannot do." Therefore we desire not any kind of framing our will to God's will, but we add: "As well in earth, as it is in heaven;" that is, Grant, O Father, that your will may be done in us earthly men, as it is done in your saints, the blessed spirits. These do not strive against your most holy will in heaven; but, being in one mind, they only will that which you wilt, Yes rather, in this one thing they are blessed and happy, that they agree and acquiet themselves in your will. Truly, it is not the least part of felicity or happiness in earth, to will that God willeth; it is the greatest unhappiness, not to will that which God willeth.

Prayer: Heavenly Father help me to mature in my faith so that I will what you will. Always. In Christ's name, Amen.

March 8

And this, truly, by infinite examples might be declared. I will allege only one, and that common too. Some one is grievously sick, and feels pains and torments scarce tolerable; but he in the mean time acknowledgeth, that he suffereth these things by the commandment and will of God, his most good, bountiful, and just Father, who wisheth him well, and has sent this grievous calamity for his salvation and for his own glory. Does not he, in the midst of his torments, by submitting himself to the will of God feel refreshing? And that which seemed most sharp and most bitter to man, by this voluntary and free submission he makes it delightful and most sweet. Again; another is sick, vexed not with a very great disease; but this man does not acknowledge this sickness to be laid upon him by the good will of God; Yes, rather thinketh that God knows not the disease, that God does not care for the disease: therefore he referreth it to divers and sundry causes, and imagineth and seeks divers means to heal it. And in these things he is wonderfully vexed and afflicted; and then, by striving so against the will of God, he feels no refreshing or comfort at all. What therefore does he else, willing that which God willeth, than (which they are wont to do), by ill means avoiding evil, double the same?

Prayer: Father grant me this day the wisdom to discern your will. And if I am uncertain, give me the wisdom to wait. But if I am certain, give me the wisdom and courage to act. Amen.

March 9

Wherefore the foundation of all happiness is faithful obedience, whereby we fully submit ourselves and whatsoever else to us belongeth to the good will of God. And therefore in this greatest petition we pray to the Father, that he would give us regeneration or newness of heart, true obedience, persevering patience, and a mind always and in all things agreeing with and obeying God.

Prayer: Heavenly Father, allow me a submissive spirit; a spirit and heart and mind willing to do your will and to prefer it to my own or any other. Amen.

March 10

The fourth petition is such: "Give us this day our daily bread." For the will of God cannot be done in us, unless we be nourished and strengthened with the bread of God. Bread, among the Hebraists, signifies all kind of meats, and the preserving or sustenance of the substance of man. Whereupon we read it said in the prophet: "I will break the staff of bread." But man consisteth of two substances, the soul and body. The soul is the spirit; the body is made of earth and other elements. Therefore it is preserved with two kinds of bread, spiritual and corporal. The spiritual meat of the soul, whereby it is preserved in life, is the very word of God, proceeding out of the mouth of God; the Lord out of the law repeating, and saying: "Man liveth not by bread only, but by every word that cometh out of the mouth of God." And for because this only sets forth to the faithful the eternal and incarnate Word of God, I mean, the very Son of God; we rightly acknowledge him to be the meat of the soul, Yes, the meat of a whole faithful man.

Prayer: Lord give me today more of your Son. Amen.

March 11

Furthermore, lest any should think himself unworthy of the daily bread, because it is due to children and not to dogs; and therefore should pray the slower, and with a more slender courage; the Lord, preventing this carefulness of the godly, addeth the fifth petition, which is this: "And forgive us our debts, as we forgive our debtors." In these words we ask forgiveness of our sins. And, that we may obtain forgiveness of our sins, it is needful that we confess ourselves to be sinners; for unless we do this, how shall we pray that our sins should be forgiven us? Truly, all the saints use this order of praying; therefore all of them acknowledge themselves to be sinners.

Prayer: Father I come so often asking you to forgive me for the same sins over and over again. I can't express how grateful I am that you are willing to hear me and to be patient enough to forgive me every time I repent even though I really am not very repentant (or I would stop doing what I do that is rebellion against you). In your Son's name, Amen.

March 12

The sixth and last petition is: "And lead us not into temptation, but deliver us from evil;" for sin is never so forgiven, that there remaineth not concupiscence in the flesh, which temptations stir up, and lead into divers kinds of sins. And these are of divers sorts. For first, God tempteth us, when he biddeth us do anything whereby to prove us, as when he bad Abraham to offer up his son; or else, when he sendeth adversity upon us, that with the fire of temptation he may both fine our faith, and cleanse away the dross of our misdeeds. These temptations of God tend to the salvation of the faithful. Wherefore we do not simply pray, not to be tempted: for the temptation of God is profitable. For that man is said to be blessed, which suffereth temptation: "for when he is tried, he shall receive the crown of life." We pray also, that we be not led into temptation: for the Devil likewise tempteth; we are tempted of the world, and of our flesh. There are temptations on our right hand and on our left; tending to this end, to overthrow us, to drown us in the bottomless pit of our sins, and thereby to destroy us: when that is done, we are not only tempted, but we are led into and also entrapped in temptation.

Prayer: I cannot stand against the wiles of the Devil alone. I must rely on you. And I do. Amen.

March 13

S uch a petition therefore we do make: If it please you, O heavenly Father, to exercise us with your wholesome temptations, we beseech you grant that we may be found tried: and suffer us not to be led by a Devilish and wicked temptation; that, leaving you, and being made bond-slaves to our enemy, and drowned in the gulf of wickedness, we be caught and kept of him in evil, sin, and in our own destruction. For now we add the contrary clause, which also expoundeth the former; which, as other say, is the seventh petition: "But deliver us from evil;" ἀπὸ τοῦ πονηροῦ; I say, from that evil, to wit, from Satan, who elsewhere is called a tempter. Deliver us from Satan, and from all evils which he sendeth: deliver us from snares, crafty practices, deceivings; from war, famine, captivity, plague; from all those things which are evil, hurtful, and dangerous. Those things that are such our heavenly Father knows very well, to whom we say here: "Give us healthful and good things; take away from us those things which you knowest to be hurtful and evil."

Prayer: Yes Father, take away those things which you know to be hurtful and evil from my life. In your Son's name and for his sake, Amen.

March 14

And so, briefly we conclude the Lord's Prayer, adding moreover, "Amen." That confirmation and giving of assent is read to have been common and usual of old; as it is to see in Deut. 27, Nehem. 8, 1 Cor. 14. The same in the beginning does express our desire; for we confess that we desire those things heartily which we pray for. Besides that, it declareth the certainty of our faith; as if we should say, I believe assuredly, that these things are granted to me of God: for "Amen" is as much as if one should say, "So be it." And the Lord in the gospel oftentimes says, "Amen, Amen, I said to you;" that is, of a certainty I tell you the truth: or, I utter and pronounce to you the undoubted truth. And so the faithful, after they have offered prayers to God, having their minds pacified, do now joyfully wait for the gifts of the Lord.

Prayer: Let my life be an Amen to your will, Lord. Amen. And Amen.

March 15

W e will say somewhat (as we have done of this) of thanksgiving, another kind of prayer. And though the same also be comprehended in the Lord's Prayer, (for it comprehendeth all things belonging to true prayer, therefore it containeth thanksgiving also;) then, after the expounding of that, I also would entreat of this by itself, lest by mingling of things there rise a confusion or disorder in our minds. And truly the Lord requires thanksgiving of us: of which thing there are extant in the holy scriptures arguments not a few. For how many praises, rejoicings, and thanksgivings, are read in the Psalms, written and left both of David and of other prophets! And in the law also the Lord instituted a peculiar kind of oblation and sacrifice, which we have said is called the Eucharist, or the sacrifice of thanksgiving. What thing else was the supper of the Passover, but a thanksgiving for the deliverance out of the Egyptian captivity? Surely, our Lord Jesus Christ, both instituting a remembrance of all his benefits and specially of the redemption purchased by his death, and knitting up all sacrifices in brevity, delivered the Eucharist, or sacrament of thanksgiving, to his church; as we will declare in place convenient, and have partly showed in our former sermons.

Prayer: Give me a thankful heart and lips of praise. And fill me with gratitude rather than allowing bitterness to take root. For Christ's sake, Amen.

March 16

Mankind in prosperity is all upon lustiness and jollity, and seldomtimes thinketh with himself, from whence prosperity cometh: so he does not set by those spiritual mysteries and benefits so much as otherwise he ought But they seem to be swine, and not men, which do not only not set by the benefits of God as they ought, but do moreover contemn them, and tread them under feet. The heavy judgment of God does tarry for them.

Prayer: The dread of judgment is overcome in Christ and for that I'm profoundly thankful. Amen.

March 17

Furthermore, the sacrifice of praise and thanksgiving is due to God only: for he is the only giver and author of all good things; though in the meanwhile he use the means and ministry of men and other creatures. Some prince sendeth to you a most royal gift; and that by a courtier not of the lowest degree, but a most chosen man: then to him, nevertheless, though he be a nobleman, you givest not thanks, but to the prince from whom the gift came: howbeit, in the mean while, you dost honestly confess, that the courtier herein bestowed his labor for your sake. But he had not bestowed it, unless his prince had so commanded: and so the whole benefit at the length redoundeth to the prince himself, even to him alone. And as all our invocation or calling upon God is acceptable to God the Father through Jesus Christ our Lord; so no thanksgiving of ours is acceptable to God, unless it be offered through Jesus Christ: for hitherto pertaineth the mystery of the altar of incense, whereof mention is made in the ceremonies of the law. But the apostle also says: "Give thanks always for all things to God the Father in the name of our Lord Jesus Christ." And again he says: "By him we offer sacrifice of praise always to God, that is, the fruit of lips confessing his name."

Prayer: Today is not going according to plan. I don't feel very much like praying so I think I'll just listen. Amen.

March 18

B ut that we may be thankful for all the benefits of God, and offer continual thanksgiving to God; it is needful first, to acknowledge, and well to weigh with ourselves, the benefits of God; for these being not then known, or rightly weighed, our mind is not set on fire to give God thanks for his benefits. And these are indeed diverse, Yes, they are infinite: for they are private and public, general and special, spiritual and corporal, temporal and eternal, ecclesiastical and political, singular and excellent. But who can reckon up all their kinds and parts? God created, beautified, garnished, and made this world fruitful for man. To the ministry of this he severally appointeth angelical spirits, whom he had created ministers for himself. He giveth us souls and bodies, which he furnisheth and storeth with infinite gifts and abilities; and, that which far passeth all other benefits, he loosed man, being entangled in sin; he delivered him, being a bond-slave to the Devil. For the Son of God sets us free into the liberty of the sons of God; by dying, he quickeneth; by shedding his blood, he purgeth and cleanseth; he also giveth us his Spirit, whereby we may be guided and preserved in this banishment, until we be received into that our everlasting and true country. They that consider these things with a true faith cannot choose but be rapt into the praise and setting forth of God's goodness, and into a wondering at a thing doubtless to be marveled at; that the gracious and mighty God has such a special care of men, than whom this earth has nothing either more wretched or miserable.

Prayer: Thank you. For forgiveness. For mercy. For grace. Thank you. Amen.

March 19

Here the saints of God are destitute of words, neither have they words meet enough for this so great a matter. David crieth: "O Lord our God, how wonderful is your name in all the world; for that you hast set your glory above the heavens;" and as it followeth in the eighth psalm. And again the same: "Who am I, O Lord God, and what is the house of my father, that you hast brought me hitherto (or so advanced me)? And what can David say further to you? for you, Lord God, knowest your servant;" and so forth, as followeth in the 2. book of Samuel, chap. 7. The same David has set down a most notable form of blessing, or praising, or giving thanks to God, in the 103 Psalm, which beginneth thus: "Bless the Lord, O my soul; and all that is within me, bless his holy name. Bless the Lord, O my soul, and forget not all his benefits; who forgiveth all your wickedness;" and so forth. But what need any more words?

Prayer: I feel very much like Bullinger felt. What need is there for words right now? Thank you for the freedom of silence in your presence.

March 20

The Lord's Prayer may be a most perfect form of praising God, and giving thanks to God for all his benefits, and serve instead of many. For as the preface and all the petitions do call to our remembrance, and absolutely set forth to us, God's greatest benefits most liberally bestowed upon us, and also upon all other: so if we consider that it is our duty to give thanks to God for every one of these, and by and by begin, even at the beginning of the Lord's Prayer, to weigh this chiefly with ourselves, that God the Father, of his unspeakable mercy to us-ward, has adopted us miserable sinners into the number of sons, by whom he will be sanctified, and in whom he will reign, and at the last also translate to his everlasting kingdom; that I may speak nothing of other petitions; what plentiful matter of praising God and giving thanks to him shall be ministered! But these things are better and more rightly understood by good, godly, and devout exercise, than by precepts, though never so diligent.

Prayer: Lord give me the good sense to pray more than I talk about or think about praying. In Jesus' name, Amen.

March 21

And the Lord does so much esteem this thanksgiving, offered to him with true humility of mind, and also faith, that he receiveth it and counteth it for a most acceptable sacrifice. Of this thing there is very often mention in the old Testament; as when it is said: "Whosoever offers me thanks and praise, he honors me. I will not reprove you because of your sacrifices. I will take no bullocks out of your house, nor goats out of your folds. Offer to God the sacrifice of praise, and pay your vows to the most Highest; and call upon me in the day of trouble; I will hear you (and deliver you), and you shalt glorify me." Again: "I will offer to you the sacrifice of thanksgiving, and I will call upon the name of the Lord." And Hosea also says: "Take these words with you, and turn you to the Lord, and say to him, O forgive us all our sins, and receive us graciously, and then will we offer the calves of our lips to you."

Prayer: Father for the remainder of the month my aim will be solely to thank you whenever I come to you in prayer. Thank you. For all you do. Thank you. Amen.

March 22

For great is the worthiness, power, and virtue, not only of praise or thanksgiving, but also of prayer wholly; I mean, of invocation also itself. Whereof although I have already spoken somewhat, where I declared that our prayers are effectual, then do I add these few words. The saints truly had a most ardent desire of praying, because of the wonderful force of prayer. For, that I may say nothing of those most ancient fathers before and anon after the flood; did not Abraham pray, when he received the promises? and as often as he changed his dwelling, did not he call upon God? At his prayer king Abimelech is delivered from death; and barrenness, which the Lord, being displeased, laid upon his house, is cured. Jacob poured forth most ardent prayers to God, and received of him inestimable benefits. In Exodus, Moses prays, not once, but often; and taketh away the plagues from the Egyptians, which the Lord by his just judgment had brought upon them. At the prayer of Moses the Amalekites turn their backs; and, when he ceased or left off, the Israelites fled away.

Prayer: Father, thank you for all you give me. Amen.

March 23

Again, when the fire of the Lord devoured the utmost parts of the tents of Israel, they cried to Moses; and Moses again cried to the Lord: and suddenly the fire that devoured them was consumed. Again, the people murmured against the Lord, and vengeance is prepared; but Moses by mild and continual prayer quencheth the wrath of God; for it is said to him: "I have let them go according to your word." Anon after, when the people began afresh to murmur against Moses and Aaron, and that the vengeance of God had already consumed fourteen thousand and seven hundred men, Aaron, at the commandment of Moses, burneth incense, and standing between the dead and those that were living, howbeit near and appointed to death, he pleadeth for and obtaineth pardon by prayers. Innumerable other of this kind are read of Moses. Joshua, Moses' successor, by prayers made the course of the sun and moon so long to stay, until he had revenged himself upon his enemies. Hannah, without any voice heard, by prayer putteth from her the reproach of barrenness, and forthwith is made a fruitful mother of very many children.

Prayer: Lord, thank you for your pardon. Amen.

March 24

Samuel, the most godly son of godly Hannah, by prayer vanquisheth the Philistines; and suddenly, in the time of harvest, raised up a mighty tempest of thunders and rain. We do also read things not unlike of Elijah. Jonah in like manner prayed in the whale's belly, and was cast on the shore safe. Jehoshaphat and Hezekiah, most religious kings, by prayers poured forth to God by faith, do triumph over their most puissant enemies. Nehemiah asked nothing of his king before he had first prayed to the Lord of heaven; therefore he obtained all things. The most valiant and man-like stomached Judith by prayer overthrew and slew Holophernes, the most proud enemy of God's people, and the terror of all nations.

Prayer: Merciful Lord, thank you for your strength each day. Amen.

March 25

And when the apostles were in dangers, the church crieth suppliantly for God's help, and presently without delay findeth succor: they receive much liberty to speak, and work very great signs and miracles among the people. Peter by an angel of God is brought out of a very strong and fenced prison. What should I speak of Paul and Silas praying and praising the Lord in prison? Is it not read, that the foundations of the prison were all shaken with an earthquake, and by that occasion the keeper of the prison was turned to God? Examples of which sort truly I could bring innumerable, but that I am persuaded that to the godly these are sufficient. And faithful men do not attribute these forces, effects, or virtues, to prayer, as to a work of ours, but as proceeding from faith; and so to God himself, which promiseth these things, and performeth them to the faithful. For the judgment of Paul touching these is known, in the 11 to the Hebrews; and that all glory is due to one God: who vouchsafe so to illuminate all our minds, that our prayer may always please him Amen.

Prayer: Father, Thank you. It's the only thing I want to say. Amen.

March 26[4]

*W*hat God is is perhaps above human understanding, but not *that* God is. For many of the wise have got so far as to have no doubt of the existence of God, though there have been some who attributed divinity to many beings—through their limited understanding, no doubt, which did not venture to attribute to one and only one being the great power and majesty that they saw must belong to divinity. There were, however, men who perceived the μικρολογία ["mean conception"] these philosophers had of God, and saw that the existence of God was less certain if divinity were attributed to many than if to one only. Therefore (whether through divine or human agency I will not now consider, as I will discuss that point presently), they arrived at the opinion that there is one and only one God, though such is the sluggishness and carelessness of the human intellect that they did not think it of any great importance to hold fast to this recognition of God, but, content to have recognized the fact and satisfied with themselves for this, they scorned to live according to His will. And this we see the general body of Christian scholars doing even now, zealously disputing about the word and the true worship of God, but in fact not becoming one whit better men.

Prayer: Father, Thank you. It's the only thing I want to say. Amen

---

[4] This and following selections are taken from Zwingli's 'Commentary on True and False Religion'.

March 27

The foundation on which they all build is what Paul wrote in Rom. 1:19: "That which is known of God is manifest in them; for God manifested it to them." Here I will treat in passing what I held back above. We here see plainly that that knowledge of God which we credit to some natural agency is really from God. "For God," Paul says, "manifested it." And what else is natural agency than the constant and uninterrupted operation of God, His disposition of all things? And whence, pray, comes our intellect but from Him, who "work-eth all things in all" [1 Cor. 12:6]? Now Paul in this passage conformed somewhat to the usage of the Gentiles in speaking of God, not because he holds the view that our knowledge of God proceeds from human reason, but because this was the view of the Gentiles, between whom and the Jews he is here acting as mediator.

Prayer: Father, Thank you. It's the only thing I want to say. Amen

March 28

Hence he carefully adds, "God manifested it to them." Following his example, I have begun with the questions of God's existence and nature, in order that I may be more easily understood by those who have derived their knowledge of God from man rather than from God. Now I come back to Paul's words, that "the knowledge of God was manifest even in the Gentiles, for God manifested it to them. For the invisible things of him," he says, "are clearly seen, being understood by the things that were made from the foundation of the world, even his power and Godhead; so that they are without excuse, because they indeed knew God, but glorified him not as God, neither were thankful; nay rather became vain in their reasonings, and their foolish heart was darkened. And though in their own judgment they were wise, they became fools, and changed the glory of the uncorruptible God for the likeness of an image not merely of mortal man, but even of birds and four-footed beasts, and creeping things, etc." Therefore, that God exists was generally acknowledged among all the heathen, but in widely different ways. Some came to the recognition of one God but did not worship Him as they ought; though of these there were very few. Others, seeing clearly a might and power grander than that of man, recognized that this was God. They did not, however, regard it as the one only Power, but turned to themselves for a conception of what kind of being God was.

Prayer: Father, Thank you. It's the only thing I want to say. Amen

March 29

S o they, first of all, divided Him into many, because they were incapable of comprehending His infinite power; and presently they clothed these many with different forms according to their own imaginations. Hence the worship of idols and spirits, who cunningly made themselves such as poor mortals in their poor wisdom had installed as gods and distinguished with various forms. Thus I think it is clearly apparent that nearly all the heathen have agreed in acknowledging that God exists, though some have made Him many, others have made Him fewer, and a very few have made Him one. Then from slowness of mind and confidence in their own wisdom they have disregarded Him, have held such views of Him as pleased them, and likewise have worshipped Him as they chose. On this subject not only our people but also the philosophers have written longer volumes.

Prayer: Father, Thank you. It's the only thing I want to say. Amen

March 30

Now the faithful (for this is the generally accepted term for believers or pious persons, or worshippers of the true God) are by virtue of this one thing faithful, because they believe in one only true and omnipotent God and have faith in Him only. Furthermore, how it comes about that the pious hold this view of God, and do not, after the fashion of the heathen, make just any unknown power God, is easy for a pious man to explain: It comes about through the power and grace of Him in whom we believe; for as far as the nature and endowment of man are concerned, there is no difference between the pious man and the impious. Accordingly, in the realm of error in regard to gods, anything that could happen to one man could happen to any other, unless there were some higher power to call and attach to itself the human heart, which has no natural aversion to those who are most completely in error. Here, then, the first traces of faith and piety disclose themselves. It is not the fact, as most men have thought, that the faithful become faithful because they hear Moses say [Gen. 1:1], "In the beginning God created the heaven and the earth"; for those are numberless who hear this but do not believe the world was made according to the Mosaic tradition.

Prayer: Father, Thank you. It's the only thing I want to say. Amen

March 31

S ince, therefore, it is clear that whoever upon hearing the words, "In the beginning God created the heaven and the earth," immediately believes that the world is the work of God does not come to this through the power of the words or of our intellect (for if the words could effect this, all would be made pious; and if our intellect could, no one who heard would be impious), it is manifest that the faithful believe that God exists, and that the world is His work, etc., just because they are taught this by God. It is of God alone, therefore, that you believe that God exists and that you have faith in Him.

Prayer: Lord if I were to spend the whole of my life thanking you I could never express my gratitude sufficiently. For all you've done, for all you do, and for all you will do, I can only and always and ever be appreciative. I am now, and will always remain, your grateful servant. Amen.

April 1

Furthermore, *what* God is, we have just as little knowledge of from ourselves as a beetle has of what man is. Nay, this infinite and eternal divine is much farther separated from man than man is from the beetle, because a comparison between any kinds of created things can more properly be made than between any created thing and the Creator, and all perishable things are nearer and more closely related to each other than to the eternal and unbounded divine, however much you may find in them a likeness and footprints, as they say, of that divine. Since, then, we can in no way attain of our own effort to a knowledge of what God is—for if, according to Solomon's words, Eccles. 1:13–18, all things (he is speaking of things under the sun) are so difficult that man cannot unfold them, what presumption it would be to try to explain what God is!—and since Isaiah, 45:15, in solemn warning says, "Verily you art a God that hidest yourself," it must be admitted that only by God Himself can we be taught what He is. For, according to the view of Paul, 1 Cor. 2:11, as no one "knows the things of a man, save the spirit of the man, which is the man himself, even so all are ignorant of the things of God save the Spirit Himself of God." We may well call it the rash boldness of a Lucifer or a Prometheus if any one presumes to know from any other source what God is than from the Spirit Himself of God.

Prayer: Father, teach me today who you are and what you wish of me so that I can be the person you wish me to be—made in your image in order to fulfill your plan and purpose. Amen.

April 2

All, therefore, is sham and false religion that the theologians have adduced from philosophy as to what God is. If certain men have uttered certain truths on this subject, it has been from the mouth of God, who has scattered even among the heathen some seeds of the knowledge of Himself, though sparingly and darkly; otherwise they would not be true. But we, to whom God Himself has spoken through His Son and through the Holy Spirit, are to seek these things not from those who were puffed up with human wisdom, and consequently corrupted what they received pure, but from the divine oracles. For when men began to disregard these, they fell into all that is fleshly, *i.e.*, into the inventions of philosophy, took to believing these, and, relying upon them, not only held such views as they liked about God, but forced others to hold the same. And this, though none of them would have permitted any one to hold such view of himself as that other, whoever he was, wished. Such is the arrogance of the flesh that gave itself out as theology. We wish to learn out of His own mouth what God is, lest we become corrupt and do abominable work.

Prayer: Gracious Lord, remind me that my own notions of you are probably false and the image I construct in my mind of you is probably an idol. So instead of coming up with truth myself, reveal your truth to me. Amen.

April 3

When Moses asked the Lord, Exod. 3:13, to declare His name to him, in order that he might be in a better position to deal with the Children of Israel, the Lord said to him, "I AM THAT I AM." In these words God disclosed Himself wholly; for it is just as if He had said, "I am he who am of myself, who am by my own effort, who am absolute being, who 'am' par excellence." And this meaning He immediately brings out by adding, "This shalt you say to the children of Israel, He that is has sent me to you." By these words He indicated that He alone is the being of all things; for unless you take it in this way, that "He that is" is, and alone is, the being of all things, the Lord would not have distinguished Himself from other things that have being, which, though they have being from Him and through Him, then still have being; and consequently God would be regarded as having evaded the question of Moses, rather than as having answered it. For suppose that neither Moses nor the Children of Israel understood the words "He that is" to mean anything different from what we mean when we say of anything that it is, what else do you suppose could have been understood both by Moses and by the Children of Israel than, "Some one has sent me to you"?

Prayer: Lord reveal yourself to me as you revealed yourself to Moses. Show me your glory. I want to see with my eyes what my heart has long believed.   Show me yourself. Amen.

April 4

For they never could have been persuaded by somebody thus casually announced to go away, leaving Egypt behind them, and to follow one whom they knew not. The same thing becomes still plainer when we examine the etymon of the supreme name of God, which the Jews pronounce as "Adonai," to be sure, in reading, in spite of the fact that the signs, *i.e.*, the letters, by no means form that word. Not that the Hebrews cannot read it according to the value of the letters, but because they think the name ineffable on account of its sanctity. For this name is derived from the word for being; or perhaps the word which to them signifies being is derived from this name. When, therefore, Moses heard the aforesaid words of God, he straightway understood that He that is, and from whom all things are, was speaking to him. And this the Lord manifested to him still more clearly, when further He bade him begin before the elders of Israel thus [Exod. 3:16]: "The Lord God of your fathers appeared to me, etc.," now plainly calling Himself "Lord" from His power and majesty, as He had just before from His being called Himself "I AM," and "He that is." By all this I wish to make this point only, that the first thing in acquiring knowledge of God is to know that He is he who is by nature, who Himself is, and who receives being from none other.

Prayer: Oh Lord, how I am reminded today of my utter dependence on you. Without you I cannot even breath or live or move. Help me give thanks that you are not dependent on me. In Jesus' name, Amen.

April 5

From this we afterwards are easily brought to see clearly that all things are from God, and that nothing we can see can have being from itself, but must have its being and existence from another, from this source and fountain of being, namely, God. He shall be, then, the only God who has His being from Himself, and who bestows being upon all, and so bestows it that they could not possibly exist a moment unless God existed, who is being and life to all, sustains all things, governs all things. This Isaiah, 40:12, has beautifully indicated, saying: "Who has measured the waters in the hollow of his hand, and weighed heaven with his palm? Who has poised with three fingers the bulk of the earth, and weighed the mountains in scales, and the hills in a balance, etc.?" This "Being" is as really good as it is being. For as it exists alone and of itself, so it is alone good, true, right, just, holy; for it is of itself good, true, right, etc. This is again clear from His own words, Gen. 1:31, "And God saw everything that he had made, and, behold, it was very good." If, therefore, such a countless brood of created things was very good, in the sense that singly and collectively they were good, it is clear that their author must be good, and in such a way good as to have his goodness from no other but his own self, and to be not only the force and essence of all things that are, but the source and fountain of all good.

Prayer: Father you are truly the source of all good things, both in this world and in my life. Thank you for all the good you send me and even more all the good you do for me, though I am unworthy, as you well know. In Christ's name, Amen.

April 6

And this Christ expresses a little more plainly, Luke 18:19, saying: "None is good, save one, that is, God." If, now, all the things which He has made are exceeding good even in His own judgment, and nevertheless none is good save God alone, it follows that all the things which are are in Him and through Him. For since all the things which are are good, and then God alone is good, all the things which are are God; *i.e.*, the reason they exist is because God exists and is their essence. This Paul expressed thus, Rom. 11:36, "For of him, and through him, and in him, are all things."

This good, therefore, is not a thing idle or inert, so as to lie torpid and motionless, moving neither itself nor other things; for we saw above that it is the essence and constitution of all things. What does this mean but that through it and in it all things are contained and live and move?

Prayer: Father It is not possible to think too much of your sustaining power. Contemplating your ability to do anything you design to is a source of great comfort to me. In you I find rest. For that, thank you. Amen.

April 7

And this, again, is made manifest by His own word, for at the beginning of the story of creation you find [Gen. 1:3]: "And God said, Let there be light: and there was light." See how light when called not only was immediately at hand, but in obedience to the command of its Creator appeared from nothing. For so great is His power that, when He calls things that are not, they obey like those that are [cf. Rom. 4:17], even if they first have to be born of nothing. And a little after He says: "Let the earth bring forth the green herb and such as yields seed, and the fruit tree bearing fruit after its kind, whose seed is in itself, upon the earth: and it was so." See how here the crude earth at the first word of command from its Creator put on a glad aspect! For when the waters had retired to their own depths and the earth had appeared in its own place, it was bare and unsightly to look upon. God was unwilling, therefore, that its bareness should be exposed to the eyes of mortals, and bade it straightway clothe itself with grass and adorn itself by producing trees, that to all the different kinds of animals, as they forthwith came into existence, it might be able to offer a shelter according to the nature of each. And not this only, but, that there might never be a scarcity of food, He conferred upon the grass and the trees the power of producing seed, so that when they had given us for the exigencies of winter all that they had, they might presently with the returning spring gird themselves again for the same task, and so on alternately without end.

Prayer: Merciful God, for your provision of all that sustains life, we give you thanks. Amen.

April 8

When we see this going on every Year in unchanging course, do we not recognize the measureless power and wisdom of the Creator, and His care and grace towards His work? For He not only spoke and it was so, commanded and the things He desired were created, but He also fed what He had created. Why, He forgot not even the raven's young [Job 38:41; Ps. 147:9; Lk. 12:24]. Since, therefore, all that moves or lives lives and moves because it has being (for unless it had being it could not move or live, and in that it has being has it in God and through God), it may be most clearly inferred that, as God is being and existence to all things, so He is the life and motion of all things that live and move. And this is beautifully shown by Paul, Acts 17:28, when after a somewhat extended discourse he sums up by saying: "For in him we live, and move, and have our being; as certain even of your own poets have said, For we are also his offspring." We see here in passing how the Apostle quotes from profane writers, not by any means using them as authorities, but, when the heavenly Spirit has willed to say anything through their mouths, showing where we may find this, so that we may not have to dig over all their filth in the search for one or two pearls. I come back to the subject.

Prayer: In consideration of your greatness, I will keep silence in your presence. Overwhelmed. Amen.

April 9

Again, He is not the life and motion of all things in such a way that either He Himself blindly puts breath or motion into them, or they which breathe and move ask blindly of Him life or motion. How could things that could not even exist unless they existed from Him ask of Him, or how ask before they existed? It is evident, therefore, that God not only is a sort of stuff, as it were, from which all things have being and motion and life, but is at the same time such wisdom, knowledge, and foresight that nothing is hidden from Him, nothing unknown to Him, nothing beyond His reach, nothing disobedient to Him. Hence not even the mosquito has its sharp sting and musical hum without God's wisdom, knowledge, and foresight. His wisdom, then, knows all things even before they exist, His knowledge comprehends all things, His foresight regulates all things. For that thing which is God would not be the supreme good unless it were at the same time supreme wisdom and foresight. For if there were anything which could be hidden from God, His wisdom and knowledge would be ineffectual to that extent, and if anything were regulated by other providence than His, then divine providence would be inert and defective in this particular, and accordingly would not be supreme nor absolute; for in as far as it failed to act it would be imperfect.

Prayer: Your wisdom is displayed, Father, in so many small ways. Forgive me for ignoring it in them and open my eyes to help me see more regularly the careful planning by which you oversee your creation. Amen.

April 10

B ut this is so far from being true of God that nothing is so at variance with His nature and character as imperfection. For that which is imperfect is not God; and, on the other hand, that alone is God which is perfect, *i.e.*, absolute, and which lacks nothing, but has everything that befits the supreme good. I am not speaking here of perfection as the theologians usually speak. Nothing, therefore, can escape God, nothing defeat or alter His purpose and ordering; and when we with more temerity than faith demand of Him a reason for His acts or designs, asking why He made the flea, the gadfly, the wasp, and the hornet, things that are a plague to man and beast, we simply display a vain and useless feminine curiosity. As if, indeed, the human mind could comprehend divine wisdom, and as if, when one or two things become known, many more would not emerge, insisting upon being known just like the first! No mind but the infinite and immeasurable mind can hold the knowledge of all these things, while one as narrow as is the human mind simply makes vain labor for itself by such inquisitiveness; as Solomon reminds us in Ecclesiastes, Chap. 1. In contemplating divine wisdom and providence poor mortals will, therefore, have to do as each does in his own sphere.

Prayer: Today, Lord, I merely contemplate, with all the Saints, your divine providence. In Jesus' name, Amen.

April 11

So, let us contemplate with reverence what God has wished disclosed to us. But what He has hidden, let us not impudently desire to touch, lest it be taken indignantly away from us, and punishment be inflicted upon us for our rashness, as was done to Prometheus of story. For the dwelling of God is large, the heaven is His abode and the earth His footstool [cf. Isa. 66:1]; and the contents are so vast and various that one who desires to know them all should rather be overwhelmed with despair than entertain the hope of comprehending them all. If you set yourself to examine one grape leaf closely and completely, you will fail. It has a stem running through the middle to the apex, and from this aortas, or principal veins, that branch out and extend to particular areas, and from these the so-called mesial or mesenteric veins, minute ducts that run out to every last particle of the blade, properly distributing the sap—just such complexity as you will find when you consider man as a whole or the entire universe. Then the workmanship in this little leaf will force you to give up before you have learned it all. See how all human wisdom, in fact, seems to amount to nothing, and is forced to confess its ignorance and lack of knowledge; but neither ignorant nor lacking in knowledge is the divine wisdom and foresight, by which all things are rightly done and regulated.

Prayer: Lord the day has been hard and racked with sorrow. Do you mind if I simply sit here in your presence and listen to your word address me? I need the balm of Gilead. Amen.

April 12

Now it is time to bring forward the witness of the word itself to everything that has been said so far about the wisdom and providence of God. Solomon, Prov. 8:22–36, has a fine description in praise of wisdom, commending it first for its antiquity, in that it was with the Lord Himself before He began to create the universe; and then because afterwards through it the poles of the world were hung in place, and all things put together. And Jeremiah, 51:15, says: "He has made the earth by his power, he has prepared the world by his wisdom, and stretched out the heavens by his understanding." But none speaks more delightfully than David in Psalm 104. He portrays both the wisdom and the providence of God so that you see God as Creator balancing the mountains in His mighty hand, putting each in its place, drawing out the valleys between and the cool streams in the valleys, spreading out the fields, thrusting back the turbulent sea into its own depths, that there may be no confusion from its unruliness, then assigning settlers to each region and adding provision abundantly.

Prayer: Thank you for your patience with us, Father. Help us to be patient with one another and rather than fight, pray. Knit us into one in the bond of love. Amen.

April 13

Now I will hasten on to the witness of the New Testament, content with the more striking passages just cited, because the whole Scripture of the Old Testament views everything as done by the providence of God. Hence the frequent appearing of angels, the many utterances of God Himself, and in time of urgent necessity the miracles. Hence the watchful care and guardianship of God over individual men dwelling among the wicked, such as Noah, Abraham, Lot, and others. Hence the sending of prophets to give warning of what was to come, and the terrible chastenings sent upon those who did not heed their warnings, the frequent victories at the hands of the Lord, if they had been obedient, the frequent defeats and disasters if disobedient.

Christ warns us distinctly, Matt. 6:25–34, not to be troubled even about the things that pertain to the body, since we can be sure that in these matters God's providence exercises care over us, from the fact that He provides so bountifully for the birds of the air, and clothes the lilies of the field so sumptuously that Solomon's gorgeous robes of state and all his adornments are mean in comparison. How much more will He give all these things to us, who are of much more value in His sight!

Prayer: Father, too often I allow trouble to eclipse the sight of you. This, I confess, is very foolish. Forgive me and aid me in rejecting shadows and holding on to just reality—the reality that is your presence. In Christ's name, Amen.

April 14

See how wide is the care of the heavenly providence, and how sure: "are all numbered," He says. What will the advocates of free will say here? Will they argue that there is a trope here? But that is just what I maintain, that the words are used τροπικῶς ["tropically"]. Must we, then, wait for them to expound the trope? Not in the least, for a child can explain the meaning of this trope: namely, that God exercises constant care over even those things that in our judgment seem hardly worthy of human care. Or is it a hyperbole? "When I feed the birds and clothe the flowers, shall I forget you? Are you not of much more value in my sight?" [Mt. 6:25–34.] But of this more when I come by and by to speak of free will. In Matt. 10:29, Christ says: "Are not two sparrows sold for a penny? and not one of them shall fall on the ground without your Father." Here no one may fairly plead a hyperbole. It is plainly an argument from the less to the greater, in which the first term must be absolutely true; otherwise the conclusion will not hold. Christ, then, means this: "Since not one of the sparrows bought for a penny falls to the ground even by accident without the Heavenly Father, how much more will you, who are of so much value in His eyes, nowhere perish without His so ordering?"

Prayer: Your care is beyond comprehension, not only for people but for everything you've made, Lord. Thank you for it. Amen.

April 15

For he said: "This sickness is not to death, but for the glory of God, that the Son of God may be glorified thereby." You see whence this sickness came? From God, surely; for He was going to use it for the glory of His Son. Christ answered his disciples in the same fashion, John 9:3, when they asked for whose sin it came about that a man who was there was born blind: "Neither did this man sin," He said, "nor his parents: but that the work of God should be made manifest in him." I will be content with these citations now, meaning to treat this topic, as I said, more fully elsewhere. Do you, good reader, remember these meanwhile, that you may not be bored to death with repetition. For the whole business of predestination, free will, and merit rests upon this matter of providence.

Prayer: Lord I'm reminded that I should wait for you to explain the things you want me to know instead of diving in the murky mud until I dredge up something unusable. Teach me patience, through trial. In your Son's name, Amen.

April 16

Now it would be vain, fruitless, and useless to mortals, if this supreme good, God, were wise for Himself alone, as is said; were goodness, life, motion, knowledge, foresight for Himself alone. For in that case He would not differ at all from mortals, whose natural characteristic is to sing for themselves, to look out for their own interests, and to wish themselves better off than others. It must be, therefore, that this supreme good, which is God, is by its nature kind and bountiful, not with that bounty with which we like to seem bountiful, looking for a return or for glory, but with a bounty that causes Him to desire the profit of those to whom He gives, with only this one thing in view, that He may belong to those things which were made by Him; for He desires to impart Himself freely. For, as He is the fountain-source of all things (for no one before he existed had any claim to be born of Him), so also is He unceasingly bountiful to those whom He begot with this one purpose, that they might enjoy His bounty. Again, things that are good merely in outward appearance desire to be sparing of themselves; for they can satisfy only a very few, being of narrow and slender compass.

Prayer: Dearest Lord, give me the tools to live a satisfied life which consists not in desiring more but in appreciating what I already have more. And those tools are, your Spirit, and your presence. Give me more of those and I will be satisfied, as I hunger and thirst not for things, but for righteousness. In your Son's name, Amen.

April 17

The whole company of created things testifies to this view. For if God had not willed that His works should enjoy Him, He never would have called them forth from nothing; for God does not enjoy them. For what purpose, then, did He create them? That they might enjoy their Creator. In Genesis 15:1, the Lord thus speaks to Abraham: "Fear not, Abraham: I am your shield, and your exceeding great reward." What, pray, is it to be shield and reward, or prize, or good, which you mayest enjoy, rich and abundant beyond what you canst imagine, but to be God? Furthermore, that He thus of His own accord discloses Himself, to whom is this not a proof that He loves to impart Himself? Isaiah, 45:1, proves clearly enough that all things are done by the providence and bounty of God, when he represents Him as talking to Cyrus. Cyrus did not know God, but God knew Cyrus, for He showered upon him victories, riches, and whole kingdoms so bountifully that the East and the West ought of right to have seen that He who gave all these things so lavishly was the one true God. After a long admonition the Lord speaks thus to him [Isa. 45:21–22] (not to write down the whole speech): "Tell you, and come, and consult together. Who has declared this from the beginning? From that time I have foretold this." (See the providence which exercises care even over the impious.) "Have not I the Lord, and there is no God else beside me?

Prayer: There is nothing beside you, nothing comparable to you. Nothing. Amen.

April 18

A just God and a Savior, there is none beside me. Be converted to me, and be you saved, all you ends of the earth: for I am God, and there is no other, etc." See the bounty with which He of His own accord invites to Himself all the ends of the earth. See also the certainty that He is the only one who dispenses all things justly, is the only Savior, and there is no God beside Him. In the same way He displays his kindness, Isa. 55:1, when He calls to Himself all who desire or need heavenly wisdom and help, thus: "All you that thirst, come to the waters, and you that have no money, make haste, buy, and eat." See how He encourages them not only to hasten, but also to drink generously. Now from the Old Covenant enough testimony has been adduced; for what is the whole gist of it but the showing that God is the only one who saves, who looks out for us, who desires that all things be asked from Him? "I, even I, am he that blotteth out your transgressions for mine own sake," Isa. 43:25. "The earth is full of the mercy of the Lord," Psalms 33:5; and [Ps. 145:15], "You givest them their meat in due season;" and [Ps. 145:16], "You openest your hand, and fillest with blessing every living creature."

Prayer: Lord we used to sing quite often a little song titled 'count your blessings'. I wish I could remember to do that every day. I'm sorry that I don't. I'll endeavor to do better. In Christ's name, Amen.

April 19

From the New Testament, what other testimony shall I bring forward than Jesus Christ, the Son of God and the Virgin, who is himself the Testament? For when we were by nature children of wrath, Eph. 2:1–7, we were restored to favor by God, who is very rich in mercy, through his Son Jesus Christ. God also appointed him a propitiator, Rom. 3:25, that they that have faith in his blood may be accounted holy and spotless before the Father. He, then, is our propitiation, therefore also our covenant and testament, which God has made with us. He is Himself the propitiator also, for through Him we have access to God, 1 John 2:1; Heb. 10:19; Eph. 2:18. Furthermore, whatever Christ is to us, He is by the bountiful gift of God; for we have not of ourselves merited that He should offer His Son for our life. If it had been possible for life to be given for our merits, there would have been no need of Christ. If there had been no need of Him, why should the Father clothe Him with flesh? The work of God is not idle, nor vain, nor superfluous, but the Son of God came into this world that we might have life and that we might have it most abundantly. Christ Himself, to reveal Himself wholly to us, cries, Matt. 11:28, "Come to me, all you that labor and are heavy laden, and I will give you rest." What, good God, is it to be bountiful and generous, if this is not?

Prayer: For the bounty that your Son is to us, we give you thanks dear Father. He is and has all we need. And we thank you. I thank you.

April 20

We all teem with evils outside and inside, to such an extent that we are weighed down under them as under a vast load. The Son of God sees this woe and calls us all to Him. And that no one's consciousness of guilt may prevent him from thinking that he may go to Him, He says distinctly, "all, both you that labor and you that are heavy laden" [Mt. 11:28]; for He had come to save sinners and to do it without recompense. This the divine prophets had foretold many ages before, especially Jeremiah, who says, 31:33–34, that it will come to pass that we shall all know the Lord on account of His bounty, with which He will be so indulgent to our sins that He will remember them and reproach us with them no more. In Rom. 8:32 Paul says that God "spared not His own Son, but delivered him up for us all," and immediately argues in this way: "How shall he not also with him freely give us all things?" By this he certainly means: Can anyone offer anything greater for a friend or brother than his only son? Now, God delivered up His Son for us. Could He have proved more clearly the bounteousness of His mercy to us? Will He who freely gave His Son be able to deny us anything? How can it be that, having given His Son, he will not with him give all things? For all things in heaven and on earth are less than the Son.

Prayer: True words are spoken by Zwingli, Father. We have already been given the greatest of all gifts. Jesus. We thank you for Him and for all he is to us. Amen.

April 21

For this purpose, then, He delivered up His Son for us, that we, seeing that what was highest as well in heaven as on earth had been made ours, might be sure that nothing could be denied us. For He who has given His Son has given His all. For the Father has nothing which the Son also has not. This will, perhaps, be enough to show the untaught that as God is the fountain-source of all good, so He is bountiful and by no means niggardly or inexorable, but is so lavish and prodigal of Himself for the benefit of those who enjoy Him that He delights to be taken, and held, and possessed by all. And He is, accordingly, so ever ready to help that He always runs to our assistance and never lags. But why should I treat at greater length of the knowledge of God, when the very words that I have quoted from His own mouth have no more value with the impious man than so-called gift goods? Anyone who casts these pearls before those swine will find he has been feeding the wind. On the other hand, the pious have in their own hearts too good and intimate a knowledge of God to get any increase of it from these words of mine.

Prayer: Lord there are few things more disappointing than sharing your Word with those who have no interest in it. Give us patience and fill us with love so that when the unbelievers are not responsive, we give them over completely to you. In Jesus' name, Amen.

April 22

Having experienced this, holy men of God have from the creation of the world called God by various names, as one may see all through both Testaments, naming Him Lord or God, Life, Existence, Father, the Mighty, Light, All-powerful, All-sufficient. Then all these names they have given Him from the faith within them, because, namely, they felt in their hearts as to God that He was their strength, life, being, father, etc. And from that faith with which they credited to Him strength, life, etc., they afterwards gave Him the names Enduring Power, Lord, Life, Strength. It must be admitted, therefore, that what I have said thus far about knowledge of God is idle unless faith be added. Hence no man can reproach me with having based my teaching about the knowledge of God upon human persuasions. For, in the first place, I have relied upon the divine utterances only; and, in the second place, I have shown without reserve that it is not through human power that we come to the knowledge and worship of God, for that "is not of him that willeth, nor of him that runneth, but of God that has mercy" [Rom. 9:16]. It is He who grants that the works of His Hand recognize Him only as true God, Lord, Savior, Helper, Strength, Life, Light, Father, the heaped-up measure of all good things, generous, kind, well-wishing, eager to impart Himself freely (for all that is what I understand by this word "God").

Prayer: Lord we, the work of your hands, confess you our Lord. And we do it every day you give us breath and life. Without you, we really are nothing. In His name, Amen.

April 23

This age has many scholars who spring up everywhere as if out of the Trojan Horse, and still more who set themselves up as censors of all things. These because of their impiety are unwilling to accept the renascent word, then make a pretense of piety and fill the ears of the pious with groundless and fictitious suspicions. Some, when we teach vigorously that all our confidence is to be placed in God our Father, spring up with the impudent suggestion that we must be guarded against; for in all our teaching, they say, our aim is that we may do away with Christ, and, after the manner of the Jews, induce all to believe in only one Person, as we believe in only one God. Others, when we show an inclination to attribute all things to Christ, say they are afraid that we too rashly attribute too much to Him. Then both make their pronouncements in such a way that you can see of yourself that they are either recklessly ignorant or knowingly impious. For they are so ignorant as to the Father, and the Son, and the Holy Spirit, in their essence, substance, divinity, power, that they do not know what you mean when you speak of one and understand all three; and their lack of knowledge is accompanied by such recklessness that what they are extremely ignorant of they all the more violently drag under suspicion.

Prayer: Father, in our time too many pretend to know you who do not know you and pretend to speak your word when they only speak their own imaginings. Give us the wisdom to distinguish between the authentic spokesperson sent by you and the inauthentic self appointed false prophet. For your Kingdom's sake, Amen.

April 24

O r they are so willingly and knowingly impious that they assail with the depravity of a perverted heart what they see is done rightly and piously, and since they despair of accomplishing anything in open warfare, they make an underground attack, alleging a fear that we are too much inclined sometimes towards the Father, sometimes towards the Son. To all such I say "fare ill." For I teach that God is to be acknowledged and embraced in such wise that whether you call Him Father, or Son, or Holy Spirit, you always conceive of Him who is alone good, righteous, holy, kind, and all the rest. On the other hand, when I attribute all things to the Son, I attribute them to Him who is what the Father is, what the Holy Spirit is, and whose are the kingdom and the power just as truly as they are the Father's and the Holy Spirit's. For He is Himself that very thing which the Father is and the Holy Spirit, though seen from a different point of view, as they say.

Prayer: Lord make this day a day holy to yourself and instruct me each moment in the right use of it. Amen.

April 25

Therefore, just as grace is first rightly known when sin has been effected through the law, as Paul says, Rom. 7:25, that is, when sin has been weighed and known through the law, so also Christ, who is the pledge of grace, nay, is grace itself, is first rightly taught and known when from close observation of sin we have learned that by its interposition the way to heaven has been closed to us. For as he that is in sound health lays no store by the physician, but he that is in a desperate condition looks upon him as a god, so Christ is not especially welcome to the whole, but to the sick he is unexpected safety sent from above. To this He Himself testifies, saying: "They that are whole need not a physician; but they that are sick," Luke 5:31; and, "I came not to call the righteous, but sinners to change their former life." In order, therefore, rightly to know Christ, we must first rightly know ourselves; for they that think themselves righteous receive not Christ, as is clear from His own words; and he that feels no sickness wants not the help of a physician.

Prayer: There isn't a single day in which I do not need a visit to the Great Physician. Thank you for always being in the office. In your Son's name, Amen.

April 26

Hence arose endless despair of ever coming to God; for how could he ever hope to be received above who by daily evils felt himself exposed to bodily death, and from a guilty conscience felt himself so removed from God that he avoided coming into His sight? But God was better, and pitied His work, and devised a plan to repair so serious a misfortune. Since His justice, being inviolably sacred, had to remain as intact and unshaken as His mercy, and since man was indeed in need of mercy but wholly amenable to God's justice, divine goodness found a way to satisfy justice and then to be allowed to open wide the arms of mercy without detriment to justice. Not that He thus took precautions against the Adversary or that the potter may not out of moistened clay make or remake any vessel He chooses [*cf.* Rom. 9:21], but that by this example of justice He might remove drowsiness and sloth from us and show us what sort of being He was—just, good, merciful; or, not to presume to say too much of His purposes, because it so pleased Him.

Prayer: Father, accept my silence. Amen.

April 27

W hile, therefore, God is alike just and merciful, though with a leaning towards mercy (for His tender mercies are over all the rest of His works), then His justice has to be satisfied that His wrath may be appeased. That, then, God's justice has to be satisfied, the theologians have rightly taught, even those of the new school. For, "if you wouldst enter into life, keep the commandments," Matt. 19:17. But how shall man satisfy the justice of God? It is so pure, so high, so far removed from any stain, while, on the contrary, any one of us is so truly nothing but sin and blemish that no one would venture to hope to reach the measure that could satisfy divine justice. For who can attain to that purity which David says ascends into the holy mountain of the Lord? In Psalm 15:1 he asks: "Lord, who shall abide in your tabernacle? or who shall dwell in your holy hill?" And he answers his own question thus: "He that walketh without blemish, and worketh righteousness and speaketh the truth in his heart. He that back-biteth not with his tongue, nor doeth evil to his neighbor, nor taketh up a reproach against his neighbors. In his eyes a reprobate is despised, but he honoreth them that fear the Lord. He that sweareth to his neighbor and deceiveth not. He that putteth not out his money to usury, nor taketh bribes against the innocent. He that doeth these things shall never be moved."

Prayer: Father, accept my repentance. I have neither kept the Commandments nor felt my own sin horribly enough. I have, as a consequence, continued to live for myself rather than for you. I am ashamed and filled with sorrow. Forgive. Forgive, please. Amen.

April 28

Who, pray, can shine with such purity as to walk without blemish and to work righteousness, when we are nothing but sin and blemish and flesh? Or who among mortals is so single-hearted that neither his heart nor his tongue has ever practiced deceit? Who has done no evil to his neighbor or not suffered others to do it unpunished? In whose eyes have the evil always been despised and the good held in high esteem? Who has not been stained with usury, perjury, and the taking of bribes against the innocent? Who on hearing these words would not tremble, despair, and make ready to flee? But God is such a pure and consuming fire that if any one is troubled with the aforesaid defects he cannot stand in His sight. This is what Isaiah had in mind, 33:14: "Who among us can dwell with the devouring fire? Who among us can dwell with everlasting burnings?" Like David, he answers: "He that walketh righteously, and speaketh truth; he that despiseth the gain of oppressions, that shaketh his hands from taking a bribe, that stoppeth his ears from hearing of blood, and shutteth his eyes from looking on evil; he shall dwell on high, etc." Since, then, this fire demands such soundness and innocence, in order, of course, that there may be no moist or earthly ingredient which must be ejected with hissing and roaring, who is there that would venture, at least if he have any sort of knowledge of himself, to aspire to the companionship of God?

Prayer: I am not innocent. I am racked by guilt. Your grace is my only cure, my only hope. I run to you and cling to you, Father. You. Amen.

April 29

Thus it becomes manifest that wherever in the Scriptures the way to heaven is shown, we are driven to despair. For who in this polluted path below can so order his life as to be able to think himself even in his own opinion worthy of dwelling with and enjoying so pure a light, especially when we have all strayed and become so unprofitable that not even one of us does good, when every man is a liar [*cf.* Ps. 116:11; Rom. 3:4], and we are all hypocrites and have all sinned and fallen short of the glory of God [*cf.* Rom. 3:23]?

But since hypocrisy is such a mighty evil that, like certain foolish sufferers who try to hide their ailment, it ventures to deny itself and tries, though in vain, to clear itself of all suspicion, it is necessary for us, after the fashion of skilful physicians, who wrest out the truth by means of various attendant circumstances and symptoms, in the same way to probe and to examine man until we turn his bold concealment into shame and frank confession. For certain clever sick persons, in order to try the skill of the physician, refuse to tell the nature of their disease until the physician pronounces them to be suffering from the very ailment of which they are themselves perfectly aware. Then they entrust themselves more securely to his care, convinced that as he knows the disease so well he will know the cure also.

Prayer: Lord forgive me of my hypocrisy. For Jesus' sake, Amen.

April 30

For "he that is spiritual judgeth all things" [1 Cor. 2:15]. For in order to make them confess what is discovered by the principles of spiritual medicine, there is need of another than a man, however expert. For man looks on the outward appearance, and God alone on the heart [1 Sam. 16:7]. Unless He excites shame in the human heart, so that it ceases to deny that of which it is conscious, and unless He so humbles it that it recognizes its eagerness for glory, it will never confess that it is such as it really is. For no one tries to descend into his secret self, no one. We come again, therefore, to the conclusion that man has as much need of God for the knowledge of himself as for the recognition of God. For no man "knows the things of a man, save the spirit of the man, which is in him" [1 Cor. 2:11], as was made plain above. But now I turn to tests by which to wrest from man the admission that he has in him what I assert is in him. I ask, therefore, first: "O you who art justified by your works, is almsgiving a good work or not?" The self-righteous answers, "It is." "In whatever way and manner it is done?" The self-righteous: "Not at all, but only when a man does as is in him" (for that is the way these people talk). "Tell me, please, what you understand by the expression 'as is in him'."

Prayer: I pray this day not for myself, but for all those who are my brothers and sisters, dear Father. I am mindful of their needs and I ask you that you use me to minster to them. Thank you, in Christ's name, Amen.

May 1

The self-righteous: "According to his powers." I answer that we beg the question in this way. For whatever the amount given and on whatever account, a man always does as is in him and always does according to his ability. Therefore all almsgiving will be a good work which will justify us. The self-righteous: "Yes." "If I give to be seen of men [*cf.* Mt. 6:1]?" The self-righteous: "I do not say that." "What, then?" The self-righteous: "I will not argue the point." There you see what this "as is in him" is. It is a figment that makes Christ quite superfluous. For in this way anybody could be justified by works done according to his powers; for anybody can do as is in him, even if in the case of many of his good deeds that be the merest trifle. But I come back to the main point. As many maladies can befall almsgiving to vitiate it as befall vineyards to destroy them. First, if the giving is not in the name of God. Those, therefore, who give only for the purpose of redeeming themselves from the punishments of hell, give in their own name, not in the name of Christ. Second, if people give with ostentation, that they may obtain glory among men, they have received their reward, Matt. 6:2. Furthermore, if they give grudgingly and dislike to give, and would not give unless they were afraid of malicious comment, they vitiate their almsgiving; "for God loveth a cheerful giver," 2 Cor. 9:7.

Prayer: Help me this day to be a cheerful giver; a person pleased and joyful returning to you, Father, through your Church, a fragment of what you give me. In His name, Amen.

May 2

If they do not give in the measure they would want given to them if they were in need, they do not give rightly; for "all things that you would that men should do to you, do you the same to them," Matt. 7:12. Nor if they give scornfully or negligently; for "cursed be he that doeth the work of the Lord negligently," Jer. 48:10. Nor if they give because overcome by the wretchedness and misfortunes of the recipient and not from the love of God and their neighbor; for "whoso has this world's goods, and sees his brother have need, we know that the love of God is not in him," 1 John 3:17. In short, so many vices are wont to attend this quite unquestionable work, that we must not expect anyone to be able worthily to perform it. For who does not give in such fashion as to keep the greater portion for himself? Who does not give either to be seen to have given or not to be seen not to have given, etc.? How, then, shall we satisfy God's justice if so pious a work is done by none in such a way that it can be reckoned worthy of reward by an impartial and pious judge? Run through in this way all the things we do, and you will see that they are subject to as great, yes, to greater, vices. Many of us pray, that we may be seen to pray, as the hypocrites do, Matt. 6:5.

Prayer: Remind me each day to enter my closet when I pray, so as not to merely pray to be seen. Such prayer is intolerable to you and so please help it be intolerable to me. Amen.

May 3

We fast in the same way, either that our frugality may be heralded [*cf.* Mt. 6:16–18], or that our thin, pale faces may indicate sanctity; or that dainties and delicacies may be brought to us fasting; or to bring back within an old garment a belly that makes too shameless a show of itself; or to save a penny, or that we may reckon as a good work the fasting which ought to be done simply for the purpose of calling us away from the flesh to the better hearing of the voice and bidding of the Spirit. Thus, I say, we measure all things with reference to ourselves, not to Him of whom and in whom we wholly are [cf. Acts 17:28], By what sacrifices or offerings, then, shall we be justified, when in our actual works we are so feeble and cold and ineffective; and this so evidently and truly that all the faithful know in their hearts it is just as I have said? For they see that this kind of disease has come to us from Adam, the original cause of this state of death; and they not only see it in the word, but in their hearts feel it true.

Prayer: Father I seldom fast but I should so that the flesh can learn to be subject to the spirit. I seldom perform many of the acts of piety which characterized my ancestors in the faith. Help me to do so. They were better Christians than I, and perhaps that's the reason why. In His name, Amen.

May 4

Here, I say, the theologians have wandered from the straight way, as I began to say a little while ago. For, weighing the justice of God accurately, as they thought, they were forced to see that it must be satisfied, but in regard to the satisfaction they failed to reckon the works of the crowd accurately, although they set a high value upon their own. For they did not rightly know man through and through and see how he is nothing but impurity and corruption and filth, so that even what he learns in its purity he puts forth corrupted. For even when through the heavenly Spirit we reach the point of delighting in that which the law commands, then the flesh is so rebellious that we accomplish no good thing, Rom. 7:18. Hence, though the justice of God is so inviolable and holy that our impurity can do nothing towards winning it, these theologians have been unwilling to learn to despair (despair of ourselves, I mean, not of the mercy of God). And this vice also came from too high an estimate of self, for it is hard for man to condemn self and to withdraw from self to such an extent as to have no sense at all of self. And here we have a strange and shameless arrogance.

Prayer: Lord help me to be in Christ what I should always be. In Christ. In His name, Amen.

May 5

In general, therefore, they have not attained a right knowledge either of God's justice or of man's injustice, and have had such an ignorant and scornful idea of Christ that they have attributed to Him little more than did the Jews. But this is not strange. For if people in general had begun to rely on Christ—that is, on the grace of God, which is obtained and confirmed through Christ—who would any longer have paid them so much for looking after his salvation? So, not without reason are they raging today; for though they have advertised themselves as agents for securing salvation, nobody hires them, and they sit all the day idle.

Prayer: Lord, keep me from living in such a way that the Gospel isn't constantly visible. Amen.

May 6

Bᵘt enough has been said about our powerlessness and about our own desperate state of mind. Now I will pass to more cheerful themes, to the gospel, namely, in which a merciful God has not only proclaimed salvation but also sent it, after it had been long foretold and promised. Since this mystery is to be treated with the greatest reverence, the greatest humility and awe, we must prostrate ourselves before the Fount of all grace, that He may so guide, so illumine, our discourse that we shall say nothing unworthy of Him. And since by human discourse, however rich, the untaught mind cannot be persuaded in the things of faith unless the Lord so teach and draw the heart that it delights to follow, we must also appeal to Him who justifieth and who calls the things that are not as though they were [Rom. 4:17], so to illumine the minds of those to whom we would communicate His gospel that they shall be able to grasp the meaning of the gospel, so to draw and to soften their hearts that they shall be able to follow. For there is nothing that He will not grant to earnest prayer [*cf.* Mt. 21:22]; and there is nothing that we ought to venture or to undertake to do without prayer. May the Lord put right words into my mouth!

Prayer: Indeed, Father, put the right words into my mouth as well! Because, when I'm left to fill my mouth myself I only ever fill it with that which displeases you. Fill my heart with your Word so that out of its abundance my mouth will speak. Amen.

May 7

Wishing at length, then, to help this desperate case of ours, our Creator sent one to satisfy His justice by offering Himself for us—not an angel, nor a man, but His own Son, and clothed in flesh, in order that neither His majesty might deter us from intercourse with Him, nor His lowliness deprive us of hope. For, being God and the Son of God, He that was sent as deputy and mediator gives support to hope. For what cannot He do or have who is God? Moreover, being man, He promises friendship and intimacy—ayou, the common bond of relationship; what, then, can He refuse who is a brother and the sharer of our weakness? Furthermore, this thing so strange and so unprecedented was conceived and prepared from the beginning of human misery. For as God created man through His Son, so He determined through Him to restore man when he had fallen into death, that the Son might be at once his creator and his restorer. For "all things were made through him," John 1:3 and Colos. 1:16–20. "All things have been created through him, and to him; and he is before all things, and by him all things consist. And he is the head of the body, the church: who is the beginning, the firstborn from the dead; that in all things he might have the preeminence.

Prayer: Today let me honor Christ preeminently. Amen.

139

May 8

Ephes. 2:18: "Through him we both" (Jews and Gentiles) "have access in one Spirit to the Father." God, then—to go back to the beginning—took pity upon man right after his fall, and when He promulgated the decision of His just judgment He took off something from the hardness of the sentence, that man might not be in utter misery forever. For when He appointed the punishment of the serpent, He made this qualification, in the interest of man: He foretold that there should sometime be seed of the woman that should bruise the head of the real serpent, the Devil, saying: "I will put enmity between you and the woman, and between your seed and her seed: it shall bruise your head, and you shalt bruise his heel." For this is the real meaning of the Hebrew, as can easily be perceived from the two pronouns, "it" and "his," which in the Hebrew are both masculine and refer to "seed," which likewise is masculine.

Prayer: Accept my silence, Father, and speak to me.

May 9

W e see it openly foretold in these words of God that from the woman should sometime proceed the seed which should bruise the head of the serpent, *i.e.*, the Devil; and that, on the other hand, the Devil would try to hurt his heel. Let us, therefore, consider briefly both prophecies. Divine Providence preserved strict verbal propriety. Having first said, "The seed shall bruise your head," He always uses the same word, "seed." For when He said to Abraham, "In your seed shall all the tribes of the earth be blessed," Gen. 15, He used the old word for him who was to be born of Abraham according to the flesh and was to enroll all the race of men among the heirs of God. His calling him "a branch" in Jeremiah 23:5 amounts to the same thing. And Paul, speaking of the same promise, says plainly: "And to your seed, which is Christ," Gal. 3:16, bearing witness that the seed of which so much is said throughout the Old Testament is Christ. Therefore this seed, Christ, crushed the head of the Devil. But the Devil himself tried so hard to hurt His heel, *i.e.*, his humanity, from vexation that it was not subject to the fall, like ours, which is conceived in sin, that he never let an opportunity slip. When Christ had marvelously sustained a fast for forty days and nights, even in the desert, the Devil demanded that he turn the stones into bread, hoping that his teeth and throat would lure him to this. Then he tempted him through the desire for power and wealth, and finally for glory [*cf.* Mt. 4:1–11].

Prayer: Father, when temptation strikes today, let me take refuge in your word. There I'll find safety from the fiery darts of evil. Thank you for that refuge. Amen.

141

May 10

When he accomplished nothing, he armed all his forces and marched out against Him. He roused the hatred of the scribes and priests against him to such a pitch that, in the words of Paul, Rom. 1:31, they were without any human kindness, friendliness, fellow-feeling, or mercifulness towards Him. And, not satisfied with having put such a load of hatred upon Him, he determined to destroy Him utterly; for he feared for his own kingdom more and more each day, seeing His unwavering devotion to the truth in His teachings and His unfailing power in healing disease. Daily he added fuel to the fire of malice, until he drove his aforementioned minions, the scribes and priests and Pharisees, to the point of forming the plan of slaying Him in any possible way. Christ was by no means unaware of this and often reproached them for their wickedness of purpose. And in the very tumult at the time of His arrest He proclaimed the wiles of the Serpent and the malignity and hatred of the priests, saying [Lk. 22:53]: "This is your hour, and the power of darkness." The Devil laid a trap for Him even when dead, demanding through his minions that the tomb be watched [Mt. 27:64–66].

Prayer: Father, I am once more amazed at your love for us in sending your Son. It remains incomprehensible. It's love incomprehensible. Thank you. Amen.

May 11

W e must, further, consider all the things done by the two Adams, that is, our parent in the flesh and Christ (for so Paul calls them both, Rom. 5:12 and 1 Cor. 15:22), that it may become clearly apparent how Christ by means of the proper antidotes restored man by satisfying the divine justice. I will compare the two in certain respects, as far as the Lord will give it me to do. Adam was placed in a garden of delights, and then because of transgressions was thrust out of his happy abode into a wild country, with which he had to struggle with spade and hoe and plough. Christ did not arrogate too much to Himself when He made Himself equal with the Father [Phil. 2:6–8], but coming down from heaven He deigned to take on our form, and in it to break with His word, as with a rod of iron, Ps. 2:9, them that were nothing but rebellious clay and flesh, that we, who through Adam were in an exile merited by his sin and our own, might through Him return to the place whence He came. The first Adam wished by knowing good and evil to become God; the second Adam deigned to put on the form and habit of ignorant man, in order to bring him back into the knowledge and favor of Him who alone is good and alone knows what good and evil are. Adam was prevailed upon by the blandishments of his wife to eat of the forbidden fruit.

Prayer: Father, I own my sins myself and am responsible for my choices. Father, help me to understand this. And help me to stop blaming others for my choices. In His name, Amen.

May 12

In Christ human weakness sometimes resisted, not knowing how to suffer, but it always came off worsted. "Let this cup pass from me!" [Mt. 26:39] cried infirmity, but the divine in Him conquered and subdued the unwilling flesh to the will of the Father. Adam stretched out his hand towards the forbidden tree, expecting to become happy and wise, Yes God. Christ stretched out all His limbs upon the ignominious cross, that we might be made happy through His sorrows, wise through His foolishness ("for the preaching of the cross is to them that perish foolishness," 1 Cor. 1:18), gods through His poverty. The author of death reached forth his hand to the deadly fruit; the author of life reached forth His hand to the saving wood of the cross. The sweetness tasted by the one brought death; the bitterness tasted by the other brought life. The one fled in the hope of hiding himself, for he was afraid to come into the sight of God. The other displayed Himself to the whole world, and submitted to the judgment and the violence of the vilest, in order to recover the lost heritage. He suffered Himself to seem a malefactor in all men's eyes, that through Him we might appear justified to the Father.

Prayer: That you would deem me worthy of being called your own is the most miraculous of all things, Father. And for it I thank you this day. Amen.

May 13

Through a tree we were bound over to slavery, because Adam was not willing to stay his hand; through a tree we were given to liberty, because Christ was willing to suffer anything rather than permit our ruin. For one of the ancient writers says: "He marked the tree at that time as the thing to do away with the damage of the tree"; showing that God at the very moment of death's origin had in view the healing by means of a tree of the disease resulting from a tree. God laughed at the transgression of Adam, and clothed him and his wife with the skins of brutes. Christ's obedience turned us from brutes into sons of God, and enwrapped us in a mantle of blessed immortality. So far are we from being scorned in the sight of God that we have even been made His heirs, and joint-heirs with Christ [Rom. 8:17]. In short, the recklessness of our first parent closed the gates of paradise; the humility of Christ opened the door of heaven. I pass over St. Paul's comparisons in Rom. 5:15–21, which all aim to make us see how our ills have been healed by corresponding remedies, and how the divine justice has been appeased for us by the righteousness of Christ alone. For His innocence, given to us, has become as much ours as the life which also we derived from Him. For "in him was life," John 1:4.

Prayer: Lord, life comes from you, and so, you have the right to determine how it's lived. Help me live my life today as you see it should be lived. Thank you, Amen.

May 14

He is "the way, the truth, and the life," John 14:6, and "in him we live, and move, and have our being," Acts 17:28. As life, I say, was given to us from Him, so also was righteousness, which has been made ours from Him and through Him; for from Him we are all that we are. He put on flesh that He might become ours. He had no need of it, but we had the greatest need of Him. To become one of us, therefore, He, great God that He is, just, holy, merciful, Creator, became man, that we through His fellowship might be raised to gods.

Prayer: You made me to be so much more than I am. In Christ, this day, help me to live up to your expectations of me. In His name, Amen.

May 15

There are also countless other prophecies in the Old Testament which so perfectly set forth His coming, career, death, and in fact His whole life and activity, that no one can deny that He is thus foreshadowed in the Scriptures, His whole activity and teaching correspond so completely with them. But since these prophecies are familiar to all, such as Isa. 11:1–2; Jer. 23:5–6, I will refrain from citing them here and content myself with citing a few figures or types. Jacob went into Mesopotamia [Gen. 28ff], and found there two wives, the elder of whom was dull-eyed, the younger of glad and beautiful countenance [Gen. 29:17]. The elder bore many children, while the younger was persistently barren. By and by the misfortune of her barrenness was changed, and the younger also began to be a mother. What could this presage but that which we see fulfilled in Christ and the Church? The synagogue of the Jews was for a long time fruitful before Christ was clothed with flesh; but after the time foreordained of God was fulfilled, the synagogue became barren and the young church of the Gentiles became fruitful. Jacob returned from Mesopotamia [Gen. 31ff], taking with him much substance, two wives, many children.

Prayer: Father remind me each day that the Jews are my brothers in the family of Abraham. Guide us all into a heart of love and mercy for your people and help us live in a way that pleases you and brings honor to your entire family. Amen.

May 16

Why should I speak of the selling of Joseph into Egypt? He is such a shining example among the clearest foreshadowings that he needs no painter's brush. And why speak of his great-grandfather, Abraham, whose faith is so proclaimed by God [Gen. 22:16–18] that he is easily seen to be happier than any Alexander or Achilles? For who ever had God as herald? Why, I say, should I speak of his rearing a son by his free wife when he was a hundred Years old, seeing that Paul in writing to the Galatians, 3 and 4, paints him as prototype in such lights and shadows that you can fairly touch him? Perez and Zerah, born of Tamar [Gen. 38:12–28], intimated the same thing. It would be tedious to enumerate all the prefigurations, since Paul says that all things happened to them by way of example, 1 Cor. 10:6.

Prayer: Lord help me to be a good example and not a bad one. A positive influence and not a negative one. A person who reflects your glory and not the world's wickedness. Amen.

May 17

He, then, through whom we were all created [1 Cor. 8:6], and through whom it pleased God to recreate and renew the world, was, when the time seemed to Him ripe, conceived in the womb of a spotless virgin without any male aid, by the fructification of the Holy Spirit (for He who was to be born thence was sent to make spiritual beings out of fleshly), and began His human life. Read Luke Chaps. 1 and 2, and Matthew 1, and John 1, that I may not have to busy myself here with such well-known facts. Christ had to be born of a virgin on two accounts: first, because His divine nature could not suffer that any stain of sin attach to it, as has been said above. For God is so thoroughly light, purity, innocence, goodness, that He cannot endure any thing that is in any respect dark, impure, denied, or evil. Therefore the birth had to be absolutely pure of every stain, because He that was born was also God. Second, on account of the nature of the sacrificial victim. For that had to be free from all blemish, as the law of Moses required, though that applied only to purity of flesh, Heb. 9:9. How much more had that victim to be absolutely spotless which made atonement for the sins not only of all who had been, but of all who were then to come! And this could not have been unless He had been born of a virgin, and without male intervention. For if the virgin had conceived from the seed of a man, would not the birth have been thereby polluted?

Prayer: Empower me today to be free of pollution and wickedness. Amen.

May 18

And if a woman who had before known a man had conceived Him, even from the Holy Spirit, who would ever have believed that the child that was born was of the Holy Spirit? For nature knows no birth that is not besmirched with stain. For, "Behold, I was shapen in iniquity; and in sin did my mother conceive me," Ps. 51:5. Virgin, therefore, she had to be, and ever virgin, too, who should bear Him in whom there could be not even the least suspicion of a blemish, much less any real blemish. Now I add evidence of these things. Of this figure I shall say nothing more, since it is perfectly clear in itself and through the notices of all who have spoken of it. Furthermore, the John who baptized the Son of God, as soon as he saw Christ coming towards him, pointed Him out to his disciples with the words: "Behold, the Lamb of God that taketh away the sin of the world!" John 1:29.

Prayer: Thank you for taking away the sin of the world. Please, take the inclination to sin out of my heart. Amen.

May 19

He taketh away, therefore, the sins of the world (for sin is used here for "offence and defect of mankind")—not the original defect only, as false religion teaches, does He atone for, nor the sins of those only who were before Him, but of the world; and not those only which the Popes direct are to be remitted by their crowd of priests, but of the world; and He takes away not only those sins which you redeem with money, but the sins of the world independently of any bargain. The sin against the Holy Ghost requires especial consideration, and I shall not go into it here. That He was born of a virgin, Matthew and Luke bear witness, as I have shown; but, lest one miss Old Testament proofs, we have Isa. 7:14 and Ezek. 44:2.

Prayer: Thank you for sending your son, conceived in sinlessness so that he might bear my sins away. For the gift of forgiveness I simply cannot thank you enough. But I'll try to each day. Amen.

May 20

What is there to wonder at, pray, if a virgin conceives? Did any woman ever conceive who had not once been a virgin, quite apart from our virgin? But the uncommon thing is that she who conceives and bears should remain a virgin. Our virgin, then, remains a virgin, and remaining a virgin is ever virgin; otherwise she would not remain a virgin. And this Ezekiel finely indicates, saying [44:2]: "This gate shall be shut; it shall not be opened, neither shall any man enter in by it; because the Lord, the God of Israel, has entered in by it, therefore it shall be shut for the prince." The objections that could be raised here as to the meaning because of the circumstances can be so easily removed that one aiming at brevity must not delay over them; for "all things happened to them by way of example, etc." False religion slips up, therefore, when she snarls out that the perpetual virginity does not hold unless it be confirmed by the decrees of the Popes. For, as they cannot by their decrees make her that is defiled undefiled, so they could not with these suspicious dicta of theirs remedy the Virgin's reproach by decreeing that she is ever virgin. For unless she were virgin in her own quality, they could not make her virgin by their decrees. Her virginity is based on the fact, not on the decrees of men.

Prayer: Lord, I admire Mary, but not as much as others do. Perhaps I'm wrong. If I am, forgive me. But if they are, forgive them. Amen.

May 21

The ever virgin, then, brought forth Christ, God's Son and hers, while on a journey to Bethlehem, according to the predictions of the prophets, Mic. 5:2, Matt. 2:6, Luke 2:7, and laid her babe in a manger, because there was no room in the inn on account of the crowd of people who had then gathered there to be taxed. Thus Divine Providence ordained that as Adam by sinning had made himself naked and exposed himself to need, so Christ, that the divine justice might be appeased, should experience want, cold, and all the ills that had been brought upon man for his sin. For this was required by justice, that He through whom we were all created, in whom there is no sin, and from whom we had gone astray, should, though innocent, bear what we had deserved through sinning, but bear it for us. For "he did no sin, neither was guile found in his mouth" [1 Pet. 2:22].

Prayer: Dearest Lord, forgive me for daily adding to the ocean of sin. Help me to stop. Help us all to stop. Amen.

May 22

For He is the true shepherd, who ever watcheth over His flock. He is circumcised on the eighth day, though unless circumcision had looked forward to Him it would have profited nothing. And He is given a name which is above every name [Phil. 2:9], and which fully signifies just what Christ is. For He is the Savior, and is called Jesus [Lk. 2:21] for the very reason that He is nothing else than Savior, for He saves the people from their sins. He grows in Years and knowledge [Lk. 2:52], that we may recognize His true humanity. He is accepted by Simeon and Hannah [Lk. 2:25–38] and is proclaimed to be the light of salvation to all nations, that His divinity also may be seen. At twelve Years of age, to the same end he sits in the midst of the doctors, talks with them, vanquishes and confutes them [Lk. 2:42–47]. And straightway, that we may not doubt His true humanity, He goes down with His mother and foster father to Nazareth and is subject to them [Lk. 2:51]. And He is so entirely subject that, following the trade of his foster father, He at length wins for Himself so famous a name in it that men say [Mk. 6:3]: "Is not this the carpenter?"

Prayer: Jesus, I'm glad you learned the trade of carpentry—it lets me know that you are qualified to build my life. Build away. Build daily. Amen.

May 23

Now He feeds hungry crowds on a few loaves [Mk. 6:34–44]; again, He gives as drink water turned into wine [Jn. 2:1–11], cleanses leprosy, drives away disease, quenches fever; endows the blind with sight, the lame with power to walk, the palsied with movement; straightens the crooked, restores the dead to life with a word [Mt. 11:4–6]; and there are no ills at all of body or mind so deep-set that He does not take them away. But when He boldly uncovers the deceits and schemes of the hypocrites, then wickedness, which like an owl cannot endure coming into the light, resists, as is its nature, and finds a way to save its reputation though at the loss of its soul. They determine, therefore, to slay Christ the innocent Son of God and the Virgin, caring nothing how much hurt they did their consciences, provided they could make the simple believe that they were just persons, and that Christ was the wicked one, in that He had unjustly heaped abuse upon the just. And since the power of trial had been taken from them, they found a way of bringing accusation against Him before the governor. But, lest something should intervene to prevent His being taken, or He should escape when taken, they made it their business to take Him themselves, thinking His destruction more certain if they brought Him in person than if they made information against Him in His absence.

Prayer: Lord of Heaven, your Son's willingness to sacrifice himself to save us is wonderful beyond words. I can't imagine doing it. Not for anyone other than my immediate family. Help me to be more like Christ. Amen.

May 24

H aving, therefore, taken Him they brought Him before the governor, and accused Him of lese majesté, declaring that He had forbidden the giving of tribute to Cæsar [Lk. 23:2]. And in order to arouse the enmity of the rabble also against Him, they suborned false witnesses to allege that He had said He had power to destroy the Temple and to build it up again in three days [Mt. 26:60f.]. In this way they hoped that, even if they found the magistrate pretty firm, His death could, nevertheless, be accomplished through the uproar and shoutings of the degraded rabble. And this is what happened. For the magistrate, as he repeatedly confessed, found no cause of condemnation in Him [Lk. 23:4, 14, 22], though he made many attempts; then, not daring to acquit Him, gave Him over to the madness of His accusers. Therefore did wickedness maltreat innocence, iniquity righteousness, the limbs of Satan God, traitors the champion of peace, ingratitude its benefactor, murderers the incarnation of life, parricides their deliverer; and did so spit upon, bruise, and buffet Him, so tear Him with thorns and scourges from the top of His head to the soles of His feet, and so utterly trample upon Him, that pitying children and women could not restrain their tears at His woe [Lk. 23:27]. But He, no way crushed by these ills, no way angered, then warned His murderers of the ills they were calling down upon themselves by a wrong so atrocious.

Prayer: Lord your Son's death ... Amen.

May 25

They, therefore, inflicted the most ignoble punishment upon Him, nailing to the cross along with murderers [Mt. 27:38] Him through whom they had life, and against whom they could have done nothing unless through Him they had received the breath of life. Never untrue to Himself when thus miserably exposed to the elements, the stars, and the derision of man, He prayed for His enemies [Lk. 23:34] that the Heavenly Father would not lay this madness to their charge; for such was their barbarity that when He thirsted amid His tortures they gave Him vinegar mixed with gall to drink [Mt. 27:34]. And when He saw that the things committed to Him by the Father were accomplished, He gave a sign, saying, "It is finished" [John 19:30]—His own work, namely, by which through His own innocence He had removed from us the claims of the Devil and of death over us. His task performed, as He was about to give up the ghost, He commended Himself to the Father thus [Lk. 23:46]: "Into your hands I commend my spirit." With these words He expired. Then suddenly all things begin to be troubled on account of the wrong to their Maker. The sun hides its brightness, that it may be apparent to the cruel murderers, as in an uprising by night, how atrocious the deed was.

Prayer: Father, give me the chance to share your love with someone today. In fact, give me a chance to share your love with everyone I meet today. And every day. But especially today. Amen.

May 26

The dead creep forth from their tombs at the commotion [Mt. 27:51–53; Lk. 23:45]. But the hearts of the impious hypocrites are unmoved. They go to the magistrate, ask him to station a watch to keep guard over the dead body, obtain their request [Mt. 27:64–66]. When the third dawn was breaking, in spite of the soldiers He came to life again through the glory of the Father. When they saw what had happened, they reported it to the priests. Bribed by them for a large sum to lie, they agreed to spread the report that the disciples had secretly taken away the body while they were asleep [Mt. 27:11–15]. Such is the course of insane madness; and hatred, ever blind, refuses to yield to the truth, and fancies that it hides itself well; nay, when it has become very deeply rooted, it has no shame, nor cares whether it is seen or not. This Solomon taught finely in Proverbs 18:3, saying: "The wicked man, when he is come into the depth of sins, contemneth." But Christ, after His triumphant return from the dead, immediately showed Himself to His disciples and, having had intercourse with them for forty days, ascended of His own motion to the Father in sight of the disciples [Acts 1:3]. All this I have briefly narrated the more willingly, in order to make clearer to every beholder the righteousness of Christ by which He healed the wound of Adam.

Prayer: The wound of Adam, sin, is cured only by you, Father. Keep me from the folly of believing that I have any part in it but am purely and simply a recipient of your kindness.

May 27

For we are still dealing with the point that Christ is our righteousness, our innocence, and the price of our redemption. For to this end He died for us and rose again, that He might declare the mystery of our deliverance and confirm the hopes which, when men saw that He had died and afterwards by His own power had become alive again, could not but be made sure in regard to life everlasting after this life. For "in that he died, he died to sin," Rom. 6:10; but not to His sin, for He was absolutely free from sin, but to ours. And He rose again in order that we may know that we have been made alive through Him.

Prayer: Alive in Him and through Him forever more. Father, there's no greater honor.   And no greater gift. Thank you.   Amen.

May 28

S in is taken in a twofold sense in the Gospel teachings: First, for that disease which we contract from the author of our race, in consequence of which we are given over to love of ourselves. Of this I spoke to the best of my ability when considering man. It is this disease that Paul has in mind when he says, Rom. 7:20: "It is no more I that do it, but sin which dwelleth in me." This sin, therefore, *i.e.*, this defect, is the disease native to us in consequence of which we shun things hard and burdensome and pursue things pleasant and agreeable. In the second place, sin is taken for that which is contrary to the Law, as through the Law comes knowledge of sin, Rom. 7:7. Any course of action, therefore, which is contrary to the Law is called sin. Let us see, then, how they are related to each other, the sin that is disease and the sin that is transgression of the Law. The disease does not know that it is disease, and thinks it has a right to do whatever it likes. God does not think so, but when the disease tries to get everything for itself and thinks all things bound to serve it and to minister to its greed, He prunes this luxuriant growth with the sickle of the Law. For the Law "was added because of transgressions," Gal. 3:19.

Prayer: Sin is such a problem for us, Lord. It's only cure is found with you. Nothing else can make us whiter than snow; there's no other place to find the new birth outside of you. Remind me today to tell others that. Amen.

May 29

For the Searcher of hearts is aware that the nature of all is the same, and that Thersites has just as much self-love as Agamemnon. Now if all were alike given loose reins, the only consequence would be that every man would subject everything to himself, according to the measure of his strength; whence a harvest of robbery, plundering, murder, parricide, and all that kind of enemy to human association would spring up. He therefore confines this far-reaching greed within fixed limits, and commands us not to do to others what we do not want done to us, and, conversely, to do to others what we want done to ourselves [Mt. 7:12]. And that we may do it more readily and recognize the wisdom of God, He sweetens this law of nature, as it is called, with the seasoning of love, saying: "You shalt love your neighbor as yourself" [Mt. 22:39]. Love is a sweet thing, but it takes even the most bitter things cheerfully, for nothing is hard to him that loveth.

Prayer: Nothing is hard to the one who loves! What a revolutionary truth. Help me love more so that I may struggle less. Amen.

May 30

The flesh, or the old Adam, I say, rebels, scorning everything but itself; for it would rather that all things should serve its own lust to their own destruction than put any limit to its greed and its passion for glory and pleasure. Hence anger against the Law and the Lawgiver, hatred and machinations—hatred, because it cannot avoid or escape the Law or the Lawgiver, for if it ascendeth into heaven, He is there, if it descendeth into hell, He is there [cf. Ps. 139:8]; machinations, because it struggles with all its might to deceive Him who then cannot be deceived; it ponders, devises, schemes, hustles about, and after many attempts comes to this conclusion: "He is a tyrant who demands these things, for how is it possible for anyone to love another as much as himself? Nevertheless, since He makes such severe demands, His vengeance must be guarded against.

Prayer: Dearest Father, let me see today how dreadful a tyrant sin is and how much it wishes to destroy everything it touches. Guard me from it. Please. In your Son's name, Amen.

May 31

T hus was the Law no more listened to, nor men's ways modeled upon it, nor the things that cause dishonor put away, but man became a god to himself; for though the Law might slay, then man none the less made himself alive in his wiles and hopes. Hence impiety gradually increased to such an extent that it said in its heart: "There is no God" [Ps. 14:1]; though by disguising its face it was openly posing as piety itself. I have spoken thus at rather great length that we might see how the sin that is transgression is born of the sin that is disease. The next thing is to show how we have been made free from the Law and from sin.

Prayer: Father, freedom from sin is not the same as being free of sin. Help me strive for the latter. Help me be as free of sin as I am in possession of freedom from sin. In Christ's name, Amen.

June 1

We have not been made free from the Law in the sense of not being bound to do what the Law bids; for the Law is the unchangeable will of God. For not one tittle of the Law shall fail, Luke 16:17. How then are we through Christ dead to the Law, so that we are subject to something other than the Law, as Paul taught by the analogy of the wife in Rom. 7:1–4? This is the way we have been made free: He that loves does all things freely, even the hardest. God, therefore, has put into our hearts a fire by which to kindle love of Him in place of love of ourselves; and He desires this fire to burn, Luke 12:49. The Baptist had promised this fire, and so had Christ Himself as He was going to heaven, Acts 1:5; which fire is love, and God is love [1 John 4:8]. If this burn in us, we shall do all things no longer from compulsion, but freely and cheerfully. For love is the completion of the law [Rom. 13:10]. For the Law was performed with repugnance and feigning, when the fire of love was not then burning; but now that that is kindled, the Law is not regarded, so far are we from fearing it; but love draws us in all things and to all things. And as we say of those who are bound by their passions that they are carried away, so those that are on fire with divine love are carried away by the spirit that burns in them.

Prayer: God, let me be consumed by the fire of your love. And give myself as a whole living sacrifice. This is the very least I can do. Amen.

June 2

W e have, therefore, one kind of freedom from the Law, that through which we do for love that which we know will please God. For Paul teaches in Rom. 12:2 that this is acceptable to God. A second kind of freedom from the Law is that the Law cannot condemn any more, which then before wrought the wrath and indignation and just vengeance of God, Rom. 4:15 and Gal. 3:10; and Deut. 27:26, where divine justice sternly thunders: "Cursed is everyone who continueth not in all things that are written in the book of the law, to do them." Christ, therefore, "redeemed us from this curse of the law, being made a curse for us," that is, being nailed to the cross for us, Gal. 3:13 and Rom. 6:10. We are no longer under the Law but under grace; and if under grace, the Law cannot condemn us, for if the Law still has the power to condemn, we are not under grace. It is, therefore, Christ who has broken the wrath of the Law (that is, who has appeased God's justice, which would have caused Him deservedly to rage against us), and who by bearing the cruelty of the cross for us has so softened it that He has chosen to make us not only free instead of slaves, but even sons. And if we are sons, as we surely are, Rom. 8:14 and Gal. 4:6, we are above the Law.

Prayer: Today, indeed, this week, Father, is a week of silence. I sit today and the rest of this week simply in your presence. The year is half done. I have spoken more than I have listened. I ask your grace to remedy that fact this week. In your Son's name, Amen.

165

June 3

"For if the Son has made us free, we are free indeed and free-born," John 8:36. We are, therefore, freed from the Law, now that love has been substituted for the fear of the Law. For since God so loved us that He gave His Son for us, has He not above all kindled a responsive love? For one might, perhaps, undergo death for a righteous friend; but God, when we were His enemies, sent His Son to free us and to make us joint heirs with Him [cf. Rom. 5:7–10]. Again, we are freed from the vengeance of the Law; for Christ has paid by His suffering that penalty which we owed for our sins. Indeed, we have been so completely freed from sin, as far as it is a disease, that it is no longer able to harm us if we trust in Christ. For "there is no condemnation to them that are in Christ Jesus, who walk not after the flesh" [Rom. 8:1]. And in so far as it is transgression, we have been freed from harm from it in the same way as from the wrath of the Law, Rom. 8:2: "For the law of the Spirit of life in Christ Jesus made me free from the law of sin and of death." For when we say, "The Law condemns," we are simply saying, "The sin which is done contrary to the will of the Law condemns." Hence I said, we must determine about freedom from sin in the same way in which we have determined about freedom from the condemnation of the Law.

Prayer: Holy silence.

June 4

When after all this we find in our own case that the disease is still so potent that we are constantly sinning, and have said that those have absolutely no hope of salvation who have not been made new men, we are, of course, driven into the old despair. Therefore, having made the needful preparations for removing this difficulty, I will now show how we are new men, even when we still are full of the old man; that is, to speak plainly, how it happens that those who are in Christ, even though they sin, then are not condemned.

Prayer: Holy silence.

June 5

In order to do this more easily and fitly, I will treat the words of Paul in Romans 7. Paul was forced to ventilate this question when he was settling the controversy about justification by faith and justification by works. One party raised the objection, Rom. 6:1, "Shall we then continue in sin, that grace may abound?" His answer to this objection he does not set forth until the eighth chapter, and I refer the diligent reader to that chapter. I shall begin with the words that seem best adapted to clearing up our problem. Paul asks, then, Rom. 7:7–8: "What shall we say then? Is the law sin? God forbid. Howbeit, I had not known sin, except through the law: for I had not known that coveting is sin" (to speak for the moment in paraphrase) "except the law had said, You shalt not covet. But sin, finding occasion, through the commandment," as with a sun-dial or a plumb line (for there is personification here), "measured out in me all manner of coveting." That is, when the Law came into sin's hands, she wanted to measure and weigh everything, and finally brought it about that I learned that all manner of human coveting is sin. For all teem with it in consequence of the disease.

Prayer: Holy silence.

June 6

But when the law, You shalt not covet, was promulgated, sin revived; not that any new change took place in me, but what I had not before known to be wicked I perceived through the Law was wicked. And as soon as I saw this, "I died." For all that I saw in me was the lust of the flesh, of the eyes, the hands, the belly, and a sort of vast pride of life. Hence nothing but despair of life could arise within me. But I must not omit to state that no one should from this death of mine accuse the Law of poisoning, so to speak, as if it killed me. The Law displayed itself to me to show me that I was dead before, but to my undoing did not understand what death or what life is; and it tried to restore me to life and innocence. But this resulted for me in death, through the fault not of the Law but of myself. For sin, being a curious but stupid evil (note the personification!), having got hold of the Law as a standard, began to measure everything. And the Law deceived me; for in great part at least I thought myself righteous, but I was mightily mistaken. Indeed, everything so teemed with sin, was so polluted and impure, that, as I said, I straightway died. For, to speak frankly, no blame for this death of mine ought to be imputed to the Law.

Prayer: Holy silence.

June 7

"The law is holy and the commandment holy, and righteous and good" [Rom. 7:12]. If you think I am now saying these things in order to defame that which is good, as if it were the cause of death to me, you are wrong. For the Law did not kill me, but at the Law's so showing I found myself dead. For [Rom. 7:13] "sin" (personification for the third time), "that it might be shown to be what it is, through the law, which is good, rendered me dead; that through the law sin" (personification again) "might make itself the greatest of sinners." That is, sin, seized with admiration of the Law, wanted to try all things by it, but only established the fact that it is itself a sinner beyond measure. This is the first part, in which we learn that we are nothing but corruption.

Prayer: Holy silence.

June 8

The second part contains the battle of the flesh and the spirit. There follows, therefore [cf. Rom. 7:14–25]: "For we know that the law is spiritual: but I," to come back to myself, whom I had begun to set before you as an illustration, "am carnal, sold under sin," like some poor, mean slave, who, like the enslaved Cappadocians, knows how to be nothing but a slave. For, that you may understand my bondage, now that I have turned to Christ I see so much of the old disease still remaining that when I begin to do anything faults immediately so assail me on all sides that there comes out a work contrary to what I desire through faith. And so it happens that "that which I do, I know not," nor approve. For what I had determined upon according to the counsel of faith, "that I do not; but, on the contrary, I rather do that which I hate." Now notice whether I accuse the Law at any point. When, as I have said, "I do that which I would not, I silently consent to the law, and bear witness to it that it is good." For I had myself determined to do what the Law bids, for the reason that it seemed to me good. When, therefore, I determine one thing according to the teachings of faith, but do a widely different thing, "it is no more I that do it, but sin that dwelleth in me," that is, the disease to which we are all subject.

Prayer: Holy silence.

June 9

"For I know that in me, that is, in my flesh, dwelleth no good thing." And think not that I mean here the flesh that we have in common with the cattle (for who does not know that there is no good thing in that?). Or what of importance would he have said who proclaimed that no good is in it? That would be too frivolous a remark for apostolic seriousness. I am speaking of the whole man, who is nothing but flesh if left to himself (as God Himself said in Genesis 6:3), and neither meditates nor determines aught that is not evil. Then if the Spirit of God comes to him to illumine him, so that man knows himself and God, the man pulls in his direction, promising nothing but pleasures, and the Spirit pulls in its direction, promising troubles but finally eternal bliss. Hence a contest arises. While I give ear to the Spirit, I excite the soul to pious living; again, when I listen to the flesh, that is sluggish and refuses to follow. Thus it happens that the will is present with me, but when I am to carry out the thing all my members are so slothful that I do nothing. "For the good that I would, I do not: but the evil which I would not, that I do" [Rom. 7:19].

Prayer: Holy silence.

June 10

When, therefore, what I would not (in so far as I obey the Spirit), that I then do, it is no more I that do it, but that violent disease of sin which dwelleth in me. I find, then, a law, that, when I would do good, evil at the same time clings very tightly to me. For I feel no little delight in the inward man—that is, the man that gives ear to the Spirit—when I hear the law of God and begin to regulate myself by it; but at once I see another law in my members, warring against the law of my mind when that would obey the Spirit, and bringing me, whether it be law or force, into captivity to the law of sin which is in my members. I am speaking to you of deep and serious matters, but in simple language, though I do my best to season it so that it will slip down successfully. I mean just this, that when with the inward man, taught by God, I consent to the law of God and begin to fashion myself according to it, the force of the old man suddenly springs up and drags me in another direction, so that I abandon my determination and desert to the camp of the flesh. I am so torn asunder, so fluctuating, so neither crow nor dove, that I am beyond measure disgusted with myself. For when my heart is given to God and I would only cling to Him and do what is pleasing to Him, straightway the violence of the flesh seizes me, like a fierce whirlwind, and throws me captive into the fetters of sin.

Prayer: Father, I experience a constant discontent—not with life or others or you, but with myself. Pressing forward is all I wish to do, so please aid me by your grace to be daily ever more like your Son. In his name, Amen.

June 11

Then do I utter without ceasing such groanings as these: "O wretched man that I am, who through the grace of God recognize what is true and right, but when I try to follow it am dragged elsewhere by this unclean way, or rather impotence and death, of the flesh! What God will grant me deliverance from this body, which should more properly be called death than body?" Thus far, dear brethren, I have been showing the discordance between the Law and the old man, and, rising from the Law and the old man to the old man and the new, I have made of one man two, the inward who obeys the Spirit and the old who never varies from his own law, that is, from self-love and self-estem. Between these you will ever find war. "For the flesh lusteth against the Spirit, and the Spirit against the flesh" [Gal. 5:17]. Hence continual battles. Sometimes the flesh wins; and though it does not rout all the forces of the Spirit, it then brings it about that we do not what we would. As a result, though nothing may happen to him from external things, the life of a Christian is then a continual battle.

Prayer: Father I am ill equipped for victory, which makes it even more meaningful that you have already defeated the foe and won the war. Thank you for being the Prince of Peace. Amen.

June 12

A nd this so often saddens and troubles me and disturbs my pious vows, that, as I have just said, I frequently cry out in impatience and on the brink of despair: "O wretched me I who will free me from this misery?" But now, in the third place, that you may have the whole matter, I will show you what conclusion comforts me in such straits. Know, therefore, that when I have battled and sweated long and much within myself in this fashion, nothing inspires me with a more grateful sense of relief than the remembrance of Christ. Laying hold on Him, I, who was very near shipwreck, joyfully make land. For I say to myself: "The God who gave His Son for you can refuse nothing, and knows your weakness [cf. Rom. 8:32]. Since, when you were once much farther away from Him, in fact His enemy, He took you back into favor, much more will He save you now that His Son has come to life again," Rom. 5:21. Then my fevers and fears begin to abate, and my soul to be at rest and my whole being to revive. And when this takes place I gird myself for the thanksgiving I would make to God, my Father, through Christ Jesus our Lord [cf. Rom. 7:25].

Prayer: Father, you are the lighthouse along the rocky and dangerous coasts of our lives. Thank you. Always. Amen.

June 13

But there are further battles—and this I mention that you may not in security and carelessness after one or two battles fall unawares into danger—and after these still others, so that the life of a Christian seems to me just like a ship that is tossed hither and thither by a great storm, which the sailors now steer for a little with the rudder, and now are compelled to let run before the fierce gale. And this I, if any man, have experienced in myself; for, in spite of what I am, I find myself serving sometimes God and sometimes the flesh. My heart persists in meditating upon those deeds which the Law of God commands; it loves God, trusts in His mercy, is eager to please Him in all things. And the flesh persists, nor changes its nature any more than does a fox or a wolf. It at last makes me sin against my will, though my heart be unwaveringly fixed upon God in unchanging hope. And I doubt not that, as what can happen to anyone can happen to everyone, your experience is the same as mine. For as no one is exempt from this disease, so, of course, none is exempt from the battle. In this matter, therefore, the sacred anchor, as it were, to which we must hold fast is in spite of everything by no means to let ourselves fall from the hope and glory of the sons and heirs of God.

Prayer: As I struggle against myself, my lower inclinations, my propensity to indulge the flesh, keep me, Father, pure. For Christ's sake. Amen.

June 14

If we hold fast firmly to this [cf. Rom. 8:1–11]—to put the finishing touch to this problem—no condemnation can touch us; but only on condition that we walk after the Spirit and not after the flesh. But, that you may understand what it is to walk after the Spirit, as far as that is granted to us while we sojourn in this world, note this: The Spirit of life in Christ, which by contrast may be called the law of the Spirit if one pleases, through which I feel in my inmost heart that I am free through Him from the just vengeance of God and made His co-heir, that Spirit, I say, has made me free from the law—*i.e.*, from the power and necessity of sin and of death. For when on account of the weakness of the flesh we could not be saved through the works of the Law, God sent His Son, clothed in flesh like to our diseased flesh in every respect except the disease; and He condemned the disease which daily called out so many sins in us; and He condemned it with His own flesh, that is, by Himself enduring death for us according to human weakness, that the righteousness of the law, which no man could fulfill, might through His help be fulfilled in us. For all that He did or bore He bore for us. Hence, also, His righteousness is our righteousness, if only we walk not after the flesh, but after the Spirit.

Prayer: All that now needs to be said, Lord, is, help me do it. Help me walk after the Spirit and not after the flesh. Trying on my own has never worked out. Amen.

June 15

The citadel must be stoutly defended, that we may not surrender ourselves wholly to the desires of the flesh. Even though we understand that, against the will of the Spirit, we are frequently drawn by it into sinning, then we must ever deny its sway, and ever open our eyes again, even though we have been blinded by the mists of the flesh seven times in the day, and ever look afresh to the Law, *i.e.*, the will of God, and struggle anew for blamelessness. We must, therefore, be on our guard vigorously against scorning the desires of the Spirit and following the flesh; for the desires and counsel of the flesh bring speedy death, whereas the counsel of the Spirit brings forth life and peace. The desires and thoughts of the flesh are enmity against God; for it in no wise obeys the law of God, nor can it be made to obey. Hence you can easily see what it is to live carnally and what spiritually. To live carnally is to be wholly given over to the sway of the flesh and to be averse to the Spirit; to live spiritually is to obey the Spirit, never to abandon faith, even though the flesh sometimes is not free from the infection of sin.

Prayer: Dearest Lord help me each day to be sensitive to the guidance of your Spirit. Amen.

June 16

Now if any man have not the Spirit of Christ, he is none of His. But when Christ is in you (to speak with perfect clearness), the body is dead because of the disorder of sin; but the Spirit is life because of righteousness, not yours but His who has been made your righteousness. Such is the Christian that with respect to the body he is ever dead; but when his heart clings to God, with respect to the Spirit he is ever living. By these words of the Apostle I think the very perplexing problem with which we are struggling is cleared up, namely, how it happens that a blamelessness is demanded which we cannot possibly offer, and then Christ is the efficient guarantee for the sins of all; because the two propositions cannot stand together, that salvation must be won by blamelessness, and that all things are condoned to the righteousness of Christ for the very reason that we cannot attain salvation of our own effort.

Prayer: Lord what I fear more than anything, I confess, is to be unright with you. Being at odds with people is bad enough; but being at odds with you is downright horrifying. Keep me ever at your side. Amen.

June 17

And although I have overcome the objection which I mentioned above, then, that certain uneducated persons may feel entirely satisfied, I will answer it again. It was objected that this magnifying of grace through Christ makes those who are called Christians frivolous and dissipated. I answer, therefore: Those who trust in Christ become new men. How? Do they lay aside their original body and take on a new body? By no means; the original body remains. Does, therefore, the disease that we have inherited also remain? Yes. What is it, then, that is renewed in us? The heart. How? In this way: Before-time it knew not God, and where there is no knowledge of God, there is nothing but flesh, sin, self-esteem; but after God is known, man sees himself within to the core, and repudiates himself thus known. As a result, he sees that all his works, even those which he had always thought were good, are of no value. When, therefore, through the enlightenment of heavenly grace the heart comes to know God, the man is made new. For he who before trusted in his own wisdom, in works or resources or strength, now puts his hope in God alone.

Prayer: Father, my only hope is you. Our only hope is you. Amen.

June 18

He who before turned all his thoughts towards securing his own interests without regard to virtue or God now devotes himself only to retaining nothing of his original habit, and to so fashioning himself according to God's will as never to offend Him. And as the body is ever bringing forth dead works, our new man is also ever bewailing this unhappy and disastrous condition: Alas! kind God, what am I but an inexhaustible sink of iniquity? I sin again and again and make no end. When wilt You set my wretched self free from this mire in which I am caught? See in passing whether the Christian life is continual repentance or not. And this despair, what is it but death? Then when in these circumstances the heart through the Spirit of God refuses to give up hope, does not the conscious self, which had just before collapsed, now revive? This, then, is the Christian life: when the hope in God through Christ never wavers, even though man through the weakness of the flesh is not without sin, then comes out victorious because he does not surrender himself to it, but as often as he falls always rises again, sure that He who said to Peter that one must be forgiven seventy times seven times [Mt. 18:22] will Himself grant the full measure of pardon that He taught.

*Prayer:	It's a fortunate truth that you forgive the repentant. And we are repentant because of your grace. In your Son's name, Amen.*

June 19

W e see, to use an illustration, that something not unlike this occurs in the grafting of trees. The husbandman digs up a wild pear, and transplants it to rich, cultivated ground. As soon as the stranger tree has taken root in the new soil, its top is cut off, and shoots of cultivated trees are grafted upon it, which then grow along with the trunk. But see what different fruit they put forth! The superior graftings bud, and render the farmer branches loaded with pears in due season. But the trunk arms itself with thorns and with rough shoots, which if not pruned away venture to produce fruit of their own; and the more you suffer them to grow, the more strength is taken from the true cultivated graft. We men are wild pears (for I do not wish, after the fashion of Paul, Rom. 11:17–24, to talk of the olive, a tree unknown to the Germans and nearly so to the French), and when we are imbued with the heavenly teachings we are planted in new earth. For he that would follow Christ must deny himself [cf. Lk. 9:23] and listen only to what He orders or suggests. And what is this but being transferred from the forest to the rich soil of a garden, transplanted from the earth to heaven?

Prayer: Plant me daily, but especially this day, in the rich soil next to the river of the Spirit, Lord. Amen.

June 20

But see what great and hard things must be done here, or we essay this planting in vain. The top must be cut off, *i.e.*, our desires, wisdom, thoughts, designs, and in their place must be grafted heavenly shoots, *i.e.*, the knowledge and hope of things divine. We are, therefore, grafted from on high; and as the trunk grows along with the grafts, so our body retains its own nature, even though the heart be changed through the heavenly Spirit. Then does the spiritual heart bring forth the fruits that Paul describes in Gal. 5:22. And the flesh puts forth its vicious growths, just as the trunk does shoots and thorns. Then, just as these are constantly cut away, so also must the faults that spring forth from the trunk of the flesh be continually and assiduously pruned off, that they may not grow to such dimensions as to be able to smother the cultivated fruit or to dwarf it by drawing away the sap. Now, the thorns are sometimes allowed to flourish on the stem that they may keep off the destructive goat until the tree grows high enough to avoid his harmful tooth. So, too, in us, when the heart is pious the sins that spring up perform some service; for "we know that to them that love God all things work together for good," Rom. 8:28. But they do not render such service that they ought to be tolerated permanently, hut only till the accomplishment of the purpose which the Lord wishes effected through them.

Prayer: Father it would be helpful if you would help me not to be so hard on myself all of the time. Instead, help me to remember that you are patient. Not rushing to punish but allowing growth. Thank you. Amen.

June 21

David [2 Sam. 24:10] had committed as shameless a sin as was ever done among the Jews, but the Lord made use of his recklessness to keep him all his life from being puffed up. So also pious men who in their hearts cling to the Lord learn through the frequent springing up of thorns, *i.e.*, through the flood of their sins, to recognize their own weakness and to be humble, lest, puffed up with their own fancied blamelessness, they fall into the snares of the Devil. Christ weaves this idea beautifully into an allegory in John 13:10, when He teaches Peter thus: "He that is bathed needeth not save to wash his feet, but is clean every whit." But, most wise Master, how is he clean or bathed who has such dirty feet that they have need of washing? Are not the feet a part of the body? How then is he clean every whit whose feet are still unclean? Christ adds, therefore: "And you are clean, but not all." "For he knew," says the evangelist, "him that should betray him." They were all clean save one, because they had remained steadfast in faith. Christ bears witness to this in Luke 22:28: "You are they that have continued with me in my temptations." But Judas was unclean; for he had already covenanted with the Jews to betray Him. The rest of the Apostles still had defects, but these could not harm them as long as the citadel of faith was held.

Prayer: Forgive my imperfections as I forgive the imperfections of those who sin against me. Amen.

June 22

When, therefore, the Apostles are pronounced clean, because they had not fallen away from their faith, even if some dust had clung to them from walking in this high road of corruption, it is quite evident that if faith in God is safe and its power unimpaired nothing that can happen can destroy. It is all washed away by that constant repentance of which I have spoken and by faith in Christ. Paul deals with the same idea in Rom. 8:10. For after having said that "the body is dead because of sin; but the Spirit is life because of righteousness" found in Christ, he adds, to prove his point: "But if the Spirit of him that raised up Jesus from the dead dwell in you, he that raised up Christ shall quicken also your mortal bodies through his Spirit that dwelleth in you." But He will only so quicken that the body be forever dead. For thus he speaks afterwards [Rom. 8:20–23]: "For the creation was subjected to vanity, not of its own will, but by reason of him who subjected it in hope, because it is itself delivered from the bondage of corruption and restored into the liberty of the glory of the children of God. For we know that the whole creation," *i.e.*, all men (for thus Christ also calls all men in Mark 16:15: "Preach the gospel to the whole creation") "alike groan and are in pain as long as they are now, *i.e.*, in this present time, living.

Prayer: Father help us to share the gospel with as much force and labor and vigor as a woman giving birth to a child. Help us to care as much about the new birth as we do the baby's birth. In Christ's name, Amen.

June 23

And a little later he explains the groaning and anguish more clearly [Rom. 8:26]: "Likewise the Spirit also aids our weaknesses." By "Spirit" here he means the spiritual man, who is so raised to God through the Spirit of God that he looks up to Him alone. This Spirit of ours, then, which is nothing else than faith in and through God, constantly grieves for our weaknesses. For we see not what we should pray for. For it often happens that we pray to be saved from poverty, illness, humiliation. Then the Spirit, that is, the faithful heart, makes intercession for us with groanings which cannot be uttered. For what great pain, think you, is begotten in the heart consecrated to God when it sees the flesh—*i.e.*, man, hopelessly subject as he is to the flesh, *i.e.*, to self-love—forever praying for those things only which it selfishly desires—vengeance, or the favor of man, or wealth? Groanings, therefore, spring up in the heart from this constant folly of the flesh, groanings which only he knows who is caught in these straits. That this is the true meaning of this passage of Paul is proved by what follows: "For he that searches the hearts knows what is the counsel or meditation of the Spirit" [Rom. 8:27].

Prayer: It seems proper, dear Father, for me to silently let your Spirit translate the deepest yearnings of my spirit to you. In Christ's name, Amen.

June 24

That Holy Spirit through which we all breathe and trust in God has no heart. Paul is speaking, therefore, of the Spirit which has a heart, *i.e.*, of the spirit of man, *i.e.*, the pious mind. And the meaning is: "Man ventures, so zealous for himself is he, sometimes to ask of God things which it is not right for Him to give or for man to receive. Then the pious mind forthwith sweats because of the recklessness of the carnal man (for Paul makes two of every man here), and cries to God with weepings and groanings inexplicable to us, grieving for its persistent folly and praying for forgiveness. And if this happens when he goes wrong in praying, how much more when he fails by sinning! The Spirit flees for refuge to God, laments the disobedience of the flesh, and is filled with shame at the constant recurrence of the weariness with life and the flesh that comes therefrom. But God, who knows the hearts, sees plainly what faith, or the pious mind, meditates: namely, that it is anxious for the salvation of the man and never ceases to cry to God in behalf of the saints, *i.e.*, of the faithful, themselves to wit. And a kind God grants that these things work together for good to them on whose behalf the pious mind is troubled." Man, therefore, is ever dead, as is shown by his works; at the same time he ever lives, as is perceived from the anguish of his soul.

Prayer: Merciful God, we humans are in a very odd condition because of sin. We are like the mythical zombie—alive, but dead. We long for eternity where we will be eternally alive. Amen.

187

June 25

Ⅰt is a most marvelous thing that even prayer has degenerated into a matter of gain. For since those were right who said that prayer is the uplifting of the heart to God, what, pray, more shameless could have been thought of than the prostituting of this union of the heart with God? Hence we cannot help seeing that the prayers we sold for a price were hypocrisy, and not a communion of the heart with God. It is, therefore, necessary for me to speak of prayer also, since the devotion of the heart has dared to sell itself as a work of merit. Prayer has been rightly defined by Augustine and others as the uplifting of the heart to God. Not that they originated the idea, but they tried to express in clearer words what everyone who was pious felt to be the case. I shall speak, first, therefore, of adoration, that thus it may become clear whence this definition of prayer arose.

Prayer: Lord, it has been another unpleasant 24 hours. Give me strength to live unhindered in your presence until the unpleasantness passes. Let me find my refuge in you.

June 26

It is about this kind of adoration that the Hebrews are speaking in Exod. 20:5. When, therefore, we say, "You shalt not adore them, nor serve them," namely idols, it would be better to say, "You shalt not serve them nor be a slave to them"; for thus we could have translated the Hebrew literally, so that we should run no risk of understanding by adoration here the devotion of the heart. Adoration is, besides, the devoting of the heart to God, that is, to the Lord who can do all things and to the Father who will. This adoration, this devotion of the heart, was bound to the elements of this world by the Israelites according to the flesh. For they ordered that it be done at Jerusalem, as the woman of Samaria complained to Christ, John 4:20. This had arisen in this way: The Lord had commanded that three times a Year all the children of Israel should assemble at the temple, or tabernacle, that was at Jerusalem [Exod. 23:14; Deut. 16:16]. This arrangement brought very much gain to the priests. Therefore they began to bind men's consciences to the place by their traditions, so that they should come oftener to Jerusalem; for it was not lawful, according to their interpretation, to appear empty-handed before God [Deut. 16:17].

Prayer: Father, Keep your servants, all of them, each and every one, from manipulating your word to their advantage. For the sake of your people. In Christ's name, Amen.

June 27

The sense is as if He were spurring on sloth and saying: "Be not reluctant to come to me, for you shall not come in vain." So in Exod. 23:15 and 34:20, although (as in Deut. 16:16, according to our version) the words seem to have the meaning, "You shalt not appear before the Lord your God empty-handed," then if you consult the Hebrew version they have exactly the meaning that I have given. For it would have smacked of the height of greed not to be allowed to appear without a gift. I am afraid that this native meaning had always been corrupted by the priests of the Jews. The priests, then, bound adoration, in the sense of devotion of the heart, to Jerusalem; and this is what our priests also, or rather those of Antichrist, have hitherto done, inviting us to pray in the temples, where we see and are seen, in order that they may conveniently inculcate the doctrine, "You shalt not appear before the Lord your God empty," though Christ bids us [cf. Mt. 6:6] go into our inner chamber, that the heart may freely lay its troubles before God. Then adoration, devotion of the heart, is free, and cannot be confined to any one place. Hence not even by these words of Christ, "Go into your inner chamber," are we to be so bound as not to be allowed to pray anywhere but in our inner chamber.

Prayer: Father help me be pious and in touch with you wherever I am and whatever I'm doing. Thank you for the freedom to be so and help all your children wherever they are obtain the same freedom. Amen.

June 28

For Paul desires "that men pray in every place, provided they lift up holy hands" to God, 1 Tim. 2:8. It is apparent, therefore, that it is no small part of prayer to lift up holy hands, which is nothing else than to be zealous in guilelessness. Christ, therefore, John 4:23, took adoration (to come to the point) for the careful guarding of faith and piety towards God, when He said: "But the hour cometh, and now is, when the true worshippers shall worship the Father in spirit and truth: for the Father seeks such to worship him. God is a spirit: and they that worship him must worship in spirit and truth." See how sharp and clear is this exposition of worship or prayer! He says God is a spirit; hence those who are to worship Him cannot do it in any better way, nor ought they to do it in any other way, than by devoting the heart to Him; not by an oath such as the monks once demanded, but by constantly increasing love, so that nothing deceitful remains in it and nothing can come out of it but what is most true and most like to God.

Prayer: Father help me fear not the fires of trial and testing. Help me fear instead disobedience. In Christ's name, Amen.

June 29

They, therefore, who have so given and devoted their hearts to God as to cleave to Him alone and to recognize Him as the one God, certainly worship Him in spirit. And when they have become thus united with Him, it follows that they speak the truth with their neighbor, which is to worship in truth; unless you prefer to understand by "worship in truth" cleaving so truly and faithfully to God that besides Him you recognize no God, that is, no helper and no spouse, so to speak. Prayer, therefore, is the conversation which as a result of faith you have with God as with a father and a most safe and sure helper. Prayer, then, is the uplifting of the heart, not of the breath or voice, to God. We pray, therefore, when the heart draws near to God, when it speaks with Him, when in sincere faith it seeks help of Him alone. Further, who could ever impute it to you as a good work that you often come to Him to ask now for money, now for clothing or food or counsel or aid?

Prayer: Lord, is it possible that one day everyone who comes to you comes with a pure heart and unmixed motives? Or at least, is it possible that I do? Help it to be so, if only in my life. In Christ's name, Amen.

June 30

Since, then, our praying to God is nothing else than a begging of aid in some matter, why do we impute it to ourselves as a work of merit, seeing that adoration, that is, the confident clinging of the heart, is nothing but the clinging of your own heart? How can you lend that to another? You can, indeed, from faith in God pray for another, but you cannot impart a portion of your faith to anyone; for faith belongs to him only who trusts, and is not a work of merit, though Christ called it a work in a sort of figurative sense, but He did that for the sake of those who still clave to works. And He called it a work in such a way as to mean to say by contrast: "You shall be blest by faith, without works" [cf. Rom. 3:28]. Adoration, then, or prayer, is nothing else than a sure confidence in the mercy of God. The consequence of this is that you come to it in every situation and appeal to it. If, therefore, you have recourse to it on account of your neighbor, it must be from love either of your neighbor or of his goods. If the first, your prayer will be answered, for love of your neighbor is based on love of God.

Prayer: We are beggars. That is always and only what we ever are. We come to you because there's no where else to go. And we are so thankful that you have received us, beggars. In Christ's name, Amen.

July 1

B ut if your prayer is inspired by eagerness to possess, you make God out impious, as if He were not accessible to all but were a sort of respecter of persons [cf. Deut. 10:17]. For if He heard your prayer but scorned your neighbor's, would He not be a respecter of persons? Furthermore, you make Him an accomplice of your greed; for if He gave to another only after that other paid you, would that not be collusion? We must admit, therefore, that these mercenary prayers are an insult to God, not an honoring of Him; for what sort of honoring is it to beseech, to importune, to complain? If we are pious, the misfortune of our neighbor hurts us, so that we run to God anxiously in his behalf; if, on the contrary, we have not this love towards our neighbor, we shall pray in vain, even if we do get a yesand bushels of gold for our praying. The Truth knows not the prayer that is made for the sake of gain. Now, we pray when we cling to God in spirit, and truly cling, so that when any evil assails us we run to Him alone, and pray that He will alleviate our affliction, but only according to the petition, "Your will be done" [Mt. 6:10].

May the Lord grant, that we may engage in contemplating the mysteries of his heavenly wisdom with really increasing devotion, to his glory and to our edification. Amen.[5]

---

[5] The prayers offered for the month of July are all from the lips of John Calvin and are drawn from his lectures on the *Twelve Minor Prophets*. They are provided in memory of the great Reformer whose birth we remember during July.

July 2

Thus all hired praying, psalms, chants, masses, vigils, fall to the ground, for what we do without love profiteth nothing, 1 Cor. 13:3. Now, when a price is received, the deed has proceeded from greed, not from love. Hence, however they snarl: "We take pay only sufficient for our maintenance, that we may pray while others on account of their labors have not time, and we pray from love," I say: "Go you also, therefore, sometime and till the fields, and let those who have hitherto labored hard while you were idle refresh themselves in your snug nests. Let us rest and labor in turn, for this is what love demands. But now, since you do not deign even to look at a church or a psalm unless because your belly makes you, and then at the same time you feign love, it is evident that you are a great hypocrite. For love sympathizes, runs to aid, lifts up; but you do none of these things, but things of no avail. If you wish to pray and sing psalms, pray and sing psalms, but without expecting pay; for the expectation of pay is inconsistent with Christian love. We cannot serve God and Mammon, *i.e.*, riches" [cf. Mt. 6:24].

Grant, Almighty God, that we may not be so hardened as to resist thy goodness, nor abuse this thine incredible forbearance, but submit ourselves in obedience to thee; that whenever thou mayest severely chastise us, we may bear thy corrections with genuine submission of faith, and not continue untameable and obstinate to the last, but return to thee, the only fountain of life and salvation, that as thou hast once begun in us a good work, so thou mayest perfect it to the day of our Lord. Amen.

July 3

I do not want to dwell at tedious length upon this matter, for I think that everybody can easily see from the meaning of religion that hired prayers and psalms are of as little use as if you should agree for a reward to be righteous for somebody else. And even those pray, I think, who when holding the plough-handle feel admiration and reverence for the power of Almighty God in the very soil, and in the seed, and who are grateful for His bounty, even though they never utter a word; for it is the heart that prays. And as to the Christians constantly praying, and praying together, in the early times, it can be done in church today also, only let it be praying and not the wanton tickling of the fancy with chanting. Let us, then, pronounce the collects plainly in the language understood by the congregation, that all may pray together following the words of him who is leading. Then, let every church have its own custom; for the same thing is not adapted to all, but everything, as far as its source is concerned, should proceed from the same piety, and what does not proceed therefrom should be quietly abolished. See now what merit amounts to. We owe blamelessness to the Lord, and even if we could offer it (which is impossible), we should still be unprofitable servants [cf. Lk. 17:10]. We are sons and heirs [cf. Rom. 8:17], not servants; we do not, therefore, serve for reward.

Grant, that we may learn to search ourselves and consider our sins, that we may be really humbled before thee, and ascribe to ourselves the blame of all our evils, that we may be thus led to a genuine feeling of repentance, and so strive to be reconciled to thee in Christ, that we may wholly depend on thy paternal love, and thus ever aspire to the fulness of eternal felicity, through thy goodness and that immeasurable kindness, which thou testifiest is ready and offered to all those, who with a sincere heart worship thee, call upon thee, and flee to thee, through Christ our

Lord.   *Amen.*

July 4[6]

D EARLY Beloved in God, after you have heard so eagerly the Gospel and the teachings of the holy Apostles, now for the fourth Year, teachings which Almighty God has been merciful enough to publish to you through my weak efforts, the majority of you, thank God, have been greatly fired with the love of God and of your neighbor. You have also begun faithfully to embrace and to take to yourselves the teachings of the Gospel and the liberty which they give, so that after you have tried and tasted the sweetness of the heavenly bread by which man lives, no other food has since been able to please you.

Grant, Almighty God, that as thou often dost justly hide thy face from us, so that on every side we see nothing but evidences of thy dreadful judgment,—O grant, that we, with minds raised above the scene of this world, may at the same time cherish the hope which thou constantly settest before us, so that we may feel fully persuaded that we are loved by thee, however severely thou mayest chastise us: and may this consolation so support and sustain our souls, that patiently enduring whatever chastisements thou mayest lay upon us, we may ever hold fast the reconciliation which thou hast promised to us in Christ thy Son. Amen.

---

[6] Excerpts following are from Zwingli's 'On the Liberty and Choice of Food'.

July 5

And, as when the children of Israel were led out of Egypt, at first impatient and unaccustomed to the hard journey, they sometimes in vexation wished themselves back in Egypt, with the food left there, such as garlic, onions, leeks, and flesh-pots, they still entirely forgot such complaints when they had come into the promised land and had tasted its luscious fruits: thus also some among us leapt and jumped unseemly at the first spurring—as still some do now, who like a horse neither are able nor ought to rid themselves of the spur of the Gospel;—still, in time they have become so tractable and so accustomed to the salt and good fruit of the Gospel, which they find abundantly in it, that they not only avoid the former darkness, labor, food, and yoke of Egypt, but also are vexed with all brothers, that is, Christians, wherever they do not venture to make free use of Christian liberty. And in order to show this, some have issued German poems, some have entered into friendly talks and discussions in public rooms and at gatherings; some now at last during this fast—and it was their opinion that no one else could be offended by it—at home, and when they were together, have eaten meat, eggs, cheese, and other food hitherto unused in fasts.

Grant, that we may not, to the last, proceed in this our wickedness, and thus provoke the vengeance thou here denouncest on men past recovery; but that we may anticipate thy wrath by true repentance, and be humbled under thy hand, yea, by thy word, that thou mayest receive us into favour, and nourish us in thy paternal bosom, through Christ our Lord. Amen.

July 6

B ut this opinion of theirs was wrong; for some were offended, and that, too, from simple good intentions; and others, not from love of God or of his commands (as far as I can judge), but that they might reject that which teaches and warns common men, and they might not agree with their opinions, acted as though they were injured and offended, in order that they might increase the discord. The third part of the hypocrites of a false spirit did the same, and secretly excited the civil authorities, saying that such things neither should nor would be allowed, that it would destroy the fasts, just as though they never could fast, if the poor laborer, at this time of spring, having to bear most heavily the burden and heat of the day, ate such food for the support of his body and on account of his work. Indeed, all these have so troubled the matter and made it worse, that the honorable Council of our city was obliged to attend to the matter. And when the previously mentioned evangelically instructed people found that they were likely to be punished, it was their purpose to protect themselves by means of the Scriptures, which, however, not one of the Council had been wise enough to understand, so that he could accept or reject them.

O grant, that we may be so preserved in obedience to thee by the teaching of thy word, that we may never turn here and there, either to the right hand or to the left, but continue in that pure worship which thou hast prescribed, so that we may plainly testify that thou art indeed our Father by continuing under the protection of thy only-begotten Son, whom thou hast given to be our pastor and ruler to the end. Amen.

July 7

W hat should I do, as one to whom the care of souls and the Gospel have been entrusted, except search the Scriptures, particularly again, and bring them as a light into this darkness of error, so that no one, from ignorance or lack of recognition, injuring or attacking another come into great regret, especially since those who eat are not triflers or clowns, but honest folk and of good conscience? Wherefore, it would stand very evil with me, that I, as a careless shepherd and one only for the sake of selfish gain, should treat the sheep entrusted to my care, so that I did not strengthen the weak and protect the strong. I have therefore made a sermon about the choice or difference of food, in which sermon nothing but the Holy Gospels and the teachings of the Apostles have been used, which greatly delighted the majority and emancipated them. But those, whose mind and conscience is defiled, as Paul says [Titus, 1:15], it only made mad.

O grant, that we may continue contented in this obedience to thee: and though Satan may, in many ways, attempt to draw us here and there, and we be also ourselves, by nature, inclined to evil, O grant, that being confirmed in faith, and united to thee by that sacred bond, we may yet constantly abide under the guidance of thy word, and thus cleave to Christ thy only-begotten Son, who has joined us for ever to himself, that we may never by any means turn aside from thee, but be, on the contrary, confirmed in the faith of his gospel, until at length he will receive us all into his kingdom. Amen.

July 8

First, Christ says, Matthew 15:17, "What goes in at the mouth defileth not the man," etc. From these words any one can see that no food can defile a man, providing it is taken in moderation and thankfulness. That this is the meaning, is showed by the fact that the Pharisees became vexed and angry at the word as it stands, because according to Jewish law they took great account of the choice of food and abstinence, all of which regulations Christ desired to do away with in the New Testament. These words of Christ, Mark speaks still more clearly, 7:15: "There is nothing from without a man, that entering into him can defile him; but the things which come out from him, those are they that defile the man." So the meaning of Christ is, all foods are alike as far as defilement goes: they cannot defile at all. Secondly, as it is written in the Acts of the Apostles, 10:10, when Peter was in Joppa (now called Jaffa), he went one day upon the housetop at the sixth hour, and desired to pray. He became hungry and wished to eat; and when the servants were making ready, he fell into a trance and saw heaven opened and a vessel descending as it were a great linen cloth held together by the four corners and let down upon earth, in which cloth were all four-footed animals, wild beasts, and creeping and flying creatures.

Grant, Almighty God, that since thou continuest daily to exhort us, and though thou seest us often turning aside from the right course, thou yet ceasest not to stretch forth thy hand to us, and also to rouse us by reproofs, that we may repent.

July 9

Then a voice spoke to him, saying: "Arise, Peter, kill and eat." But Peter said, "No, Lord, for I have never eaten forbidden or unclean food." Then again the voice spoke to him, saying: "What God has purified, shalt you not consider forbidden or unclean." Now, God has made all things clean, and has not forbidden us to eat, as his very next words prove. Why do we burden ourselves wilfully with fasts? Here answer might be made: This miracle, shown to Peter, meant that he should not avoid the heathen, but them also should he call to the grace of the Gospel, and therefore material food should not be understood here. Answer: All miracles that God has performed, although symbolical in meaning, were still real occurrences and events. As when Moses struck the rock with his staff and it gave forth water, it was symbolical of the true Rock of Christ, from which flowed, and ever shall flow for us all, the forgiveness of sins and the blessings of heavenly gifts, but none the less was the rock really smitten and gave forth water. And so here, although this miracle was symbolical, still the words of God's voice are clear: What God has cleansed, shalt you not consider unclean. Until I forget these words I shall use them.

O grant, that we may not be permitted to reject thy word with such perverseness as thou condemnest here in thine ancient people by the mouth of thy Prophet; but rule us by thy Spirit, that we may meekly and obediently submit to thee, and with such teachableness, that if we have not hitherto been willing to become wise, we may not at least be incurable, but suffer thee to heal our diseases, so that we may truly repent, and be so wholly given to obey thee, as never to attempt any thing beyond the rule of thy word, Amen.

July 10

Thirdly, Paul writes to the Corinthians (1., 6:12): "All things are lawful to me, but all things are not expedient: all things are lawful for me, but I will not be brought under the power of any. Meats for the belly and the belly for meats: but God shall destroy both it and them." That is, to me are all things free, although some things are rather to be avoided, in case they offend my neighbor too much. (About the troubling of one's neighbor, I shall speak specially later on). And therefore no one can take from me my freedom and bring me under his authority. Food is taken into the belly to sustain life. As now the belly and the food are both to be destroyed, it makes no difference what one eats or wherewith one nourishes his mortal body.   Fourthly, Paul says, 1 Corinthians 8:8: "But meat commendeth us not to God: for neither, if we eat, are we the better; nor, if we eat not, are we the worse." This word Paul speaks of the food which was offered to the idols, not now of daily food. Notice this, however, to a clearer understanding. At the time when Paul wrote the epistle, there were still many unbelievers, more indeed, it seems to me, than Christians.

O grant, that when thou warnest and wouldest restore us to the right way, we may at least be pliant, and without delay attend to the scourges of thy hand, and not wait for extreme severity, but timely repent; and that we may truly and from the heart seek thee, let us not put on false repentance, but strive to devote ourselves wholly to thee, through Jesus Christ our Lord. Amen.

July 11

These unbelievers offered to their idols, according to custom, animals, such as calves, sheep, and also other forms of food; but at these same offerings, a great part, often all, was given to eat to those that made the offerings. And as unbelievers and Christians lived together, the Christians were often invited to partake of food or meat, that had been sacrificed to the honor of the idols. Then some of the Christians were of the opinion, that it was not proper to eat this food; but others thought that, if they ate the food of the idols, but did not believe in them, such food could not harm them, and thought themselves stronger in their belief, because they had been free to do this thing, than those who from faint-heartedness and hesitation did not venture to eat all kinds of food. To settle this difference, Paul uses the above words: "No kind of food commends us to God." Even if one eats the food of the idols, he is not less worthy before God, nor then more worthy, than one who does not eat it; and whoever does not eat it is no better. Indeed that will seem very strange to you, not only that meat is not forbidden, but also that even what has been offered to idols a Christian may eat.

O grant, that we, being renewed by thy Spirit, may not only remain constant in the fear of thy name, but also advance more and more and be established; that being thus armed with thy invincible power, we may strenuously fight against all the wiles and assaults of Satan, and thus pursue our warfare to the end,—and that being thus sustained by thy mercy, we may ever aspire to that life which is hid for us in heaven, through Jesus Christ our Lord. Amen.

July 12

Fifthly, Paul says in the First Epistle to the Corinthians, 10:25: "Whatsoever is sold in the shambles, that eat, asking no questions for conscience' sake." These words are clear and need no explanation, except that they are among other words about the offence caused by the food of idols. But do not let yourself err. From the pulpit I shall speak sufficiently of giving offence, and perhaps more clearly than you have ever heard. Sixthly, Paul also says, Colossians 2:16: "No man shall judge you in meat or in drink, or in respect of a holy day." Again you hear that you are to judge no man either as good or bad from his food or drink; he may eat what he please. If one will, let him eat refuse. Here it should be always understood that we are speaking not of amount but of kind. As far as kind and character of food are concerned, we may eat all foods to satisfy the needs of life, but not with immoderation or greediness.

O grant, that by the direction of thy Spirit, we may at length so return to thee, that we may never afterwards fall away, but be preserved in pure and true obedience, and thus constantly continue in the pure worship of thy majesty and in true obedience, that after this life past, we may at last reach that blessed rest, which is reserved for us in heaven, through Jesus Christ our Lord. Amen.

July 13

S eventhly, Paul says again, 1 Timothy 4:1: "Now the Spirit speaketh expressly, that in the latter times some shall depart from the faith, giving heed to seducing spirits, and doctrines of Devils; speaking lies in hypocrisy; having their consciences seared with a hot iron; forbidding to marry and commanding to abstain from meats, which God has created to be received with thanksgiving of them which believe and know the truth. For every creature of God is good, and nothing to be refused, if it be received with thanksgiving: for it is sanctified by the word of God and of prayer." These are all the words of Paul. And what could be more clearly said? He says that God's Spirit spoke this as a warning, that they might withstand this, who had no fixed strong belief, and who did not put trust in God, but in their own works which they themselves chose as good. And that such things are placed in them by seducing spirits and Devils, that inspire men with hypocrisy, that is, with the outward form, lead men away from trust in God to confidence in themselves. And then the same will always surely realise in themselves, that they act dishonorably toward God, and they always feel the pain of it, and know their disgraceful unfaithfulness in that they see only their own advantage or desire and greed of heart. Still they are willing to sell themselves, as though they did it not for their own sakes, but for God's.

O grant, that, being fortified by invincible faith against these so many temptations, we may persevere in true religion, until we be at length gathered to Christ our King, under whom, as our head, thou hast promised that we shall ever be safe, and until we attain that happy life which is laid up for us in heaven, through the same Christ our Lord. Amen.

July 14

That is having a conscience branded on the cheek. Then he recounts what they will forbid to do as bad. They shall not enter into marriage or wed. Know too that purity so disgracefully preserved had its original prohibition from the Devil, which prohibition has brought more sin into the world than the abstinence from any food. But this is not the place to speak of that. Likewise it is forbidden that one should eat this or that food, which God created for the good and sustenance of men. Look, what does Paul say? Those that take from Christians such freedom by their prohibition are inspired by the Devil. "Would I do that?" said the wolf, as the raven sat on the sow's body. Now God placed all things under man at the head of creation, that man might serve him alone. And although certain foods are forbidden in the Old Testament, they are on the contrary made free in the New, as the words of Mark 7:15, clearly show, quoted in the first article above, as also Luke 16:15. "For that which is highly esteemed among men is an abomination in the sight of God." The law and the prophets were only a symbol, or have lasted only to John. Hear now, that which seemed great to men was detested by God (the word is *abominatio*), and as far as the law is ceremonial and to be used at court, it has been superseded.

O grant, that we may not become hardened in our wickedness, but seasonably repent, and that we may not be drawn away after the inventions of our flesh, nor seek ways to flee away from thee, but come straight forward to thy presence, and make a humble, sincere, and honest confession of our sins, that thou mayest receive us into favour, and that being reconciled to us, thou mayest bestow on us a larger measure of thy blessings, through Christ our Lord. Amen.

July 15

Hear then that whatever a man eats cannot make him evil, if it is eaten in thankfulness. Notice that proper thankfulness consists in this, that a man firmly believe that all our food and living are determined and continued by God alone, and that a man be grateful for it; for we are more worthy in the sight of God than the fowls of the air which he feeds: us then without doubt he will feed. But the greatest thanks is a conscientious recognition that all our necessities are provided by him. Of these words nothing further. Eighthly, after Paul shows Titus (1:15) that there are many disobedient, many vain talkers and deceivers, which one must overcome, he adds: "To the pure all things are pure: but to them that are defiled and unbelieving is nothing pure; but even their mind and conscience is defiled." Here you see again he did not desire Jewish wiles heeded; this is plainly shown by the words next preceding, where he says: "Wherefore rebuke and punish them sharply (of course with words), that they may be sound in the faith, not listening to Jewish fables and human commandments, that pervert the truth."

O grant, that Satan may not thus perpetually harden and fascinate us; but that we, being at length awakened, may feel our evils, and be not merely affected by outward punishments, but rouse ourselves, and feel how grievously we have in various ways offended thee, so that we may return to thee with real sorrow, and so abhor ourselves, that we may seek in thee every delight, until we at length offer to thee a pleasing and acceptable sacrifice, by dedicating ourselves and all we have to thee, in sincerity and truth, through Jesus Christ our Lord. Amen.

July 16

But they desired to draw the new Christians into abstinence from food, pretending that some food was unclean and improper to eat; but Paul showed that they were wrong, and said: To those of a pure belief, all things are pure, but to the unbelievers nothing is pure. Cause: their hearts and consciences are defiled. They are unbelievers that think the salvation, mercy, and freedom of Christ are not so great and broad as they really are, as Christ chide his disciples, saying that they were of little faith, Matthew 16:8, and 6:30. In these passages we are certainly taught that we are not only fed each day by him, but also controlled and instructed with fatherly fidelity, if we console ourselves confidently alone in his word and commands. Wherefore every Christian should depend alone upon him and believe his words steadfastly. Now if you do that, then you will not believe that any food can defile a man; and if you surely believe it, then it is surely so, for his words cannot deceive. Accordingly all things are pure to you. Why? You believe, therefore all things are pure to you. The unbeliever is impure. Why? He has a doubting heart, which either does not believe the greatness and freedom of God's mercy, or does not believe these to be as great as they are. Therefore he doubts, and as soon as he doubts, he sins, according to Romans 14:23.

Grant, Almighty God, that as thou shinest on us by thy word, we may not be blind at mid-day, nor wilfully seek darkness, and thus lull our minds asleep: but that exercising ourselves in thy word, we may stir up ourselves more and more to fear thy name, and thus present ourselves, and all our pursuits, as a sacrifice to thee, where there is reserved for us eternal rest and glory, through Jesus Christ our Lord. Amen.

July 17

Ninthly, Paul says to the Hebrews (13:9): "Be not carried about with divers and strange doctrines. For it is a good thing that the heart be established with grace; not with meats, which have not profited them that have been occupied therein." In these words see first that we should not be carried about with many kinds of doctrines, also that without doubt or suspicion the Holy Gospel is a certain doctrine, with which we can console ourselves and on which we can surely depend. Accordingly it is best to establish the heart with grace. Now the Gospel is nothing but the good news of the grace of God; on this we should rest our hearts—that is, we should know the grace of the Gospel to be so certain and ready, and trust it, so that we may establish our hearts in no other doctrine, and not trust to food, that is, to eating or abstaining from eating (so also Chrysostom takes these words) this or that food; for that such oversight and choice of food was not of profit to those that have clung thereto is clear enough.

Grant, Almighty God, that inasmuch as thou hast freely embraced us in thy only-begotten Son, and made us, from being the sons and race of Adam, a holy and blessed seed, and as we have not hitherto ceased to alienate ourselves from the grace thou hast offered to us,—O grant, that we may hereafter so return to a sound mind, as to cleave faithfully and with sincere affection of heart to thy Son, and so retain by this bond thy love, and be also retained in the grace of adoption, that thy name may be glorified by us as long as we sojourn in this world, until thou at length gatherest us into thy celestial kingdom, which has been purchased for us by the blood of thy Son. Amen.

July 18

These announcements seem to me to be enough to prove that it is proper for a Christian to eat all foods. But a heathen argument I must bring forward for those that are better read in Aristotle than in the Gospels or in Paul. Tell me which you think more necessary to a man, food or money? I think you will say that food is more useful than money, otherwise we should die of hunger with our money, as Midas died, who, according to the poets, desired that everything he touched be turned to gold. And so food is more important to preserve life than money; for man lived on food before money was invented. Now Aristotle says that money is indifferent—that is, it is neither good nor bad in itself, but becomes good or bad according to its use, whether one uses it in a good or bad way. Much more then is food neither good nor bad in itself (which I, however, for the present omit), but it is necessary and therefore more truly good. And it can never become bad, except as it is used immoderately; for a certain time does not make it bad, but rather the abuse of men, when they use it without moderation and belief.

O grant, that we may not bring forth wild grapes, and that our fruit may not be bitter and unpleasant to thee, but that we may strive so to form our whole life in obedience to thy law, that all our actions and thoughts may be pleasant and sweet fruits to thee. And as there is ever some sin mixed up with our works, even when we desire to serve thee sincerely and from the heart, grant that all stains in our works may be so cleansed and washed away by the sacrifice of thy Son, that they may be to thee sacrifices of sweet odour, through the same, even Christ Jesus, who has so reconciled us to thee, as to obtain pardon even for our works. Amen.

July 19

No Christian can deny these arguments, unless he defends himself by denying the Scriptures: He is then, however, no Christian, because he does not believe Christian doctrine. There are nevertheless some who take exception to this, either to the times, or the fasting, or human prohibitions, or giving offence. All these I will answer from the Scriptures later with God's help. At first then they object to the time: Although all things are pure, still they are not so at all times; and so during the fasts, quarter fasts, Rogation-day week, Shrove-Tuesday, Friday, and Saturday, it is improper to eat meat. During fasts also eggs, milk, and milk products are not proper. Answer: I do not say that these are not forbidden by men; we see and hear that daily. But all of my efforts are directed against this assumption, that we are restrained at this and that time by divine law. Let each one fast as often as the spirit of true belief urges him. But in order to see that according to the law of Christ we are free at all times, consider as follows.

Grant, Almighty God, that as thou hast once appeared in the person of thy only-begotten Son, and hast rendered in him thy glory visible to us, and as thou dost daily set forth to us the same Christ in the glass of thy gospel,—O grant, that we, fixing our eyes on him, may not go astray, nor be led here and there after wicked inventions, the fallacies of Satan, and the allurements of this world: but may we continue firm in the obedience of faith, and persevere in it through the whole course of our life, until we be at length fully transformed into the image of thy eternal glory, which now in part shines in us, through the same Christ our Lord. Amen.

July 20

First, Mark 2:23, once when Christ was going through the cornfields, his disciples began to pluck the ears (and eat). But the Pharisees said to him: "Lo, what are your disciples doing that is not proper on the Sabbath day?" And Christ said to them: "Have you not read what David did when he had need, when he and they with him were hungry; how in the days of Abiathar, the high priest, he went into the house of God and ate the bread that was offered to God, which it was improper for any one to eat but the priests, and gave also to those with him, saying to them, "The Sabbath was made for man, and not man for the Sabbath: Therefore the Son of man is also Lord of the Sabbath." Notice here that need is superior not only to human but also to divine law; for observing the Sabbath is divine law. And still the hunger of the disciples did not observe the Sabbath. Notice again that no place withstands need, and that David in need might go into the temple. Notice also that the matter of persons is not respected in need; for David and his followers were not priests, but ate the food proper only for priests to eat. This I show you now that you may learn that what is said of one circumstance is said in common of all circumstances in the Scriptures, if anything depends on circumstances or is deduced from circumstances. Circumstances are where, when, how, the person, or about whom.

O grant, that we may, in a spirit of meekness, at length turn to thy service, and fight against the hardness and obstinacy of our flesh, till we render ourselves submissive to thee, and not wait until thou puttest forth thy hand against us, that thou mayest show thyself to us not only as our Lord, but also as our Father, full of mercy and kindness, through Christ our Lord. Amen.

July 21

Thus Christ says, Matthew 24:23: "Then if any man shall say to you, Lo, here is Christ, or there; believe it not." See, this is the circumstance where, or the place. The meaning is that God is not revealed more in one place than in another. Indeed, when the false prophets say that, one is not to believe them. In this way you should understand the circumstance of time, and other circumstances, that not more at one time than at another God is revealed as merciful or as wroth, but at all times alike. Else he would be subject to the times which we had chosen, and he would be changeable who suffers no change. So also of the matter of persons; for God is not more ready or open in mercy and grace to a person of gentle birth than to the base born, as the holy Peter says, Acts 10:34: "Of a truth I perceive that God is no respecter of persons." But we do not need this proof here, where we wish to prove that all time is free to men. For the words of Christ are of themselves clear enough, when he says: the Sabbath is made for man and not man for the Sabbath; the Sabbath is in the power of man, not man in the power of the Sabbath. In a word, the Sabbath and all time are subject to man, not man to the Sabbath.

O grant, that we may not be unmindful of so many and so singular benefits, but respond to thy holy calling, and labour to devote ourselves wholly to thee, and labour, not for one day, but for the whole time designed for us here, both to live and to die according to thy good pleasure, so that we may glorify thee to the end, through our Lord Jesus Christ. Amen.

July 22

Now if it is true that the Sabbath which God established is to be subject to us, then much more the time which men have imposed upon us. Indeed, not only the time but also the persons, that have thus fixed and established these particular times, are none other than the servants of Christ and co-workers in the secret things of God, not revealed to men. And these same co-workers should not rule Christians, commanding as over-lords, but should be ready only for their service and for their good. Therefore Paul says, 1 Cor. 7:35: "I say this for your good, not that I would put a noose about your necks"—that is, I would not seize and compel you with a command. Again he speaks, 1 Cor. 3:21: "All things are yours; whether Paul, or Apollos, or Peter, or the world, or life, or death, or things present, or things to come; all are yours." Here you see that all things are intended for men or for the service of men, not for their oppression, yes, the Apostles themselves are for men, not men for the Apostles.

O grant, that we may thus come to thee, that through him we may certainly know that thou art our Father, so that the covenant thon hast made with us may never fail through our fault, even this, that we are thy people, because thou hast once adopted us in thy only-begotten Son, our Lord Jesus Christ. Amen.

July 23

O overflowing spring of God's mercy! how well Paul speaks when he says, that these things are known but through the Spirit of God. Therefore we have not received the spirit of this world, but the spirit that is from God, because we see what great things are given us by God. You know your liberty too little. Cause: the false prophets have not told you, preferring to lead you about rather as a pig tied with a string; and we poor sinners cannot be led to the love of God any other way but by being taught to summon to ourselves the Spirit of God, so that we may know the great things which God has given us. For who could but be thankful to God, so kind, and who could but be drawn into a wonderful love of him? Here notice too that it is not the intention of Christ, that man should not keep the Sabbath (for us Christians Sunday is ordained as the Sabbath), but where our use or need requires something else, the Sabbath itself, not only other times, shall be subject to us.

O grant, that we may entirely devote ourselves to thee, and truly render thee that free service and obedience which is due to a Father, so that we may have no other object in life but to confirm that adoption, with which thou hast once favoured us, until we at length, being gathered into thy eternal kingdom, shall partake of its fruit, together with Christ Jesus thy Son. Amen.

July 24

Here you are not to understand either the extreme necessity, in which one would be near death, as the mistaken theologians dream, but ordinary daily necessity. For the disciples of Christ were not suffering extreme necessity, when on the Sabbath day they plucked the ears, else they would not have answered Christ as they did, when he asked them, Luke 22:35: "When I sent you without purse and scrip, lacked you anything?" For the disciples answered: "Nothing." From this we understand that Christ never allowed his disciples to fall into such dire extremity, but that the need, which they felt on Sunday, was nothing but ordinary hunger, as also the word "need" as we use it does not mean the last stages of necessity, but has the usual meaning; as when one says, "I have need," he does not refer to the last or greatest want, but to a sufficiency of that which daily need demands. Then as far as time is concerned, the need and use of all food are free, so that whatever food our daily necessity requires, we may use at all times and on all days, for time shall be subject to us.

Secondly, Christ says, Luke 17:20: "The kingdom of God cometh not with observation: neither shall they say, Lo! here, lo! there."

O grant, that we may be wholly given to the contemplation of thine image, which thus shines before us; and that we may in such a manner be transformed into it, as to make increasing advances, until at length, having put off all the filth of our flesh, we be fully conformed to that pure and perfect holiness which dwells in Christ, as in him dwells the fulness of all blessings, and thus obtain at last a participation of that glory which our Lord hath procured for us by his resurrection. Amen.

219

July 25

This word observation, Latin *observatio*, has this meaning, as if one carefully watched over something that had its time and moment, and if one did not take it then, it would pass away, as fishermen and fowlers usually watch, because fish and fowl have certain times and are not always to be caught. Not thus the kingdom of God, for it will not come with observation of time or place. Since now the mistaken theologians say that we ourselves deserve the kingdom of God with our works, which we choose of our own free will and complete according to our powers, the words of Christ, who cannot lie, answer: if the kingdom of God cometh not with observation or watching (of time, or place, or of all circumstances, as is proved in the above paragraph), and if at any time the prohibiting of the food which God has left free is nothing else but observation, then the kingdom of God will never be made ready by the prohibition of food. Now it must be that abstinence cannot avail anything as to time, and you are always to understand that it is not our intention to speak here of amount, but only of kind, neither of the times which God has set, but of those which men have established.

O grant, that we may not transfer to others the glory due to thee, and that especially since we are daily admonished by thy word, and even severely reproved, we may not with an iron hardness resist, but render ourselves pliable to thee, and not give ourselves up to our own devices, but follow with true docility and meekness, that rule which thou hast prescribed in thy word, until at length having put off all the remains of errors, we shall enjoy that blessed light, which thou hast prepared for us in heaven, through Jesus Christ our Lord. Amen.

July 26

Thirdly, Paul writes to the Galatians (4:9): "But now after you have known God, how turn you again to the weak and beggarly elements, whereto you deserve to be again in bondage? You have expectation, or you keep day and month, time and Year." Here you hear the anger of Paul at the Galatians, because after they had learned and known God (which is nothing else but being known or enlightened of God), they still returned to the elements, which he more closely describes in Colossians 2:20. But since we must use these words later more accurately and must explain them, we shall now pass them over, satisfying ourselves with knowing what the weak elements are. In Latin and Greek the letters were called elements, for the reason that as all things are made up and composed of elements, so also each word was made of letters. Now the Jews and heathen have always clung closely to the letter of the law, which oppresses much, indeed kills, as Paul says. Not only in the Old Testament, but also in the New, it oppresses much. Is that not a severe word which is found in Matthew 5:22?

Grant, Almighty God, that as them dost so kindly call on us daily by thy voice, meekly and calmly to offer ourselves to be ruled by thee, and since thou hast exalted us to a high degree of honor by freeing us from the dread of the devil, and from that tyranny which kept us in miserable fear, and hast also favoured us with the Spirit of adoption and of hope. Amen.

July 27

" "B ut I say to you, that whosoever is angry with his brother shall be in danger of the judgment." So it is, if taken literally, indeed impossible for us weak mortals to keep. And therefore Christ has given it to us that we might recognise our shortcomings therein, and then take refuge alone in him, who mercifully pitied our shortcomings when he said, Matthew 11:28: "Come to me, all you that labor and are heavy laden, and I will give you rest." But whosoever does not know and will not know this narrow way to the mercy of God through Christ, undertakes with his own powers to fulfill the law, sees only the letter of the law and desires with his might to fulfill that, prescribing for himself this and that chastisement and abstinence at certain times, places, and under other circumstances, and after all that he still does not fulfill the law, but the more he prides himself on having fulfilled the law, the less he has fulfilled it, for in his industry he becomes puffed up in himself.

Grant, Almighty God, that as thou hast given us thy only-begotten Son to rule us, and hast by thy good pleasure consecrated him a King over us, that we may be perpetually safe and secure under his hand against all the attempts of the devil and of the whole world. Amen.

July 28

As the Pharisee, that boasted of the elements—that is, of the works which he had literally fulfilled, said, "I thank you, O God, that I am not as other men are; I fast," etc. Consider the over-wise piety that exalts itself at once above other men, from no other reason than that according to his advice or opinion, and powers, he is confident to have fulfilled the law; and, on the other hand, consider the publican hoping for nothing but the rich mercy of God, and counting his own works nothing, but only saying: "O God, be merciful to me, a sinner!" Is not, then, the publican considered more righteous before God than the Pharisee? From all this you see that the weak elements are nothing else than human wisdom and conception of happiness, for man either purposes to wish and to be able to keep the letter of the law or else prescribes for himself some work to do, which God has not commanded but left free, and therefore likes to think the works prescribed by himself to be a sure road to blessedness, and clings to his opinion to his own injury.

O grant, that we may ever by faith direct our eyes towards heaven, and to that incomprehensible power, which is to be manifested at the last day by Jesus Christ our Lord, so that in the midst of death we may hope that thou wilt be our Redeemer, and enjoy that redemption, which he completed when he rose from the dead; and not doubt but that the fruit which he then brought forth by his Spirit will come also to us, when Christ himself shall come to judge the world; and may we thus walk in the fear of thy name, that we may be really gathered among his members, to be made partakers of that glory, which by his death he has procured for us. Amen.

July 29

A nd for just this reason Paul complains of the Galatians, that having been mercifully enlightened of God they turned again to their own devices, that is, to the weak elements, to which the Jews and heathen held, and had not so strong a belief in God, that they trusted alone in him and hoped alone in him, listened alone to his ordinances and will, but foolishly turned again to the devices of men, who, as though they desired to improve what had been neglected by God, said to themselves: "This day, this month, this time, wilt you abstain from this or that," and make thus ordinances, persuading themselves that he sins who does not keep them. This abstaining I do not wish to condemn, if it occurs freely, to put the flesh under control, and if no self-confidence or vainglory, but rather humility, results. See, that is branding and injuring one's own conscience capriciously, and is turning toward true idolatry, and is, as David says, Psalm 81:12, "walking in one's own counsels." But this God desired to prevent by the words of David, who says: "Hear, O my people, I will testify to you, Israel (that is, he sees God and trusts him so thoroughly that he is possessed of him), if you wilt hearken to me; there shall no strange god be in you; neither shalt you worship any strange god.

Grant, Almighty God, that as thou invitest us daily with so much kindness and love, and makest known to us thy paternal goodwill, which thou didst once show to us in Christ thy Son. Amen.

July 30

O Christian of right belief, consider these words well, ponder them carefully, and you will see that God desires that we hearken to him alone! If now we are thoroughly imbued with him, no new god will be honored within our hearts, no man instead of God, no feeling of our own instead of God. But if we do not hear the true warnings of God, he will let us walk according to the desires and devices of our own hearts. Do we not see that consolation oftener is sought in human hearts than in God; that they are more severely punished who transgress human laws than those who not only transgress but also despise and reject God's laws? Lo, these are the new idols which we have cast and chiseled in our hearts. Enough has now been said about these words of Paul, and it is authority enough to prove that we are as little forbidden by God to eat at certain times as we are now forbidden by him to eat certain sorts and kinds of food.

Grant, Almighty God, that as thou seest us so foolish in nourishing our vices, and also so ensnared by the gratifications of the flesh, that without being constrained we hardly return to thee,—O grant, that we may feel the weight of thy wrath, and be so touched with the dread of it, as to return gladly to thee, laying aside every dissimulation, and devote ourselves so entirely to thy service, that it may appear that we have from the heart repented, and that we have not trifled with thee by an empty pretence, but have offered to thee our hearts as a sacrifice, so that we and all our works might be sacred offerings to thee through our whole life, that thy name may be glorified in us through Christ our Lord. Amen.

July 31

T hey will now raise as objections the fasts, or all fast days, saying that people will never fast if they are allowed to eat meat. Answer: Have you heretofore fasted because you were not allowed to eat meat, as naughty children that will not eat their broth, because they are not given meat? If any one desires to fast, has he not as much the power to do so, when laborers eat meat, as when they are forced to fast with the idle, and are thus less able to do and to endure their labors? In a word, if you will fast, do so; if you do not wish to eat meat, eat it not; but leave Christians a free choice in the matter. You who are an idler should fast often, should often abstain from foods that make you lustful. But the laborers' lusts pass away at the hoe and plough in the field. You say, the idle will eat meat without need. Answer: The very same fill themselves with still richer foods, that excite more than the highly seasoned and spiced. And if they complain of the breaking up of the custom [of fasting], it is nothing but envy, because they dislike to see that considered proper for common men, for which they can well find a substitute without difficulty and without weakening the body, on the contrary, even with pleasure; for fish eating is surely everywhere a pleasure. You say that many cannot endure this liberty in eating, not from envy, but from fear of God.

Grant, Almighty God, that as we continue to excite thy wrath against us, and are so insensible, though thou exhortest us daily to repentance. Amen. [7]

---

[7] The prayers of Calvin from his lectures on the minor prophets are concluded.

August 1

L ikewise, if you are so concerned about others, as to what they should not eat, why will you not note their poverty and aid it? If you would have a Christian heart, act to it then. If the spirit of your belief teaches you thus, then fast, but grant also your neighbor the privilege of Christian liberty, and fear God greatly, if you have transgressed his laws, nor make what man has invented greater before God than what God himself has commanded, or again I will turn out a hypocrite of you, if you are such a knotty block, twisted in yourself and depending upon your own devices.

Prayer: Dear Lord help me to be as gracious to others as I am to myself; and as forgiving. Amen.

August 2

Is one not to keep the feasts? Answer: Who says or teaches that? If you are not content with the fasts, then fast also Shrovetide. Indeed, I say that it is a good thing for a man to fast, if he fasts as fasts are taught by Christ: Matthew 6:16, and Isaiah 58:6. But show me on the authority of the Scriptures that one cannot fast with meat. Even if it could be shown, as it cannot, still you know very well that laborers are relieved of the burden of fasting, according to your laws. Here I demand of you to show me where meat is forbidden to him not under obligation to fast. Thus they turn away from the observance of the fast, and at last they all come to the canonical law, fourth chapter, "Denique," etc., and when you ask for a wagon, they offer you a chopping-knife. The chapter beginning "Denique" does not command you to forbid laymen to eat meat; it shows that at these same times the laymen fill themselves with meat on the Sundays in the fast more than on other days.

Prayer: I have never, Lord, been one to fast. Perhaps that's why my devotion is oftentimes as weak as it is. Perhaps I need to restrict the flesh more so that the spirit may flourish. Help me know. In Christ's name, Amen.

August 3

After that they come with Thomas Aquinas, as though one single mendicant monk had power to prescribe laws for all Christian folk. Finally they must help themselves out with custom, and they consider abstinence from food to be a custom. How old the custom is supposed to be, we cannot really know, especially with regard to meat, but of abstinence from eggs the custom cannot be so very old, for some nations even to-day eat eggs without permission from Rome, as in Austria and elsewhere. Milk food became a sin in the Swiss Confederation in the last century and was again forgiven. And since I have chanced upon this matter, I must show you a pretty piece of business, so that you may protect yourselves thus from the greed of the powerful clergy. Our dear fellow Swiss purchased the privilege of using milk food from the Bishop of Rome in the last century: Proof, the documents about it at Lucern. Go back now before the time of these letters and think what our forefathers ate before the indulgence, and you cannot say that they ate oil, for in the Bull the complaint was made that people in our country are not accustomed to eat oil, that they ate the foods usual there, milk, whey, cheese, and butter. Now if that was a sin, why did the Roman bishops watch so lazily that they allowed them to eat these fourteen hundred Years? If it is not a sin, as it is not, why did they demand money to permit it?

Prayer: Heavenly Father, use whomsoever you wish to teach me your truth today. Whether they be learned or foolish. In your Son's name, Amen.

August 4

Say rather this, I see that it is nothing but air, see that the Roman bishops announced that it was a sin, when it became money to them: Proof, as soon as they announced it as a sin, they immediately sold it for money, and thus abused our simplicity, when we ought fairly to have seen that, if it was sin according to God's law, no man can remit it, any more than that one might murder a man, which is forbidden by divine law, could be permitted by any one, although many distasteful sins of this kind are committed. From all these remarks you notice also that abstinence from meat and drink is an old custom, which however later by the wickedness of some of the clergy came to be viewed as a command. So if the custom is not bad or dishonorable, one is to keep it properly, as long and as thoroughly as the greater part of men might be offended by its infringement.

Prayer: Father the Church in many places is beset by the most terrible of difficulties. Please help me to be in constant remembrance for my brothers and sisters in distress. In Christ's name, Amen.

August 5

Offence or vexation, Greek, *skandalon*, is understood in two ways: first, when one offends others, so that they sin in judgment or decision, and become worse; and of these we desire to speak first; second, offence occurs, although not in the Scriptures, but here as accepted by us, when a man in himself becomes more sinful or worse, or when a whole parish is purposely brought into a worse condition.   First, Christian love demands that every one avoid that which can offend or vex his neighbor, in so far, however, as it does not injure the faith, of course you are to understand. Since the Gospel has been preached frequently in these Years, many have therefore become better and more God-fearing, but many on the contrary have become worse. And since there is much opposition to their bad opinion and plans, they attack the Gospel, which attacks the good cannot endure but oppose. From which reason the bad cry out saying: "I wish the Gospel were not preached. It sets us at variance among ourselves." Here one should not yield for that reason, but should keep close before his eyes what Christ says, Matthew 10:32: "Whosoever therefore shall confess me before men, him will I confess also before my Father which is in heaven.

Prayer: Father if it comes to a choice of having to offend you or offend another, I will have to become an offense to others rather than to you.   It's more important to please you than all the world.   Grant me the courage to live accordingly. Amen.

August 6

In these words Christ gives us strength not to consider the vexation of those who will not be convinced of the truth; and, even though they are our nearest and dearest, we are not to be worried, if they separate from us, as he says later, Matt. 10:37: "Whosoever loves father and mother more than me, he is not worthy of me; whoever loves his son or daughter better than me, he is not worthy of me, and whoever does not take his cross and follow me, he is not worthy of me." And also Luke 14:26. So wherever it is a matter of God's honor, of the belief or of hope in God, we should suffer all things rather than allow ourselves to be forced from this. But where a thing cannot harm the belief, but offends one's neighbor, although it is not a sin, one should still spare his neighbor in that he should not injure him; as eating meat is not forbidden at any time by divine law; but, where it injures or offends one's neighbor, one should not eat it without cause. One should make those of little faith strong in the faith.

Prayer: Indeed Lord, help me rather to suffer all things than disappoint you and offend your glory. Strengthen me, and all your children, this day. Amen.

August 7

But when one (thirdly) will not be referred to the divine truth and the Scriptures, when one says: "I firmly believe that Christ has never forbidden me any food at any time," and when the one of little faith will not grant it or believe it, although one shows him the Scriptures about it, then the one who believes in liberty shall not yield to him, although he should yield the matter of eating meat in his presence, if it is not necessary; but he should cleave to the Scriptures and not let the sweet yoke of Christ and the light burden become bitter, so that it may not be unpleasant to men or please them less, and thereby show that it is a human and not a divine prohibition. Thus a burgomaster gives an answer, in the name of the Council, and after the answer adds something harsh and hard, which the Council did not command him to say and did not intend. He says: "This I say of myself; the Council has not commanded it."

Prayer: All has not been well this day, Father. So I need, I must receive, a special portion of your kindness. The world can be exceedingly harsh and your people sometimes too. Help me avoid being like the world. Amen.

August 8

This also, all those that teach in God's name should not sell their commands, ordinances, and burdens as God's, so that the yoke of his mercy should not become unpleasant to any one, but should leave them free. That I shall prove by the opinion of Christ: Matthew 24:49, and Luke 12:45, where he does not want one to trouble one's fellow servants—that is, one's fellow Christians. "But if that servant say maliciously in his heart, 'My Lord delayeth his coming,' and shall begin to beat his fellow servants and to eat in excess and to drink with drunkards, the Lord of that servant will come on a day when he looketh not for him, and at an hour when he is not watching, and will cut him in sunder, and will appoint the share of the bad servant to the Pharisees." Here open your eyes and see whether the servant, to whom it was given to pasture the sheep of Christ, has not now for a long time beaten his fellow servants—that is, fellow Christians; whether he has not eaten and drunk excessively, and, as though there was no God, run riot, and troubled Christians with great burdens (I speak of bad bishops and priests— take it not of yourself, pious man) so that the sweet yoke of Christ has become to all Christians a bitter herb.

Prayer: As Shepherds, Father, help your Pastors to treat the flock as you would treat it. Let them never take advantage, or mislead, or abuse your good flock. In Christ's name, Amen.

August 9

O
n the other hand, see how the Lord has come with his light and illuminated the world with the Gospel, so that Christians, recognizing their liberty, will not let themselves be led any more behind the stove and into the darkness from which a schism has come about, so that we really see that God has uncovered the Pharisees and hypocrites and has made a separate division of them. Yes, in that case I venture to command you to fight against those who prefer to keep the heavy yoke of the hypocrites rather than to take the sweet yoke of Christ upon themselves, and in thus doing to be careful to offend no one, but, as much as is in them, to keep peace with all men, as Paul says. Not every one can do this, or knows how far to yield or to make use of Christian liberty, therefore we will hear the opinion of Paul about offence.

Prayer: Keep me from hypocrisy today, and every day, Lord. Amen.

August 10

Secondly, Paul teaches in the Epistle to the Romans 14 and 15, how one should avoid giving offence; these words I translate into German and give more according to the sense than the letter. Him, he says, that is weak in the faith, help, but do not lead him into the trouble of still greater doubt. One believes that it is proper for him to eat all things; but the other, weak in faith, eats only herbs. Now the one who is certain that he may eat all things, shall not despise him who does not venture to do such (understand, from little faith); and he who ventures not to eat all things shall not judge the eater, for God has accepted and consoled him. You weak man, who are you that you judge another man's servant? He will stand upright or fall for his own master, still he will be supported or held up, for God can well support or hold him up.

Prayer: As I go about my tasks today, Lord, help me to be a helper to those who are weak in faith and when one stronger in faith than I comes my way, help me abandon pride and receive the help they offer. Amen.

August 11

One man esteems one day above another, another esteems all days alike. Let every man be fully persuaded in his own mind, that he who regards one day above another may do so to the honor of God, and that he who regards not one day above another does the same to the honor of God (understand that he has so strong a faith that he certainly does not believe himself at any time freed from God's rule, for the greatest honor to God is to recognise him aright and those things which are given us by him: John 17:3, and 1 Corinthians 2:12); also that he who eats all kinds of food, does the same to the honor of the Lord, for he gives the Lord thanks, and he who does not eat, does it also to the honor of God, and is also thankful to God, for no one among us lives for himself or dies for himself. Whether we live, let us live for the Lord, or whether we die, let us die for the Lord; and therefore whether we live or die, we are the Lord's. For to that end Christ died, arose, and lived again, that he might be Lord of the living and the dead. But, you weak man, why do you judge your brother? Or, you stronger man who eat, why do you despise your brother? For we shall all stand before the judgment seat of Christ.

Prayer: As I live in preparation for my appearance in your presence, help me live in preparation for my appearance in your presence. Amen.

August 12

Therefore shall each one of us render God an account. Thus let us not judge one another, but be this our judgment, that no one displease or offend his brother. I know and am taught in Jesus Christ that nothing is unclean of its nature, except that it is unclean to him who considers it unclean. But if your brother is offended or injured on account of food, you do not act according to love (that is, you do not give up the food which injured your brother before he has been correctly instructed). Vex and injure and offend not with food your brother, for whom Christ died, and in return your goodness (that you do all things in your faith, you eat, you keep fast, or not) shall not be despised. For the kingdom of God is not food or drink, but piety, peace, and joy in the Holy Ghost. Whoever serves Christ in these things, is pleasing to God and approved before men. Let us then strive to do the things which lead to peace; and that we may edify one another (that is, properly instruct), do not make God's work (piety, peace, and joy, as is written above) of no avail on account of food. All things are clean, but it is bad that a man eat with vexation and offence as a result. It is proper and good that a man eat no meat and drink no wine, indeed eat nothing, whereby your brother is vexed or offended or whereby he is made ill.

Prayer: Lord keep me always sensitive to those around me; thinking not only of my needs but of theirs as well, and more. In Christ's name, Amen.

August 13

You who are stronger, if you have faith, have it in you before God. Happy is he who does not doubt that which he considers certain; but whoever doubts and, in doubt, eats the meat about which he doubts, he is condemned, for the reason that he did not eat from belief; for what is done not in belief, is sin. Also thus should we, who are strong in belief, be patient with the timidity of the weak, and not please ourselves, but each of us please his neighbor by edifying and doing him good; "for even Christ pleased not himself; but, as it is written, " 'The reproaches of them that reproached you fell on me.' " All these are words of Paul, from which you will shortly conclude three things. First, that he who firmly believes that it is proper for him to eat all things, is called strong; and secondly, that one who has no belief is called timid or weak; thirdly, that the strong should not let the weak remain always weak, but should take him and instruct him, that he become also strong, and should yield a point to the weak and not vex him maliciously. How we are to yield a point to the weak, you shall hear.

Prayer: If my Lord, Father, didn't live to please himself, how much more important is it that I not? Help me on this day to live like Christ. In His name, Amen.

August 14

Thirdly, Paul says of vexation, 1 Corinthians 8:1, to those who were present: They might eat of that which had been offered to the idols, for this reason: they well knew they believed not in the idols, and therefore without soiling their consciences they might eat such food, in spite of those who were badly offended by it; indeed to them he speaks thus: "We know that we all have understanding or knowledge of the food which is offered to the idols. Knowledge puffeth up and makes conceited, but love edifieth." Here Paul means, that you, although you, a man firm in faith, know you do not sin, when you eat the food of the idols, should, if you love your neighbor, favor him fairly, so that you offend him not; and when in time he is better instructed, he will be greatly edified, when he sees that your Christian love overlooked his ignorance so mercifully. After Paul has said that those well taught in the faith know well there is no idol but only one true God and one Lord Jesus Christ, it is further mentioned that not every one is so well taught as the first mentioned; for some eat the food of the idols in such manner that they still hold to them somewhat, and also that food does not commend us to God (as is shown above in the first part of the fourth division).

Prayer: Lord it's sometimes hard to be as patient as we must, so we need your help. A lot. Please. In Christ's name, Amen.

August 15

Indeed after all that he says further: "See that your power or freedom does not vex the weak, for if one of them sees you sitting knowingly at a table where the food of idols is eaten, will not his conscience be strengthened or encouraged to eat the food of idols? And then your weak brother through your knowledge and understanding perishes, for whom Christ died." See how strongly Paul opposes wanton treatment of the weak. It follows further on that when you thus sin against your brethren, frightening and striking their weak consciences, you sin against Christ; therefore, if food offends my brother I will rather never eat meat than that I make my brother offend. Here notice that, although the foregoing words are spoken of the food of idols, they still show us in a clear way how we should conduct ourselves in this matter of food, namely, that we should abstain in every way from making to offend, and that he is not without sin, who acts against his brother, for he acts also against Christ, whose brother each Christian is. But you say, "What if my brother from stubbornness will not at all be taught, but always remains weak?" The answer will follow in the last part.

Prayer: Indeed, Lord, what should I do with those who wish to stubbornly remain spiritual infants? Teach me how to proceed when I do not know how to. For your Kingdom's sake. Amen.

August 16

Fourthly, Paul writes in the above mentioned epistle, 1 Corinthians 10:23: "All things are lawful for me, but all do not result in usefulness." Let no one seek his own good, let each seek, that is, strive for, the advantage of the other. Eat all that is sold in the shambles, not hesitating for conscience' sake; for the earth is the Lord's (as it reads in Psalm 24:1), and all the fulness of the earth, or all that is in the earth. If an unbeliever invites you and you want to go with him, eat all that is placed before you (that is, as far as the kind of food is concerned; otherwise he would be a faithless glutton, if he ate all) not doubting for conscience' sake. But if one said to you: "That is from the sacrifice to the idols," eat it not for the sake of him who thus points it out to you, and for conscience' sake. I say not for *your* conscience' sake but for the sake of *another's* conscience.

Prayer: Father, again, help me to keep others in view as I act, speak, and work. Help me to put others before myself. Amen.

August 17

For why is my liberty judged by the conscience of another, if I eat with gratitude? Therefore, whether you eat or drink or whatever you do, do it to the honor of God; do not offend Jews or heathen and God's Church, just as I endeavor to please all men, not regarding myself, but the many, that they be saved; they are my followers as I am a follower of Christ.

Prayer: Thank you. Thank you for allowing all who will to be a part of your purpose. Thank you.

August 18

Here you see, first, that we should avoid for the sake of another what otherwise would be proper; secondly, that all things are proper for us to eat, that are sold in the shambles, without violence to the conscience; thirdly, how one should act about eating forbidden food after the manner prescribed for the food offered to idols; for although our proposition and the one here in Paul are not wholly alike, still a good rule is to be derived therefrom; fourthly, that although your liberty cannot be judged according to another's conscience, nor you yourself condemned, still you should always consider the honor of God, which honor, however, grows the greater among men, if they see you for the sake of the honor of God not using your liberty; fifthly, that all things can take place to the honor of God, indeed the daily custom of eating and drinking, of working, trading, marrying, if a man cleaves to God in all his doings, and trusts that he is called to, and chosen for, the work by God.

Prayer: Give my hands your work this day Father. Amen

August 19

A nd do not let this idea, which may occur to you, trouble you: "Then I will blaspheme, gamble, commit adultery, do other wrongs, and think I am called to this by God." For such things do not please the man who trusts in God. The tree is now good, let it produce only good fruit. And if one lives not in himself, but Christ lives in him so thoroughly that, although a mistake escapes him, he suffers from that hour for it, he is ashamed of his weakness. But those who thus speak are godless, and with such words insult God and those who have the Spirit of God. Listen to a striking example. No respectable and pious wife, who has a good husband, can allow one to report that which is dishonorable to her husband or let a suspicion arise of a misdeed, which she knows is displeasing to him. So man, in whom God rules, although weak, still cannot endure to be shamefully spoken of against his will. But a wanton likes to hear the disgrace of her husband and what is against him. Thus also those, who speak thus, are godless; otherwise, if they had God in their hearts, they would not willingly hear such disgraceful words.

Prayer: Lord, give us the grace to avoid chatter which falsely represents others.   And help us live the kind of lives that glorify you and don't call our love into question. Amen.

August 20

Fifthly, Paul had Timothy circumcised, although the circumcision was of no service, that he might not offend the Jews, who at that time still believed that one must keep the Old Testament with its ceremonies together with the New Testament; and so he had it done, as it is written in Acts 16:3. Sixthly, Christ himself did not wish to offend any one; for, when at Capernaum Peter was asked, Matthew 17:24, whether his master paid tribute, Peter answered, "Yes." And after they had entered the house, Christ anticipated Peter (who doubtless was about to ask him something about tribute) and said: "Simon, what thinkest you? Do the kings of this world take tribute and custom of their children or of strangers?" Peter answered him: "Of strangers." Jesus said to him: "Then are the children free. But lest we should offend them, go to the sea and cast a hook, and the first fish that comes up take; and when you hast opened his mouth, you shalt find a coin (it was a penny, that could pay for them both, but was worth much more than the real tax pennies, wherefore I think it was a tribute which they collected from Christ), take it and give it for you and me."

Prayer: Lord it's one of those days when I can only be silent—heavy laden with despair. Boost my spirit and empower me to be governed by love rather than fear. Amen.

August 21

Thus Christ did not desire to vex the authorities, but rather to do what he might otherwise refuse. This paragraph I would not have added, had not my opponents represented it thus: Christ, they said, desired himself to avoid taxation. For this article is more against them than for them; thus, if you spiritual teachers in the flesh are all so inclined to avoid vexation, why do you not then also help to bear the common burden, when you see that the parish is badly vexed about it and cries out: "You go lazily away from our work. Why do you not help us carry the burden?" Hear also that Christ gave the tribute money, in order not to arouse any one to anger. Loose the knot. There are more places still in the Gospel in which the word *skandalon* is written; but it means there either disgrace, or if it means offence, it is used in the following sense: disgrace and contempt, Matthew 18:7. "Woe to the world because of offences"—that is, woe to the world on account of disgrace and contempt, since one despises, refuses, and rejects the simple (who is, however, as much God's as the highest), which the following words mean, when he says: "Take heed lest you offend one of the least of these." Thus it is also to be understood, Luke 17:1, which also is clear from what precedes about the rich man, who did not let poor Lazarus have the crumbs.

Prayer: Lord give me the strength to carry the load you assign and do it without grumbling or complaining or attempting to shirk my duty to you and others. Amen.

August 22

From the above mentioned arguments one can readily learn that one should carefully avoid offence. But still I must think that, as one should forgive the weak, one should also in forgiving teach and strengthen him, and not always feed him with milk, but turn him to heartier food; for Christ says, Matthew 13:41: "The Son of man shall send forth his angels (that is, messengers), and they shall gather out of his kingdom all things that offend and them which are not God-fearing and do iniquity, and shall cast them into a furnace of fire." Are his angels to do that? Yes. Then it is better that we should do it ourselves; then it will not be done by God and punished so severely, as Paul teaches us, 1 Corinthians 11:31: "For if we would judge ourselves, we should not be judged." If we ourselves take the offence, it must not be taken with the judgment of God, to which now St. Paul arouses us.

Prayer: If I offend anyone today Father please forgive me and please help me avoid giving offense. Even when I want to strike back and retaliate for perceived wrongs. In His name, Amen.

August 23

First, Christ says, Matthew 5:29: "If your right eye offend you, pluck it out, and cast it from you: for it is profitable for you that one of your members should perish, and not that your whole body should be cast into hell. And if your right hand offend you, cut it off, and cast it from you: for it is profitable," etc., as above. The same is also said in Matthew 18:8, except that he adds the foot. Who is now the eye, the hand, the foot, which, offending us, shall be cast away? Every bishop is an eye, every clergyman, every officer, who are nothing more than overseers; and the Greek word *episkopos* is in German an overseer, to which the words of St. Paul refer, Acts 20:28, where he says to the bishops of Ephesus: "Take heed therefore to yourselves, and to all the flock, over which the Holy Ghost has made you bishops (that is, overseers or shepherds), to watch and feed the Church of God, which he has bought with his own blood." Here you see briefly what their duty is: overseeing the sheep, feeding, not flaying and shearing too closely and loading them with unbearable burdens, which is nothing else than giving offence, pointing out sins that are not present, so that weak consciences are troubled and made to despair; this is offending God's little ones: Matthew 18:6.

Prayer: Oh Father, spare me from hurting new believers or even older ones. Nothing could be more terrible than driving someone from you. In Jesus' name, Amen.

August 24

But you see yourself, according to the words of Isaiah 56:10, that his watchmen have become blind, all ignorant, stupid dogs, that cannot bark, taught in loose things, lazily sleeping and dreaming, indeed, preferring dreams to the truth, the most shameless dogs, which cannot be satisfied: shepherds which have no reason, each following his own way or capricious desires, all avaricious, from the highest to the lowest, saying: "Let us drink good wine and become full, and as we do to-day, so shall we do to-morrow, Yes, still more." These all are the words of Isaiah, and little is to be added. Do you not see that such eyes offend men much, and, although Christ tells us to pluck them out, we suffer them patiently? Understand also hand and foot which are so nearly related to you, as your own members; indeed, even if they are necessary to you for support and strength as a hand or a foot, still one is to remove them if they abuse their superiority. Now this paragraph is placed here by me to prove that offence should be avoided, and that one should not always endure it, but that everything should take place with timely counsel and reason, not with any one's own assumption and arrogance. If they do not do that, who ought to do it?

Prayer: Heavenly Father send us Pastors who are not cowards. Send us Pastors who are willing to speak the truth. Send us Pastors who will not bow to the winds of popular opinion. Amen.

August 25

We should recognise that our sins have deserved of God this, that such blind eyes lead us, the blind, astray and rule us. Nehemiah 9:30: "You hast warned them in your spirit through your prophets, and they have not followed, and you hast given them into the hand of the people of the earth"—that is, into the hands of the unbelievers. Also Isaiah 3:4: "And I will give children to be their princes (note this well), and old women shall rule them." Secondly, the words of Paul are to be considered, Romans 14:1, where it is mentioned above in the second article on giving offence, in which place he says: "Him that is weak in faith receive you, but not to doubtful disputations." See you, the weak is not to be allowed to remain weak, but is to be instructed in the truth, not with subtle arguments, by which one becomes more doubtful, but with the pure, simple truth, so that all doubt may be removed. Therefore I could well endure that those who are considered steadier and stronger in belief, also understood how to make Christians strong in belief, and gave them really to understand what has been given and left to them by God; but they do exactly the contrary. If anything is strong, they wish to make the same again weak and timid.

Prayer: Father as we look around today and observe what's happening in and to your Church, we can only plead with you to send awakening to your people. Too long have they slumbered. Wake them up. Before there's no waking to be done. Amen.

August 26

Woe to them, as Christ spoke to the Pharisees, Matthew 23:13: "For they closed the kingdom of God to men, for they neither go in themselves nor let other people go in." By means of these words of Christ and of Paul, I think I have excused my arrogance, of which certain hypocrites accused me—that is, of having preached upon freedom concerning food on the third Sunday of this fast, when they thought that I ought not to do it. Why? Should I snatch from the hand of those who cling to the Scriptures, which I myself have preached, their means of defence, and contradict the Scriptures and say they lie? And should I have in my hands the key of God's wisdom, as Christ says, Luke 11:52, and not open to the ignorant, but also close it before the eyes of the knowing? Do not deceive yourself that you have persuaded me to this, you vain, loose hypocrite. I will rather take care of my soul, which I have laden with enough other misdeeds, and will not murder it outright with a suppression of the truth.

Prayer: Keep me from hypocrisy! I understand that I ask this regularly but it's only because that's my greatest threat. Amen.

August 27

Thirdly, it is true that Paul had Timothy circumcised, Acts 16:3. But on the other hand, as he says, Galatians 2:3, he did not have Titus circumcised: "Titus, who was with me, did not want to be forced to circumcision. He had this reason: False brethren have slipped unseen among us, who are come into our midst to spy out our liberty, which we have in Jesus Christ, that they might make us again slaves and subjects, to whom we yielded not a moment, that the truth of the Gospel might continue with you." Those who protect the liberty of the Gospel put this up before the ceremonies as a shield and bulwark. If Paul circumcised Timothy, still he did not, on the contrary, have Titus circumcised, although much reproach came to him on that account. What is to be done with him? Is Paul inconsistent with himself? No. If he had Timothy circumcised, it was because he could not keep him from it on account of the great disturbance of the Jews who were Christians. But afterwards, those of the Jews who had become Christians were better taught, so that he was able to spare Titus and protect him without great uproar; and, although some demanded his circumcision, and, when it did not happen, were greatly offended at it, he considered the truth and Christian liberty more than any strife that arose against it from bad feeling.

Prayer: Father, renew and revitalize your Church.   And begin here, with me.   Amen.

August 28

Fourthly, Paul writes, Galatians 2:12, that Peter ate with the Christians, who had become believers from heathendom; indeed, he ate with the heathen. But when some came from Jerusalem to Antioch who were also Christians but converted from Judaism, he fled from the heathen, so that the Jews might not be offended. Paul did not desire him to do that, but chide him in these words: "You teach the heathen to live as Jews, because you are a Jew by birth"; that is, if you flee from the heathen on account of the Jews, you raise a suspicion against the heathen, that they were not really Christians, or they would have to keep human fasts, as the Jews, or else sin. And about this he said: "When I saw that he did not walk uprightly, I withstood him to his face." At this place you find Paul, who teaches diligently, not offending, not caring if a few want to be offended, providing he could keep the greater multitude unaffected and unsuspicious. For if even the Jews, on whose account Peter fled from the heathen, became offended, still Paul gave them no attention, so that the heathen Christians (thus I call them that were converted from heathendom) could remain free and would not be brought under the oppression of the law by Jewish Christians.

Prayer: Help me live out the spirit and intent of the Law in the power of Christ. Not to gain favor but to live rightly. Not because I must, but because, with His help, I can. Keep me far from libertinism. In Christ's name, Amen.

August 29

hen Christ spoke to the Pharisees, Matthew
15:11, "Not that which goeth into the mouth
defileth a man," his disciples said to him:
"Knowest you that the Pharisees who heard these words
were offended and angered?" Christ answered them: "Let
them go, they be blind leaders of the blind." See that here
Christ's meaning is, as it seems to me, that the disciples
should let the Pharisees go and should live according to
their liberty and custom in spite of them; for they were
blind and saw not the truth of liberty; were also leaders of
those who erred as they did. Since now in the above two
articles, I have spoken enough of offence and of the doing
away with offence, it seems to me good to bring together in
short statements all that touches upon offence, so that each
may know where he shall yield and where not.
I. What clearly affects the divine truth, as the belief and
commandments of God, no one shall yield, whether one is
offended or not. Psalm 145:18; 1 Corinthians 2:2; Matthew
5:10: "Blessed are they which suffer for righteousness'
sake." 2 Corinthians 13:8: "For we can do nothing against
the truth, but for the truth."

*Prayer: Father help me be flexible when I need to be and
unwavering when I need to be. And five me the wisdom to
know the difference. Amen.*

August 30

On account of all this they complain very bitterly who have learned the acceptance of virtues rather from Aristotle than from Christ: saying that in this way all good works, as not eating meat, abstaining from labor, and other things which I shall not mention, are done away with. To these I answer as follows: Many mistakes are made as to the choice of good works, although we might well hear what St. James says, 1:17, that all good gifts and presents come from above from the Father of lights. From this we can conclude that all good which pleases God must come from him; for if it came from any other source, there would be two or more sources of good, of which there is however only one; Jeremiah 2:13: "They have forsaken me the fountain of living waters, and hewed them out cisterns, broken cisterns, that can hold no water." Notice the fountain; notice the broken cistern. Thus Christ speaks to the young man who called him good, in order to do him eye-service: "God alone is good." If he alone is good, without doubt no good fruit can come from any source except from the tree which alone is good. Then notice the angels and you will find that, as soon as they depended somewhat upon themselves, they fell. Thus also man, as soon as he depended somewhat upon himself, fell into the trouble that still follows us. See, those are the bad, false, broken cisterns, which are dug and thrown up only by men, not real natural fountains.

Prayer: Lord help me do much more than serve for appearance-sake. Help me serve from the heart. For your Son's Kingdom's sake. Amen.

August 31

Thus they thought that that would seem good to God and please Him, which they had attempted and which resulted in great disadvantage to them, from no other reason, as I think, than that they had assumed to know the good or the right, and did not depend alone on God and trust alone in him. Not that I mean to say that abstinence from food is bad; indeed, where it comes from the leading and inspiration of the Divine Spirit, it is without doubt good; but where it comes simply from fear of human command, and is to be considered as a divine command and thus trusted in, and where man begins to please himself thereby, it is not only good but also injurious; unless you show me from the Holy Writ that our inventions must please God. I shall also not be worsted, if you say to me: "Still the assembly of a church may set up ordinances which are kept also in heaven." Matthew 16:19, and 18:18: "Verily I say to you whatsoever you shall bind on earth shall be bound in heaven; and whatsoever you shall loose on earth shall be loosed in heaven." That is true, but the observance is not made by the whole Christian Church, indeed only by certain bishops, who had for a time undertaken to place upon Christians certain laws, without the knowledge of the common people.

Prayer: Today I give myself to you anew and afresh. For your service. For your work. For your will. Use me as you see fit. In any way. For anything. Amen.

September 1

Also if you should say that silence is a form of consent, I answer: The pious simplicity of Christians has kept silence in many things from fear, and that no one has told them of their liberty coming from the Scriptures. For example, whom did it ever please that the Pope conferred all benefices on his servants? Indeed, every pious man everywhere has said, "I do not believe it is right." But the people kept still about it with much pain, till the Gospel truth gave forth light, when for the first time the mask was taken from it. Thus also here the clergy have taken a hand to control everything, after they have seen Christians willingly following them. Why? They fear us for the reason lest he who transgresses the command be obliged to give us money. Then it all would have had no success, if such oppressive regulations were not given out as being divine. We sold them for that, and where the agreement was of that kind, after the truth had come to light, you can see what kind of an agreement it was. But we will hear what Paul says of works.

Prayer: Father as I share the Gospel today with whomsoever you send my way, help me to share it rightly and truthfully and accurately. And not Pharasaically. Amen.

September 2

To the Colossians, 2:16 (which passage I have quoted above), he writes: "Let no man judge you in meat, or in drink, or in respect of a holyday, or of the new moon, or of the Sabbath days: which are a shadow of things to come; but the body is of Christ. Let no man beguile you of your reward in a voluntary humility and worshipping of angels, intruding into those things which he has not seen, vainly puffed up by his fleshly mind, and not holding the Head, from which all the body by joints and bands having nourishment ministered, and knit together, increaseth with the increase of God. Wherefore if you be dead with Christ from the rudiments of the world, why, as though living in the world, are you subject to ordinances (touch not, taste not, handle not: which things are all to perish with the using) after the commandments and doctrines of men? Which things indeed have a showing of wisdom in will-worship, humility, and neglecting of the body; not in any honor to the satisfying of the flesh." All these are the words of Paul, which in Latin are not at all intelligible, but in Greek are somewhat clearer. But that each may well understand them, I shall briefly paraphrase them.

Prayer: Father help us all abstain from legalism. But help me remain faithful even if I am accused of being legalistic. Help me value your opinion of me more than I value the opinion of anyone else. Amen.

September 3

No one shall reject you or consider you good on account of any food, or holyday, whether you rest or not (always excepting Sundays, after God's Word has been heard and communion administered). Let the new moon fast and the Sabbath go; for these things have become only symbolical of a Christian holiday, when one is to cease and leave off sinning, also that we, repenting such works, become happy only in the mercy of God; and, as Christ has come, the shadows and symbols are without doubt done away with. One thing more, notice as to the time: It surely seems to me (I cannot help thinking so) that to keep certain times with timidity is an injury and harm to unchanging and everlasting justice, thus: simple people think that everything is right, if only they confess the fasts, fast, enjoy God (*i.e.*, take the sacrament), and let the whole Year pass away thus; whereas one should at all times confess God, live piously, and do no more than we think is necessary in the fast. And Christ says again, Matthew 25:13: "Watch therefore, for you know neither the day nor the hour."

Prayer: Today teach me to wait. I await your help to that end. Amen.

September 4

Further, he reminds them that they shall not allow themselves to be beguiled by those who pretend humility. What is beguiling but disregarding the simple meaning of God and wanting to find or show to the simple another shorter way to happiness, and to seek therewith wealth, name, and the reputation of a spiritual man? Therefore Paul advises against this and warns us that we should not allow ourselves to be beguiled—that is, not allow ourselves to be deceived. For the same hypocrites will falsely assert that angels spoke with them and revealed something to them, and will elevate themselves on that account. Listen, how well he paints them in their true colours, and then we do not want to recognise them. Why do you dream here of the doctrines and ordinances which are chattered out at the pulpit in the cloisters? And why of the crows which nip the ears of some of you? Do you not now hear that all such things are suggested by the flesh, and not by the spirit? For the same depend not on the head of Christ, from which all other members being arranged, co-ordinated, and united, receive their nourishment or support of heavenly life, and progress in a growth that pleases God. Notice here in the spiritual growth and increase a different method than in the bodily. In the body all members grow from the sustenance of the belly, but in the spirit from the head of Christ.

Prayer: Let me grow in Christ this and every day, loving Father. Let me become more like him, by the hour, by the day, by the week, my entire life. Please. Amen.

September 5

Consider now human doctrines: if they are like the opinion of the head, they are sustained by the head; if they are not like it, they come from the belly, O you bellies! But if we are dead with Christ to the rudiments of the world—that is, if Christ by his death made us free from all sins and burdens; then we are also in baptism—that is, in belief, freed from all Jewish or human ceremonies and chosen works, which he calls the rudiments. If we are now dead to the rudiments, why do we burden ourselves with fictitious human ordinances? Just as though God did not consider and think enough, did not give us sufficient instruction and access to blessedness and we make ourselves ordinances, which oppress us saying: "Touch not, taste not, handle not"; which touching or eating does not serve to injure or disturb the soul. For only for this purpose have the false teachers pretended that this was injurious, that with simple-minded people they might have the name of being wise and godly, indeed also with those who prescribe for themselves their own religion, saying: "Is not such abstinence and purification of the body a good thing? Is it not a good thing to prevent sin by good ordinances?"

Prayer: Lord, my sin won't be lessened by my efforts or wishes. It can only be solved in faithfulness to Christ. Lend me aid in achieving more faithfulness today. In your Son's name, Amen.

September 6

Hear how much weight Paul gives this folly. He says these things have only the form of the good. It is a Greek word, and means the honor or fear of God, which one has chosen for himself and to which he stubbornly clings: as, for example, many will not cut the beard on Friday and think they greatly honor God thereby; and, when they transgress this, they greatly sin in thus doing, and consider the rule that they themselves have set up so important, that they would three times sooner break their marriage vows, than to do anything against their reputation for wisdom. Indeed, deceive not yourself that things are with God as you have persuaded yourself; that is true superstition, a stubborn self-chosen spirit. Here in the words of Paul consider the greater part of the ordinances and rules, and you will find pretty things.

Prayer: Heavenly Lord, I believe that I need to simply be silent once more this week in our time together. Silent and receptive. Amen.

September 7

All food is created for the support of man; as far as it only affects bodily use it is of no moment, whether you eat this or that food. Go rather again to the clearer words of Paul and read them again, and they will be much clearer to you and worthier in your heart. Pious servants of Christ, these are the opinions, which I have preached from the Holy Writ, and have again collected for no other purpose than that the Scriptures might be forcibly brought to the notice of those ignorant of the same, and as Christ commands that they might rather search them, and that you and your people may be less reviled by them. For as far as I am concerned, it was entirely against my will to write of these things, for the reason that, even if winning by the aid of the Scriptures, as without doubt I shall win with God's help, still I have gained nothing, except that according to divine law no kind of food is forbidden to man at any time; although among the right and humbly thankful this writing of mine causes great joy of conscience, in which they rejoice in freedom, even if they never eat meat at forbidden times. And as a result I must have a worse time avoiding offence than if I had left the world in the belief that it was a divine ordinance, which, however, I could not do.

Prayer: Heavenly Lord, I believe that I need to simply be silent once more this week in our time together. Silent and receptive. Amen.

September 8

What has been written above, I am responsible before God and man to account and answer for, and I also desire of all who understand the Scriptures, in case I have misused the same, to inform me of this either orally or by letter, not disgracing the truth by shameless clatter behind one's back, which is dishonorable and unmanly. I desire to be guided everywhere by the New and Old Testaments. But what follows, I only wish to view as submitted, still with proof from the Scriptures, and let each one judge of it in secret for himself.

Prayer: Heavenly Lord, I believe that I need to simply be silent once more this week in our time together. Silent and receptive. Amen.

September 9[8]

We who are preaching the Gospel in the cities of a Christian State, were anxiously awaiting, O Charles, holy Emperor of justice, the time when an account of our faith, which we both have and confess, would be asked of us also. While we are standing in readiness for this, there comes to us the report, more by rumor than by definite announcement, that many have already prepared an outline and summary of their religion and faith, which they are offering you. Here we are in a great dilemma; for, on the one hand, love of truth and desire for public peace urge us all the more to do ourselves what we see others doing; but, on the other hand, the shortness of the time deters us, not only because all things must be done very speedily and as it were superficially, on account of your haste, (for this also rumor announces); but also because we, who are acting as preachers of the Divine Word in the cities and country districts of the State already mentioned, are settled and separated too far apart to be able to assemble in so brief a time, and deliberate as to what is most fitting to write to your Highness.

Prayer: Heavenly Lord, I believe that I need to simply be silent once more this week in our time together. Silent and receptive. Amen.

---

[8] Excerpts following are from Zwingli's 'An Account of the Faith'.

September 10

Moreover, as we have already seen the confession of the others and even their refutation by their opponents, which seem to have been prepared even before a demand was made for them, I believed that it would not be improper if I alone should forthwith submit an account of my faith, without anticipating the judgment of my people. For if in any business one must make haste slowly, here we must certainly make haste swiftly, since by handling this matter with careless neglect we run into the danger of being suspected because of silence or of being arrogant because of negligence. To you then, O Emperor, I offer a summary of my faith, with this condition, that at the same time I declare solemnly, that I entrust and permit the judgment not only of these articles, but of all that I have ever written or, by the grace of God, shall then write, not to one man only, nor to a few merely, but to the whole Church of God, as far as it speaks by the command and inspiration of the Word and Spirit of God.

Prayer: Heavenly Lord, I believe that I need to simply be silent once more this week in our time together. Silent and receptive. Amen.

September 11

First of all, I both believe and know that God is one and He alone is God, and that He is by nature good, true, powerful, just, wise, the Creator and Preserver of all things, visible and invisible; that Father, Son and Holy Spirit are indeed three persons, but that their essence is one and single. And I think altogether in accordance with the Creed, the Nicene and also the Athanasian, in all their details concerning the Godhead himself, the names or the three persons. I believe and understand that the Son assumed flesh, the human nature, indeed the whole man, consisting of body and soul, which He truly assumed of the immaculate and perpetual virgin Mary; but this in such a manner, that the whole man was so assumed into the unity of the hypostasis or person of the Son of God, that the man did not constitute a separate person, but was assumed into the inseparable, indivisible and indissoluble person of the Son of God.

Prayer: Heavenly Lord, I believe that I need to simply be silent once more this week in our time together. Silent and receptive. Especially on this day of all days. Amen.

September 12

And, although both natures, the divine and the human, have so preserved their character and peculiarity that both are truly and naturally found in Him, then the distinct peculiarities and activities of the natures do not separate the unity of the person any more than in man soul and body constitute two persons. For as these are of the most diverse nature, so they function by diverse peculiarities and operations; nevertheless man, who consists of them, is not two persons, but one. So God and man is one in Christ, the Son of God from eternity and the Son of Man from the time appointed; one person, one Christ; perfect God and perfect man; not because one nature becomes the other, or because the natures are fused together, but because each remains its peculiar self; and then, the unity of this person is not broken by this retention of the peculiarities.

Prayer: Heavenly Lord, I believe that I need to simply be silent once more this week in our time together. Silent and receptive. Amen.

September 13

Hence one and the same Christ, according to the character of the human nature, cries in infancy, grows, increases in wisdom [Luke 2:52], hungers, thirsts, eats, drinks, is warm, is cold, is scourged, sweats, is wounded, is cruelly slain, fears, is sad and endures what else pertains to the penalty and punishment of sin, though from sin itself He is most remote. But according to the peculiarity of the divine nature, with the Father He controls the highest and the lowest [*i. e.*, heaven and earth], he pervades, sustains and preserves all things, gives sight to the blind, restores the lame, calls to life the dead, prostrates His enemies with His word, when dead resumes life, ascends to heaven and sends from His home the Holy Spirit. All these things, however diverse in nature and character, the one and the same Christ does, remaining the one person of the Son of God, in such a way that even those things that pertain to His divine nature are sometimes ascribed, on account of the unity and perfection of the person, to the human nature, and those things that pertain to the human nature are sometimes attributed to the divine. He said that He was the Son of Man in heaven, [John 3:13], although He had not then ascended into heaven with the body. Peter asserts that Christ suffered for us [1 Peter 2:21], when the humanity alone could suffer. But on account of the unity of the person it is truly said both that: "The Son of God suffered" [Lk. 9:22], and that "the Son of Man forgives sins" [Mk. 2:10].

Prayer: Heavenly Lord, I believe that I need to simply be silent once more this week in our time together. Silent and receptive. Amen.

September 14

It is just as when we say that a man is wise, although he consists of body no less than soul, and the body has nothing to do with wisdom, nay rather is a poison and an impediment to knowledge and intelligence; and again we say that man is torn with wounds, when his body alone can receive wounds, but his soul in no way. Here no one says that two persons are made of the man, when to each part that is attributed which belongs to it; and vice versa no one says that the two natures are fused when that is predicated of the entire man which, because of the unity of the person, belongs indeed to the entire man, but because of the peculiar qualities of the parts to one only. Paul says: "When I am weak, then I am strong" [2 Cor. 12:10]. But who is it that is weak? Paul. Who at the same time is truly strong? Paul. But is not this contradictory, inconsistent, intolerable? Not at all. For Paul is not one nature, although one person. When, therefore, he says, "I am weak," the person who speaks is undoubtedly Paul, but what he says is neither predicated nor understood of both natures, but of the weakness of the flesh only.

Prayer: As, Father, I think about my faith and ponder its meaning in the hallowed shadow of Christian Doctrine, help me always think clearly and help me as well never exalt reason about your revelation of yourself. Amen.

September 15

And when he says, "I am strong and well," undoubtedly the person of Paul speaks, but only the soul is meant. So the Son of God dies, He who according to the unity and simplicity of His person, undoubtedly is both God and man; then He dies only with respect to His humanity. Thus not I alone do believe, but all the orthodox, whether ancient or modern, did likewise so believe regarding the deity, the divine persons as well as the assumed human nature. So also believe those who today acknowledge the truth.   Secondly—I know that this supreme Deity, which is my God, freely determines all things, so that His counsel does not depend upon the contingency of any creature. For it is peculiar to defective human wisdom to reach a decision because of preceding discussion or example. God, however, who from eternity to eternity surveys the universe with a single, simple look, has no need of any reasoning process or waiting for events; but being equally wise, prudent, good, etc., He freely determines and disposes of all things, for whatever is, is His. Hence it is that, although having knowledge and wisdom, He in the beginning formed man who should fall, but at the same time determined to clothe in human nature His Son, who should restore him when fallen. For by this means His goodness was in every way manifested.

Prayer: Father thank you for Jesus and for his bridging the gap between heaven and earth. Give me a chance today to tell someone about him. Thank you. In His name, Amen.

September 16

Since this goodness contained mercy and justice within it, He exercised justice when He expelled the transgressor from the happy home of Paradise, when He bound him to the mill of human misery and by fetters of disease, when He shackled him with the law, which, although it was holy, he was never able to fulfill. Here, twice miserable, man learned that not only his flesh had fallen into tribulation, but that his mind also was tortured by the dread of the law he had transgressed. For he saw that, according to its intent, the law is holy and just and a declaration of the divine mind, so that it enjoined nothing but what equity taught, then he saw at the same time that by his deeds he could not satisfy the intent of the law. Being thus condemned by his own judgment, having abandoned all hope of attaining happiness, and departing in despair from God's sight, he had no prospect but that of enduring the pains of eternal punishment. All this was a manifestation of the justice of God.

Prayer: The weight of my sin weighs heavy on my heart and yet I am free of its penalty. I regret my rebellion and I am grateful, this day, for your salvation. Amen.

September 17

Then, when the time came to reveal His goodness, which He had determined from eternity to display no less than His justice, God sent His Son to assume our nature in every part, except as far as it inclined to sin, in order that, being our brother and equal, He could be a mediator, to make a sacrifice for us to divine justice, which must remain holy and inviolate, no less than to His goodness. Thereby the world might be sure both of the appeasing of the justice and of the presence of the goodness of God. For since He has given His Son to us and for us, how will He not with Him and because of Him give us all things [Rom. 8:32]? What is it that we ought not to promise ourselves from Him, who so far humbled himself as not only to be our equal but also to be altogether ours? Who can sufficiently marvel at the riches and grace of the divine goodness, whereby He so loved the world, *i. e.*, the human race, as to give up His Son for its life [John 3:16].

Prayer: Thank you for reminding me of the gift of salvation, purchased by your Son for my sake and the world's. Give us all listening ears so that we might hear him. Amen.

September 18

This I regard as the heart and life of the Gospel; this is the only medicine for the fainting soul, whereby it is restored to God and itself. For none but God himself can give it the assurance of God's grace. But now God has liberally, abundantly and wisely lavished it upon us that nothing further remains which could be desired; unless someone would dare to seek something that is beyond the highest and beyond overflowing abundance. Thirdly—I know that there is no other victim for expiating sin than Christ (for not even was Paul crucified for us); no other pledge of divine goodness and mercy more certain and undisputable (for nothing is as certain as God); no other name under heaven whereby we must be saved than that of Jesus Christ [Acts 4:12]. Hence there is left neither justification nor satisfaction based on our works, nor any expiation nor intercession of all saints, whether on earth or in heaven, who live by the goodness and mercy of God. For this is the one, sole Mediator between God and men, the God-man Christ Jesus. But the election of God remains firm and unchangeable. Those whom He elected before the foundation of the world He elected in such a manner as to make them His own through His Son; for as He is kind and merciful, so also is He holy and just. All His works, therefore, savor of mercy and justice.

Prayer: Father when we go into the world today remind us to share Christ where and when we can—he is their only hope. He alone can bring us to God and he can alone offer us release from the power of sin. Thank you for his justifying love. Amen

September 19

Fourthly—I know that our primeval ancestor and first parent, through self-love, at the pernicious advice suggested to him by the malice of Satan, was induced to desire equality with God. When he had determined upon this crime, he took of the forbidden and fatal fruit, whereby he incurred the guilt of the sentence of death, having become an enemy and a foe of his God. Although He could therefore have destroyed him, as justice demanded, nevertheless, being better disposed, God so changed the penalty as to make a slave of him whom He could have punished with death. This condition neither Adam himself nor anyone born of him could remove, for a slave can beget nothing but a slave. Thus through his fatal tasting of the fruit he cast all of his posterity into slavery. Hence I think of original sin as follows: An act is called sin when it is committed against the law; for where there is no law there is no transgression, and where there is no transgression there is no sin in the proper sense, since sin is plainly an offense, a crime, a misdeed or guilt. I confess, therefore, that our father [Adam] committed what was truly a sin, namely an atrocious deed, a crime, an impiety. But his descendants have not sinned in this manner, for who among us crushed with his teeth the forbidden fruit in Paradise?

Prayer: Lord I wasn't in the Garden and I didn't eat the forbidden fruit—but I have sinned by breaking your law. I have sinned by rebellion. Like Adam, I have disregarded your will. Forgive, cleanse, and make me whole this day. For Christ's sake, Amen.

September 20

Hence, willing or unwilling, we are forced to admit that original sin, as it is in the children of Adam, is not properly sin, as has been explained; for it is not a misdeed contrary to law. It is, therefore, properly a disease and condition—a disease, because just as he fell through self-love, so do we also; a condition, because just as he became a slave and liable to death, so also are we born slaves and children of wrath [Eph. 2:3] and liable to death. However, I have no objection to this disease and condition being called, after the habit of Paul, a sin; indeed it is a sin inasmuch as those born therein are God's enemies and opponents, for they are drawn into it by the condition of birth, not by the perpetration of a definite crime, except as far as their first parent has committed one.

Prayer: Merciful Father, forgive, again, me of these crimes against you. Thank you for Jesus, who eases my burden and guilt. Help me cling always nearer to him. Amen.

September 21

The true cause, therefore, of discord with God and of death is the crime and offense committed by Adam, and this is truly sin. But that sin which attaches to us is in reality a disease and condition, involving indeed the necessity of death. Nevertheless, this would never have taken place through birth alone, unless sin had vitiated birth; hence the cause of human misery is sin and not birth; birth only in as far as it follows from this source and cause. This opinion can be supported by authority and example. Paul in Romans 5:17 says: "If by one man's sin death reigned by one, much more," etc. Here we see that the word "sin" is properly used. For Adam is the one by whose fruit death hangs upon our shoulders. In chapter 3:23 he says: "For all have sinned and come short of the glory of God," *i. e.*, the goodness and liberality of God. Here sin is understood as a disease, condition and birth, so that we all are said to sin even before we come forth to the light, *i. e.*, we are in the condition of sin and death, even before we sin in act.

Prayer: For deliverance from sin, we thank you Lord. We thank you. Amen.

September 22

This opinion is irrefutably strengthened by the words of the same writer, Rom. 5:14, "Death reigned from Adam to Moses, even over them that had not sinned after the similitude of Adam's transgression." See, death is our lot, even though we have not sinned as Adam. Why? Because he sinned. But why does death destroy us when we have not sinned in this way? Because he died on account of sin and, having died, i. e., being condemned to death, he begat us. Therefore we also die, by his guilt indeed, then by our own condition and disease, or if you prefer, by our sin, improperly so called. The example [we spoke of] is as follows: A prisoner of war by his perfidy and hostile conduct has deserved to be held as a slave. His descendants become serfs or slaves of their master, not by their own fault, guilt or crime, but by their condition which was the result of guilt; for their parent of whom they were born had merited it by his crime. The children have no crime, but the punishment and requital of a crime—namely a condition, servitude and the workhouse.

Prayer: Father remind me today that what I do affects all those around me. Help me not to forget that. Any day. And today. Amen.

September 23

I f it please someone to call these a crime, because they are suffered for a crime, I do not object. I acknowledge that this original sin, through condition and contagion, belongs by birth to all who are born from the love of man and woman; and I know that we are by nature children of wrath, but I doubt not that we are received among the sons of God by grace, which through the second Adam, Christ, has repaired the fall. This takes place in the following manner:
Fifthly—It is evident, if in Christ, the second Adam, we are restored to life, as in the first Adam we were delivered to death, that in condemning children born of Christian parents, nay even the children of heathen, we act rashly. For if Adam by sinning could ruin the entire race, and Christ by His death did not quicken and redeem the entire race from the calamity inflicted by the former, then the salvation conferred by Christ is no longer a match for sin. Moreover (which God forbid) the word is not true: "As in Adam all die, even so in Christ shall all be made alive" [1 Cor. 15:22].

Prayer: Father all are brothers and sisters potentially. May every person accept your Son's gift so that they may eternally belong to your family. In you Son's name, Amen.

September 24

B ut, whatever must be the decision about the children of heathen, this we must certainly maintain that, in view of the efficacy of the salvation procured through Christ, those go astray who pronounce them subject to an eternal curse, not only on account of Christ's reparation already mentioned, but also on account of God's free election, which does not follow faith, but faith follows election, about which see the following article. For those who have been elected from eternity have undoubtedly been elected before faith. Therefore those who because of their age have not faith, should not be rashly condemned by us; for although they do not as then have it, then God's election is hidden from us. If before Him they are elect, we judge rashly about things unknown to us. However, regarding the children of Christians we judge differently— namely, that all children of Christians belong to the church of God's people and are parts and members of His Church. This we prove in the following way: It has been promised by the testimonies of almost all the prophets that the Church is to be gathered from the heathen into the Church of the people of God. Christ himself said: "They shall come from the east and west, and shall sit down with Abraham, Isaac and Jacob" [Matth. 8:11], and, "Go you into all the world," etc. [Matth. 28:19].

Prayer: Help us never take for granted that we and our children belong to your family. Help us instead to teach all that they must individually and personally receive your gift through your Son. Help us never to presume, or assume. In Jesus' name, Amen.

September 25

B ut to the Church of the Jews their infants belonged as much as the Jews themselves. No less, therefore, belong our infants to the Church of Christ than did, in former times, those of the Jews; for if it were otherwise the promise would not be valid, as then we would not sit down with God on the same terms as Abraham. For he, with those who were born of him according to the flesh, was counted as in the Church. But if our infants were not thus counted with the parents, Christ would be sordid and envious towards us in denying us what He had given to the ancients, which it would be impious to say. Therefore, since the infants of Christians no less than the adults, are members of the visible Church of Christ, it is evident that they no less than the parents are of the number of those whom we judge elect. How godlessly and presumptuously do those judge who surrender to perdition the infants of Christians, when so many clear testimonies of Scripture contradict it, which promise not merely an equal but even a larger Church from the Gentiles compared with that of the Jews.

Prayer: We honor and respect those who have come before us, Lord. But we honor you more and respect your word more. When we encounter those whose words we trust help us never exalt even our dearest friend's words above yours. Amen.

September 26

We thus think, namely, that the word "Church" in the Scriptures is to be taken in various meanings. It is used for the elect, who have been predestined by God's will to eternal life. Of this church Paul speaks when he says that it has neither wrinkle or spot [Eph. 5:27]. This is known to God alone, for according to the word of Solomon [Prov. 15:11], He alone knows the hearts of the children of men. Nevertheless those who are members of this church, since they have faith, know that they themselves are elect and are members of this first church, but are ignorant about members other than themselves. For thus it is written in Acts [13:48]: "And as many as were ordained to eternal life believed." Those, therefore, that believe are ordained to eternal life. But no one, save he who believes, knows who truly believe. He is already certain that he is elect of God. For, according to the apostle's word [2 Cor. 1:22], he has the seal of the Spirit, by which, pledged and sealed, he knows that he has become truly free, a son of the family, and not a slave. For the Spirit cannot deceive.

Prayer: We rejoice in your providing us with a family and yourself as our Father. Dear Lord, without you and one another, we would be orphans. Thank you, from the bottom of my heart, for including me. Amen.

September 27

If He tells us that God is our Father, and we confidently and fearlessly call Him Father, untroubled because we shall enter upon the eternal inheritance, then it is certain that God's Spirit has been shed abroad in our hearts. It is therefore settled that he is elect who has this security and certainty, for they who believe are ordained to eternal life. Then many are elect who as then have no faith. For the mother of God [Mary], John and Paul, did not believe while infants, and then they were elect, even before the foundation of the world. But this they knew not, either through faith or revelation. Were not Matthew, Zacchaeus, the thief on the cross and Magdalene elect before the foundation of the world? Nevertheless, they were ignorant of this until they were illumined by the Spirit and drawn to Christ by the Father. From these facts it follows that this first church is known to God alone, and they only who have firm and unwavering faith know that they are members of this church.

Prayer: Dear Father thank you for choosing me. I believe, without a shred of doubt, that you have done so. I thank you for also electing those I love most in this world. And I pray that all who have been chosen are properly grateful. I pray I am properly grateful too. Amen.

September 28

A gain, the "Church" is taken in a general sense for all who are rated as Christians, *i. e.*, those who have enlisted under His name, a large number of whom acknowledge Christ publicly by confession or participation in the sacraments, and then at heart shrink back from Him or are ignorant of Him. To this Church, we believe, belong all those who confess Christ's name. Thus Judas belonged to the Church of Christ and all those who turned away from Christ. For by the apostles Judas was regarded as belonging to the Church of Christ no less than Peter and John, although it was by no means the case. Christ knew who were His and who were the Devil's. This church, therefore, is visible, albeit it does not assemble in this world. It consists of all who confess Christ, even though among them are many reprobates. Christ has depicted it in the charming allegory of the ten virgins, some of whom were wise and others foolish [Matth. 25]. This church is also sometimes called elect, although it is not like the first without spot. But as it is considered by men the Church of God, because of known confession, so for the same reason it is styled elect.

Prayer: Lord help us all be kept from Satan's grasp and secure in your care. But more than that, help us not to wander from you and endanger myself and others by drawing near to him. In Christ's name, Amen.

September 29

Finally, the "Church" is taken for every particular congregation of this universal and visible Church, as the Church of Rome, of Augsburg, of Lyons. There are still other meanings of the word "church," which it is not necessary to enumerate at present. Hence I believe that there is one Church of those who have the same Spirit, through whom they are made certain that they are the true children of the family of God; and this is the first fruits of the Church. I believe that this Church does not err in regard to truth, namely in those fundamental matters of faith upon which everything depends. I believe also that the universal, visible Church is one, while it maintains that true confession, of which we have already spoken. I believe also that all belong to this Church who give their adherence to it according to the rule and promise of God's Word. I believe that to this Church belong Isaac, Jacob, Judah and all who were of the seed of Abraham, and also those infants whose parents in the first beginnings of the Christian Church, through the preaching of the apostles, were won to the cause of Christ. For if Isaac and the rest of the ancients had not belonged to the Church, they would not have received the Church's token, circumcision.

Prayer: Rest, Lord, is what I need today. Rest in you. Rest from labor. I need your refreshing spirit. In His name, Amen.

September 30

These are the grounds for baptizing and commending infants to the Church, against which all the weapons and war engines of the Anabaptists avail nothing. For not only are they to be baptized who believe, but they who confess, and they who, according to the promise of God's Word, belong to the Church. For Simon the impostor, Ananias, Judas, and no one knows who, were baptized when they declared their adherence to Christ, even though they did not have faith. On the other hand, Isaac was circumcised as an infant without declaring his adherence or believing, but the promise acted in his behalf. But since our infants are in the same position as those of the Hebrews, the promise also declares their adherence to our Church and makes confession. Hence, in reality baptism, like circumcision (I am speaking of the sacrament of baptism) pre-supposes nothing but one of two things, either confession, i. e., a declaration of allegiance or a covenant, *i. e.*, a promise. All of which will become somewhat clearer from what follows.

Prayer: Father your promises are as certain as your love. Allow us to be at peace with them and with you and with those around us as we see them worked out in our lives. Give us the peace that is the sister of promise. We thank you for it. In Christ's name, Amen.

October 1

Seventhly—I believe, indeed I know, that all the sacraments are so far from conferring grace that they do not even convey or dispense it. In this matter, most powerful Emperor, I may seem to you perhaps too bold. But my opinion is firm. For as grace comes from or is given by the Divine Spirit (when I speak of grace I use the Latin term for pardon, *i. e.*, indulgence or spontaneous favor), so this gift pertains to the Spirit alone. Moreover, a channel or vehicle is not necessary to the Spirit, for He Himself is the virtue and energy whereby all things are borne, and has no need of being borne; neither do we read in the Holy Scriptures that visible things, as are the sacraments, carry certainly with them the Spirit, but if visible things have ever been borne with the Spirit, it has been the Spirit, not the visible things that have done the bearing. Thus when the rushing of the mighty wind took place [Acts 2:2] at the same time the tongues were conveyed by the power of the wind; the wind was not conveyed by the power of the tongues. Thus the wind brought the quails and carried away the locusts [Nu. 11:31ff; Ex. 10:4ff]; but no quails nor locusts were ever so fleet as to bring the wind.

Prayer: Lord send your Spirit to bear me through life. It's too perilous a pilgrimage to undertake on my own. And awaken those who try to do it to the folly of their ways. Amen.

October 2

Thus the Truth [Christ] spake. Therefore, the Spirit of grace is conveyed not by this immersion, not by this drinking, not by that anointing. For if it were thus, it would be known how, where, whence and whither the Spirit is borne. If the presence and efficacy of grace are bound to the sacraments, they work whithersoever they are carried; and where they are not used, everything becomes feeble. Nor can theologians plead that the proper disposition of the subject is demanded as a prerequisite [for the right use of the sacraments]. If he prepares himself, we can do something of ourselves and prevenient grace is nothing. If he is prepared by the Spirit for the reception of grace, I ask whether this be done through the sacraments as a channel or independent of the sacraments? If the sacraments mediate, man is prepared by the sacrament for the sacrament, and thus there will be a process ad infinitum; for a sacrament will be required as a preparation for a sacrament. But if we be prepared without the sacrament for the reception of sacramental grace, the Spirit is present in His goodness before the sacrament, and hence grace has been shown and is present before the sacrament is administered.

Prayer: Lord we thank you for the signs of your presence—both in the Supper and in Baptism. You unite us with yourself in both. Nothing could be more wonderful. In Christ's name. Amen.

October 3

From this it follows (as I willingly and gladly admit in regard to the subject of the sacraments) that the sacraments are given as a public testimony of that grace which is previously present to every individual. Thus baptism is administered in the presence of the Church to one who before receiving it either confessed the religion of Christ or has the word of promise, whereby he is known to belong to the Church. Hence it is that when we baptize an adult we ask him whether he believes. And only when he answers "yes," then he receives baptism. Faith therefore, has been present before he receives baptism, and is not given by baptism. But when an infant is offered, the question is asked whether its parents offer it for baptism. For when members of the Church offer it, the infant is baptized under the law that, since it has been born of Christians, it is regarded by the divine promise among the members of the Church. By baptism, therefore, the Church publicly receives one who has previously been received through grace. Hence baptism does not convey grace but the Church certifies that grace has been given to him to whom it is administered.

Prayer: The year is drawing to an end. Through the Fall and Winter keep our souls warmed by your presence. Please. Keep me from growing cold. In Christ's name, Amen.

October 4

I believe that a sacrament is a sign of a sacred thing, *i. e.*, of grace that has been given. I believe that it is a visible figure or form of the invisible grace, provided and bestowed by God's bounty; i. e., a visible example which presents an analogy to something done by the Spirit. I believe that it is a public testimony. Thus when we are baptized the body is washed with the purest element; by this it is signified that by the grace of divine goodness we have been gathered into the assembly of the Church and of God's people, wherein we should live upright and pure. Thus Paul explains the mystery in Romans VI. The recipient of baptism testifies, therefore, that he belongs to the Church of God, which worships its Lord in soundness of faith and purity of life. For this reason the sacraments, which are sacred ceremonies (for the Word is added to the element and it becomes a sacrament) should be religiously cherished, *i. e.*, highly valued and treated with honor. For though they are unable to bestow grace, they nevertheless associate visibly with the Church us who have previously been received into it invisibly; and this should be regarded with the highest veneration, since with their administration the words of the divine promise are declared and pronounced.

Prayer: Lord help us to treasure your gifts to us. Amen.

October 5

For if we think otherwise of the sacraments, namely that their external use cleanses internally, it would be but a return to Judaism, which believed that, by various anointings, oblations, offerings, sacrifices and feasts, sins could be atoned and grace could be purchased and secured. Nevertheless, the prophets, especially Isaiah and Jeremiah, always most steadfastly urged in their teaching that the promises and benefits of God are given by God's free goodness, and not with respect to merits or external ceremonies. I believe also that the Anabaptists in denying baptism to infants are entirely wrong; and not here only, but also in many other points, of which this is not the place to speak. That men might avoid their folly and malice, I have been the first to teach and write against them, not without danger, but relying on God's help, with the result that now, by God's goodness, this plague among us has greatly abated. So far am I from receiving, teaching or defending anything of this seditious faction.

Prayer: Father as we speak your word let us all, each of us, speak it truthfully and well as we are aided by your power. Hinder us from misspeaking or misrepresenting your word and truth in any way. In Jesus's name, Amen.

October 6

Eighthly—I believe that in the holy Eucharist, *i. e.,* the supper of thanksgiving, the true body of Christ is present by the contemplation of faith. This means that they who thank the Lord for the benefits bestowed on us in His Son acknowledge that He assumed true flesh, in it truly suffered, truly washed away our sins by His blood; and thus everything done by Christ becomes as it were present to them by the contemplation of faith. But that the body of Christ in essence and really, *i. e.,* the natural body itself, is either present in the supper or masticated with our mouth and teeth, as the Papists or some who look back to the fleshpots of Egypt assert, we not only deny, but constantly maintain to be an error, contrary to the Word of God. [I will make my points as follows]: First, by citing the divine oracles; secondly, by attacking the opponents with arguments derived therefrom, as with military engines; lastly, by showing that the ancient theologians held our opinion. Meanwhile, you Creator, you Spirit, be present, enlighten the minds of your people, and fill with grace and light the hearts that you hast created!

Prayer: Lord of all, teach your people the meaning of the Supper, how it is to be observed, and what impact it should have on their lives. Use your pastors and teachers to instruct the world rightly. Amen.

October 7

Christ Himself, the mouth and wisdom of God, says: "The poor you have always with you; but me you have not always" [John 12:8]. Here the presence of the body alone is denied, for according to His divinity He is always present, because He is always everywhere, according to His other word: "Lo, I am with you always, even to the end of the world" [Matth. 28:20], viz., according to divinity, power and goodness. Augustine agrees with us. Neither is there any foundation for the assertion of the opponents that the humanity of Christ is where-ever the divinity is, otherwise the person is divided; for this would destroy Christ's true humanity. Only the deity can be everywhere. An example is the sun, whose body is in one place, while his power pervades all things. The human mind also surmounts the stars and penetrates the underworld, but the body is nevertheless in one place.

Prayer: For your abiding presence we give you thanks dear Lord. What could we do without your help? Where could we flee but to you for aid? Thank you. In Christ's name, Amen.

October 8

C hrist says also: "Again I leave the world and go to the Father" [John 16:28]. Here the word "to leave" is used, just as "to have" before, so that the opponents cannot say: "We do not have Him visibly." For when He speaks of the visible withdrawal of His body, He says: "A little while and you shall not see me," etc. [John 16:16]. Neither would we maintain anything but a delusion if we were to contend that His natural body were present, but invisible. For why should He evade sight, when He nevertheless would be here, who so often manifested himself to the disciples after the resurrection? "But, it is expedient for you," He says, "that I go away" [John 16:7]. But if He were here, it would be expedient that we should see Him. For as often as the disciples thought about seeing Him, He manifested Himself openly, so that neither sense nor thought might suffer in aught. "Handle me," He says; and "Be not afraid, it is I," and "Mary, touch me not," etc. [Lk. 24:39; John 6:20; 20:17].

Prayer: Lord I so look forward to the day when, in heaven, I can embrace my Lord and my God. I cannot wait to thank and worship you in person. Thank you, in advance, for the honor. Amen.

October 9

And that we may know when He took His departure—not, as they invent rather than explain, when He made Himself invisible—Luke says: "While he blessed them he was parted from them, and carried up into heaven" [Lk. 24:51]. He does not say: "He vanished," or "rendered himself invisible." About this Mark says: "After the Lord had spoken to them he was received up into heaven, and sat at the right hand of God" [Mk. 16:19]. He does not say: "He remained here, but rendered his body invisible." Again Luke says in Acts: "When he had said these things, as they were looking, he was taken up; and a cloud received him out of their sight" [Acts 1:9]. A cloud covered Him, of which there would have been no need if He had only removed His appearance but otherwise had continued to be present. Nor would there have been any need of removal and elevation. Again: "This same Jesus, who was taken up from you into heaven, shall so come in like manner as you beheld him going into heaven" [Acts 1:11]. What is clearer than this? "From you," he says, "he was taken up;" therefore, He was not with them visibly or invisibly, according to His human nature. When, then, we shall see Him return as He departed, we shall know that He is present. Otherwise He sits, according to His human nature, at the right hand of His Father until He will return to judge the quick and the dead.

Prayer: Come quickly Lord Jesus! Come today! Amen.

October 10

B ut since there are some who deprive the body of Christ of restriction to a place and say that He is not in a place, let them see how clearly, and with closed eyes, they oppose the truth. He was in the manger, on the cross, at Jerusalem when his parents were on their journey home; in the sepulcher and out of the sepulcher; for the angel says: "He is risen, he is not here: behold the place where they laid him" [Mk. 16:6]. And that they may not be able to say that His body is everywhere, let them hear: "When the doors were shut, Jesus came and stood in their midst" [John 20:19]. What need had He of coming if His body was everywhere, but invisible? It would have been enough to come, but merely as one who was present to manifest Himself. But let such sophistical trifles be gone, which rob us of the truth both of Christ's humanity and of the Holy Scriptures.

Prayer: Father, we praise you for Jesus, the God Man. The Son of the Father. We appreciate his assumption of flesh and we appreciate his subjection to death.   In Jesus's name, Amen.

October 11

These testimonies deny the presence of Christ's body anywhere but in heaven, scripturally speaking, *i. e.*, as far as Scripture tells us about the nature and properties of the body assumed by Christ. And however far the contradictions, which are involved in our propositions regarding the power of God, drive us, we ought not to wrest it to such a point that we believe that God acts contrary to His Word. That would be a sign of impotence, not of power. Moreover, that the natural body of Christ is not eaten with our mouth, He Himself showed us when He said to the Jews, disputing about the corporeal eating of His flesh: "The flesh profiteth nothing" [John 6:63], namely, eaten naturally, but eaten spiritually it profits much, for it gives life. "That which is born of the flesh is flesh; and that which is born of the Spirit is spirit" [John 3:6]. If, therefore, the natural body of Christ is eaten with our mouth, what else than flesh can come out of flesh, eaten naturally? "That which is born of the Spirit is spirit." Therefore, that which is spirit, is born of the Spirit. If then the flesh is salutary to the soul, it should be eaten spiritually, not carnally. This applies also to the sacraments, that spirit is born of Spirit.

Prayer: Is it ever tiresome, Lord, for you to hear us thank you for your Son and the visible reminders of his covenant with us? Or do we fail to thank you enough? Nonetheless, thank you. Amen.

October 12

Paul announces that if he once knew Christ according to the flesh, henceforth he would know Him no more after the flesh [2 Cor. 5:16]. In view of these passages we are compelled to confess that the words: "This is my body," should not be understood naturally, but figuratively, just as the words: "This is Jehovah's Passover" [Ex. 12:11]. For the lamb that was eaten every Year with the celebration of the festival was not the passing over of the Lord, but it signified that such a passing over had formerly taken place. Besides there is the temporal succession, in that the Lord's Supper followed the eating of the lamb; which reminds us that Christ used words similar to those employed at the Passover, for succession leads to imitation. Moreover, the arrangement of the words is the same. The time affords an additional argument, since in the same evening meal the Passover was discontinued and the new act of thanksgiving was instituted. A further consideration is the characteristic of memorials, in that they take the name from the thing which they commemorate.

Prayer: Lord remind us to commemorate your Son's death in our lives each day. Help us. In Christ's name, Amen.

October 13

Thus the Athenians named removal of debts not as though the debts were remitted every Year, but because what Solon once did they continually celebrate; and this their celebration they dignify with the name of the thing itself. Thus those things are called the body and blood of Christ which are the symbols of the true body. Now follow the proofs: As the body cannot be nourished by a spiritual substance, so the soul cannot be nourished by a corporeal substance. But if the natural body of Christ is eaten, I ask whether it feeds the body or the soul? Not the body, hence the soul. If the soul, then the soul eats flesh, and it would not be true that spirit is only born of Spirit.

Prayer: I think I need to once more spend this time in silence, Father. Thank you for the gift of simply sitting in your presence wordless. Amen.

October 14

In the second place, I ask: What does the body of Christ, eaten naturally, bring about? If it be the forgiveness of sins, as one party claims, then the disciples obtained forgiveness of sins in the Lord's Supper, and therefore, Christ died in vain. If that which is eaten imparts the virtue of Christ's passion, as the same party claims, then the virtue of the passion and redemption was dispensed before it had taken place. If the body is fed for the resurrection, as another [Luther] very ignorantly asserts, much more would the sacrament heal our body and deliver it from sickness. But Irenaeus wants to be understood differently, when he says that our body is nourished by Christ's body for the resurrection. For he desires to show that the hope of our resurrection is strengthened by Christ's resurrection. Behold, what an appropriate figure of speech!

Prayer: Silence, Lord. Amen.

October 15

Thirdly—If the natural body of Christ was given to the disciples in the Supper, it necessarily follows that they ate it as it then was. But it was then capable of suffering; hence they ate a vulnerable body, for it was not then glorified. For if they say: They ate the same body, then not as it was capable of suffering, but the same as it was after the resurrection, I reply: Either He had two bodies, one not then glorified and another glorified, or one and the same body was at the same time capable of suffering and incapable. And so, since He dreaded death so much He was doubtless unwilling to suffer, but wanted to make use of that bodily endowment, by virtue of which He was free from pain. Therefore He did not truly suffer, but only by appearance; in this way Marcion is again brought back by these blindfolded gladiators.

Prayer: Silence, Lord. Amen.

October 16

By Ambrose, who in the [Commentary on the] First Epistle to the Corinthians says concerning the words: "You do show forth the Lord's death," etc.: "Mindful that by the Lord's death we have been freed, we signify in our eating and drinking the flesh and the blood which were offered for us," etc. By this we plainly see that whatever the ancients said so excellently concerning the Supper, they thought not of the natural but of the spiritual eating of Christ's body. For since they knew that the body of Christ must be in one place, and that it is at the right hand of God, they did not withdraw it thence to submit it for mastication to the foul teeth of men.

Prayer: Silence, Lord. Amen.

October 17

L o, a key for us whereby we can unlock all the declarations of the ancients concerning the Eucharist! That which is only a sign of the body, he says, is called the body. Let them who wish go now and condemn us for heresy, only let them know that by the same process they are condemning the opinions of the theologians, contrary to the decrees of the Pontiffs. For from these facts it becomes very evident that the ancients always spoke figuratively when they attributed so much to the eating of the body of Christ in the Supper; meaning, not that sacramental eating could cleanse the soul but faith in God through Jesus Christ, which is spiritual eating, whereof this external eating is but symbol and shadow.

Prayer: Silence, Lord. Amen.

October 18

And as bread sustains the body and wine enlivens and exhilarates, thus it strengthens the soul and assures it of God's mercy that He has given us His Son; thus it renews the mind by the confidence that, by His blood, the sins with which it was being consumed were destroyed. With these passages we shall now rest content, although any one could compile whole volumes in expounding and confirming the fact that the ancients are of our opinion. Neither let the pamphlet recently published concerning the opinions of the ancients, which it expressly promised to defend, move any one. For in a very short time we shall see the refutation of our very learned brother Oecolampadius, the object of whose exordium it was to defend the opinion of the ancients. But what things should be required in this matter for its clearer exposition and the refutation of the opponents we who hold this opinion have shown, I believe, abundantly, in many books, written to different persons.

Prayer: Silence, Lord. Amen.

October 19

Ninthly—I believe that ceremonies which are not through superstitious use contrary either to faith or to God's word (although I do not know whether such be found) can be tolerated by charity until the light of day shines clearer and clearer. But at the same time I believe that by virtue of the same charity the ceremonies mentioned should be abolished when it can be done without great offense, however much the evil minded may clamor. For Christ did not forbid Mary Magdalene to pour out the ointment, although the dishonest and evil minded Judas made an ugly disturbance. Images, however, which are misused for worship, I do not count among ceremonies, but among the number of those things which are diametrically opposed to the Word of God. But those which do not serve for worship and in whose cases there exists no danger of future worship, I am so far from condemning that I acknowledge both painting and statuary as God's gifts.

Prayer: Lord of all, keep me from worshiping anything or anyone but you. Especially myself. Yes Father, especially myself. Help me never to exalt my will above yours. Please. If I do, I only wreck my life. In Christ's name, Amen.

October 20

Tenthly—I believe that the work of prophesying or preaching is most sacred, so that it is a work most necessary, above all others. For to speak scripturally or strictly, we see that among all nations the outward preaching of apostles, evangelists and bishops preceded faith, which nevertheless we attribute to the Spirit alone. For alas! We see very many who hear indeed the outward preaching of the Gospel, but believe not, because there is a lack of the Spirit. Whithersoever, then, prophets or preachers of the Word are sent, it is a sign of God's grace, that He wishes to manifest a knowledge of Himself to His elect; and to whom they [the preachers] are denied, it is a sign of His impending wrath. This can be inferred from the prophets and the example of Paul, who was sometimes forbidden to go to some, and again called to others. But also the laws themselves and the magistrates can be assisted in maintaining public justice by no other means more effectually than by preaching. For in vain is that which is just taught unless they upon whom it is enjoined have a regard for what is just and love equity. But for this prophets prepare minds as ministers, and the Spirit as leader both of teachers and hearers.

Prayer: Lord fill the mouths of your preachers with your word and nothing else. Fill their hearts so with your Spirit that there is no room left for anything else. In this way alone can they bring your word to your people—and your people need it desperately. In Jesus's name, Amen.

October 21

This kind of ministers, namely those who teach, comfort, alarm, care for and faithfully watch, we acknowledge among Christ's people. That also we recognize, that they baptize, and in the Lord's Supper administer the body and blood of Christ (for thus we also call figuratively the holy bread and wine of the Supper), visit the sick, feed the poor from the resources and in the name of the Church; finally this that they read the Scriptures, interpret them and make a public profession, by which either they or others are prepared for presiding at some time over the churches.

Prayer: For faithful Pastors Lord we give you thanks. And we pray that you would send more. Amen.

October 22

Eleventh—I know that the magistrate when lawfully installed, holds God's place no less than the prophet. For as the prophet is a minister of heavenly wisdom and goodness, as one who teaches faithfully and brings errors to light, so the magistrate is the minister of goodness and justice. Of goodness, in that with fidelity and moderation, like God, he both hears and determines concerning the affairs of his people; of justice, in that he breaks the audacity of the wicked and protects the innocent. If a prince have these endowments, I believe that no fear need be entertained for his conscience. If he lack these, though he make himself an object of fear and terror, his conscience can in no way be cleared, upon the ground that he has been lawfully installed. Then, at the same time I believe, that a Christian should obey such a tyrant, until that time comes whereof Paul says: "If you canst become free, use it rather" [1 Cor. 7:21]. Nevertheless, I believe that this time is indicated by God alone, and not by man; and this is done not obscurely but as openly as when Saul was rejected and David became his successor. Regarding tribute and taxes, to be paid for protection, I am of the same opinion as Paul, Romans 13.

Prayer: Lord if ever we needed godly government it is now. Touch the lives of our leaders in the secular realm and give them the gift of insight so that they are equipped to lead your nations as you wish them to be led. Send a spirit of peace into all their hearts. Amen.

October 23

Twelfthly—I believe that the figment of purgatorial fire is as much an affront to the redemption of Christ freely granted to us as it has been a lucrative business to its authors. For if it be necessary by punishments and tortures to expiate the guilt of our crimes, Christ will have died in vain and grace will have lost its meaning. Can anything more wicked be imagined in Christianity? Or what sort of a Christ do they have who wish to be called Christians and then dread this fire, which is no longer fire, but smoke? There is a hell, where the unbelievers, disobedient and public enemies are forever punished. For when the Truth [Christ] speaks of the universal judgment, He asserts that after this judgment some will go into everlasting fire. [Matth. 25:41]. After the universal judgment, therefore, there will be everlasting fire.

Prayer: Heavenly Lord, we give you praise for your goodness to us and for your Son's willingness to pay fully the price we owe for our sins. Thank you that the very notion that somehow or other we would need to, or even be able to atone for ourselves was invented by persons fleecing the flock and not based in your word. In Jesus's name, Amen.

October 24

The above [twelve points] I firmly believe, teach and maintain, not by my own utterances, but by those of the Word of God; and, God willing, I promise to do this as long as the mind controls these members, unless someone from the declarations of Holy Scripture, properly understood, explain and establish the reverse as clearly and plainly as we have established the above. For it is no less agreeable and delightful than fair and just for us to submit our judgment to the Holy Scriptures, and the Church, deciding in harmony with these by virtue of the Spirit. We could have explained everything more amply and exhaustively, but since opportunity is lacking, we are content with these points, which we consider such that, while someone may readily pick flaws, which today is so common and easy, none will be able to pick it to pieces. If nevertheless anyone will attempt it, he will not do it unpunished. Then we shall perhaps draw forth what ammunition we have in reserve.

Prayer: Lord, for your Word, we give praise and thanks to you for providing such a gift—your Word, Jesus. And your word, the Bible. In your Son's name, Amen.

October 25

Howver, to come to what we are aiming at, we have for many Years made such studies in sacred and likewise in profane letters, that what we teach is not done thoughtlessly. May we also be permitted to praise the grace and bountifulness of God, so liberally bestowed upon our churches! Truly, the churches that hear the Lord God through us have so received the Word of God that falsehood and dishonesty are diminished, pride and luxury subdued, and violence and wrangling have departed. If these are not truly fruits of the divine Spirit, what are they then? Consider indeed, most excellent Emperor, and all you princes and nobles, what good fruit the so-called "human doctrine" has produced for us! The masses that were bought increased the lust and the impudence of both princes and people. Likewise they introduced and increased the luxury of the pontiffs and the excesses of the ministrants of the mass. Yes, what wicked deeds have they not kindled? For who can distribute the wealth accumulated through the mass, unless we tie up the veins, so to speak, and stop them flowing?

Prayer: Father we ask that you keep your Church from falling into manipulations and tricks to enrich itself. Thank you. Amen.

October 26

May God, therefore, who is far better than all of you—whom we both gladly call and believe to be most excellent men—grant that you may undertake to cut the roots of this and all other errors in the Church, and to leave and desert Rome with her rubbish which she has thrust upon the Christian world, and especially on your Germany. Moreover, whatever force you have exerted against the purity of the Gospel may you direct against the criminal attempts of ungodly Papists, that justice, which has been banished by your indifference and our innocence, which has been obscured by artful misrepresentations, may again be restored to us. There has been enough cruelty, unless it be not savage and cruel to issue unjust commands, to condemn, Yes to slaughter, kill, rob and outlaw. Since this way has not been successful, we must certainly go another way. If this counsel is from the Lord, do not fight against God; but if from elsewhere, it will fall to the ground by its own rashness. For this reason permit the Word of God to be freely disseminated and to sprout, O children of men, whoever you be, who cannot forbid even a grain from growing. You see that this seed is abundantly watered by the rain from heaven, neither can it be checked by any heat from men so as to become parched.

Prayer: Father, let the Gospel light shine unhindered and undimmed from my life, from our lives, for Christ's sake, Amen.

October 27[9]

I did in my last Sermon, dearly beloved, declare to you, by what means goods are rightly gotten, and how many kinds of theft there be, and sundry sorts of getting wealth unlawfully. There is then behind another treatise for me to add, and therein to teach you what is the true use of goods rightly gotten, and how we may lawfully possess them, and justly spend and dispose them in this transitory life. For justice doth not only not defraud any man, but doth, so much as it may, endeavor itself to do good to all men; neither is it enough for a godly man not to hurt anybody, unless also he do good to all that he can. And in this point do many men sin, while they are persuaded that they have done all the duty that they owe, if they hurt no man, and if they possess that which they have without trouble to any man; although in the meanwhile they have no regard, whether they help or do good to any man, or no. And he sins as greatly in the sight of the Lord, which doth not use rightly goods justly gotten, as he that has heaped up wealth in wickedness and naughty means. I will tell you therefore, so far as God shall give me grace, how, and in what sort, godly men may holily possess and dispose these earthly goods.

Prayer: Lord we very much need to know how to use the things you allow us to have rather than them using us. Forgive us for our rank materialism. Amen.

---

[9] Excerpts following are from *The Decades of Henry Bullinger: The Third Decade.*

October 28

First of all, that the use of worldly wealth may be healthful to the owner, holy men have a diligent care, that nothing of another man's remain in their possession: that is, they do carefully separate wealth rightly come by from unjust-gotten goods, and do faithfully restore whatsoever they find, in that which they have, to belong of right to other men. For they are thoroughly persuaded, and do verily believe, that by this means the wealth that is left them, although by restitution it be somewhat diminished, will then notwithstanding prosper the better, endure the longer, and be far more fruitful to them.

Prayer: Lord never allow me to keep something not rightfully mine nor accept anything gotten immorally. And help the Church to do the same. In Jesus's name, Amen.

October 29

Now this restitution is flatly commanded, and also very necessary to be put in practice: for the Lord in the law doth by sundry means, and that very carefully, give charge of it too, as is to be seen in the twenty-second of Exodus. Moreover, so often as the just and holy commandment of God was, through the covetousness and wickedness of mankind, cast off and neglected, the Lord raised up grievous and almost unspeakable evils against the despisers thereof, and scattered abroad the unjust-gotten goods by wars, mishaps, and divers calamities. For the prophet Isaiah crieth, saying: "The Lord shall enter into judgment with the elders and princes of his people, and shall say to them, It is you that have burnt up my vineyard, the spoil of the poor is in your houses." And Amos in the third chapter of his prophecy crieth: "They store up treasures in their palaces by violence and robbery. Therefore thus says the Lord God: Miseries shall invade you on every side of the land, and your enemies shall bring down your strength, or riches, from you, and your palaces shall be spoiled." We read therefore in the gospel, that Zachaeus, of his own accord, promised restitution four-fold double, that is, a full and absolute recompence of whatsoever he had taken wrongfully away; and it is assuredly certain, that he performed that promise: for he understood by the inspiration of the Holy Ghost, that a restitution of his ill-gotten goods was especially necessary, and that he should never be happy until he had made a full amends for all his wrongful dealings.

Prayer: Merciful God, help me make amends for my sins and not simply accept the notion that saying I'm sorry is enough. Help all of us take repentance as seriously as Zachaeus did. Amen.

October 30

But touching the time, when restitution ought to be made, the example of Zachaeus teacheth us; who, so soon as he was received to the favor of Christ, and did understand the works of truth and equity, did immediately promise restitution, and out of hand perform the same. Wherefore we must not foad off from day to day to make restitution. No man has need to double his offence. For you needest not by your morrow and over-morrow delays to augment his discommodity and hinderance any longer, from whom you hast, by your subtle means and wicked violence, wrested the goods that he has; considering, that he to his loss has lacked them long enough, and been without them too long, God wills.

Prayer: Dearest Lord, let me have a sense of urgency in regards to penitence and lead me to perform today the deeds of restitution needed today. In the name of Christ, Amen.

October 31

If you demandest, to whom you oughtest to make restitution? I answer, to him from whom you tookest it, if you knowest from whom you hast had it, and who it is whom you hast defrauded. But by that means, sayest you, I shall bring myself into obloquy and infamy. I bid you not do so: but, if you didst invent a means to take it, then find out some handsome way to restore it again, whereby you mayest escape and not incur the note of infamy. And pray to the Lord, that he will vouchsafe to show you a ready way and apt for to accomplish the thing that you mindest. If you meanest in good sadness to make true restitution, you shalt undoubtedly find a way to do it without reproach and obloquy. But if you dost but dally and jest with the Lord, you wilt not be without a thousand excuses, the best and the soundest whereof will never set your conscience at quiet liberty. Neither is God mocked. I cannot tell, sayest you, from whom I have taken it, and therefore I know not to whom I should restore it. If in very deed you knowest not from whom you hast taken it; then hast you the poor and needy, on whom to bestow it: to those you oughtest to deal your unjust-gotten goods, and not to superstition, or the ministers thereof.

Prayer: Oh Father, how much we justify our actions when they benefit us is a horrible thing to behold. Deliver us from this self-love and help us instead to love you and one another. Amen.

November 1

Now, let every one make restitution of so much as he has taken away; or at the least, of so much as he is able to restore. For many have spent, and so prodigally wasted other men's goods, that they are not able to make restitution of any thing again. Let such fellows acknowledge their fault, and repent their folly, from the bottom of their hearts. And if it happen at any time afterward that they come by goods, then let them be so much more liberal of their own, as before they were prodigal in spending other men's. But if all the riches which you possessest be other men's goods, and gotten of you by theft and robbery, so that, if you madest a full restitution, there should no penny be left for you, but that you must needs go beg; then art you verily hard bestead, and in too woeful a taking; Yes, you art mad and far beside yourself, if you wilt not stick, but still go on to paint your pride, and maintain a port with other men's pence, and satisfy your lust in the bowels, blood, and sweat of poor men's brows. Why dost you not rather abase yourself to poverty, and use your unjust-gotten goods, as needy people use their alms? For you livest of that that should be the poor's.

Prayer: Lord we live in a time when the rich are rich precisely because they take advantage of the poor. Give us eyes to see the truth and hearts to repent the evil. In Christ's name, Amen.

November 2

Therefore lay down your pride, and forsake your ruffling riot. Consider with yourself, who you art, and whereupon you livest: and still do your endeavor to make restitution, so far as you canst; and let it grieve you to see yourself not able to restore the whole again. If it be not a grief to you for a time to suffer poverty, to labor and faithfully to exercise some honest occupation, and to train up your children, leading them as it were by the hand, to work; then you shalt not want whereon to live, although you restorest all, whatsoever you hast, of other men's goods. But there is very small and almost no faith at all in many men; whereby it cometh to pass, that very few, or none, can be persuaded to make true restitution. To this I add (before I go any further) that they ought especially to think of a restitution, which have with evil words corrupted the minds of simple souls; with privy backbiting raised slanders on other men; or with perverse counsel stirred up the mightier men against the weaker sort: for these things do pass and are far above all earthly riches.

Prayer: It is sadly true, Lord, that most lack the faith to act restoratively. Let me be one of the few who will. Give me the strength I frequently lack to live the Gospel in its fullness. In Christ's name, Amen.

November 3

Thus much have I said hitherto touching restitution, of which other men have left very ample discourses. I for my part do see, that to a godly mind this work of restitution is short and plain enough; and therefore have I spoken of it so shortly as I have. For a godly and well disposed man doth with all his heart desire and seek to obey the law of God; and therefore, by calling to God for aid, he shall easily find a way to work justice and equity. As for those whose desire is rather to seem just men than to be just indeed, and do love this world more than it becometh them to do; they, with their over many questions and innumerable perchances and putcases, do make the treatise of restitution so tedious and intricate, that no man shall ever be able to make it so plain that they will understand it. I will not therefore answer them anymore, but only warn them to examine their own conscience, and see what that doth bid them do. Now I would have that conscience of theirs to be settled in, and be mindful of, the general law, which says: "Whatsoever you wouldest have done to yourself, that do you to another; and whatsoever you wouldest not have done to yourself, that do not you to another."

Prayer: Give the Spirit and infuse me with love so that I do indeed do to others what I wish done to myself. Heavenly Father, if you would. Amen.

November 4

After this now I will somewhat freely discourse upon the just possessing, using, or disposing of well-gotten earthly substance. First of all, no man must put any confidence in riches, which are indeed things transitory and do quickly decay: we must not settle our minds upon nor be in love with them; but by all means take heed that they drive us not to idolatry, nor hinder the course that we have to pass. Heaven is the goal whereat we run. Here again we must all give ear to the divine and heavenly words uttered by the prophet David, who said: "Put your trust in God always, pour out your hearts before him; for God is our refuge. As for the children of men, they be but vain: the children of men are deceitful upon the weights, they are altogether lighter than vanity itself. Trust not in wrong and robbery, give not yourselves to vanity: if riches increase, set not your hearts upon them." The apostle Paul, being endued with the same spirit, biddeth us to use the world and worldly things, as though we used them not. Again, he calls covetousness the worshipping of idols; and chargeth rich men not to put their trust in uncertain riches, but in the living God, who ministereth to all creatures living sufficiently enough. And therefore the Lord in the gospel forbids to heap up treasures upon earth.

Prayer: Lord of All, I thank you for all your blessings. But I am especially grateful for your gift of salvation, which eclipses all the rest. In Jesus's name, Amen.

November 5

Now, on the other side, we are not bidden by the apostles to spend our goods prodigally, in riot and wantonness. For we may not abuse the wealth, that the Lord has lent us, in pride and luxury, as many do, who lash out all in dicing, sumptuous building, strange clothing, excessive drinking, and over-dainty banqueting. The end and destruction of such kind of people the Lord doth very finely, though not without terror to them that hear it, set down in the parable of the rich glutton, who, after his delicate fare and costly apparel, was after this life tormented in hell with unspeakable thirst, and toasted there with unquenchable fire. Therefore these temporal goods must be rightly, holily, and moderately used, without excess.

Prayer: When you bless me materially, Father, also bless me with the wisdom of right use. Keep me from sin in this matter. Amen.

November 6

Every man must acknowledge these terrestrial goods to be the mere and free gifts of our bountiful and heavenly Father, and not to be given for our deserts, or gotten by our might. For we have of God's liberality all things necessary to maintain our lives. It is the Lord which blesseth and doth prosper our labor. Finally, they are not evil, but the good gifts of God, which he giveth to the maintenance of our lives, and not to our destruction: the fault is in ourselves, that riches are a snare to bring many men to evil ends. Moreover, the Lord himself requires, and in his word commandeth us, to be thankful to him for his good benefits bestowed on us; to use them with thanksgiving; to praise his name for all things; and to rejoice in his fatherly goodness showed to us. For thus doth Moses, the servant of God, in Deuteronomy, charge the Israelites: "When you hast eaten therefore, and filled yourself, then thank the Lord your God in that good land which he has given you.

Prayer: All good things come from your loving hand, Lord. Hinder me from boasting and thinking otherwise, as though what I have I somehow merit. In Jesus's name, Amen.

November 7

S ay not then in thine heart, My power and the might of mine own hand has prepared me this abundance. Remember the Lord your God: for it is he that giveth you power to get substance, etc." Moreover Paul the apostle says, that all the creatures of God are good, created to the good and preservation of us men; and biddeth us use them with the fear of God and giving of thanks. And again: "Whether you eat or drink, or whatsoever you do, do all to the glory of God." And in another place: "Let your manners be far from covetousness; and be content with the things that you have: for he has said, I do not forsake, nor leave you. So that we may boldly say, The Lord is my helper, I will not fear what man can do to me." Let earthly goods also serve our necessity. Now necessity requires a commodious dwelling-place, so much victuals as are sufficient, comely apparel, and honest company-keeping with our neighbors and equals. Let every man measure and esteem these circumstances, first by his own person, then by his family or household. For an householder must warily provide and foresee, that no necessary thing be wanting in his family.

Prayer: God, as this day proceeds, help me expend energy and effort to provide for my family, my friends, and my community. In that order. And help me be liberal with those things you have entrusted to me. Amen.

November 8

A nd thus far verily, and to this end or purpose, it is lawful for any man to lay somewhat up in store against years to come. The man, whose charge is much in keeping a great house, has need of the more to maintain it withal: and he, whose family is not so big, needeth so much the less as his house is the smaller. And one state of life, and a greater port, becometh a magistrate; when another countenance, and a lower sail, beseemeth a private person. But in these cases let every man consider what necessity requires, not what lust and rioting will egg him to. Let him think with himself, what is seemly and unseemly for one of his degree.

And then we do not in this treatise make so strict a definition of necessity, as that thereby we do utterly condemn all pleasure and moderate liberty for sensuality and luxury. For I know that God has granted and given to man, not only the use of necessity,—I mean, the use of those things which we as men cannot be without,—but also doth allow him all moderate pleasures wherewithal to delight him. Let no man therefore make scruple of conscience in the sweet and pleasant use of earthly goods, as though with that sweet pleasure which he enjoins he sinned against God; but let him which makes conscience, make it rather in the just and lawful use of those terrestrial riches.

Prayer: Thank you Lord for today and thank you Lord for your theologians who teach us things such as these. Indeed, help this day as I strive to live with what I need and not simply fill my life with things which I desire. As well, thank you for the pleasures of life! Amen.

November 9

For the Lord has in no place forbidden mirth, joy, and the sweet use of wealth, so far forth that nothing be done indecently, unthankfully, or unrighteously. For the prophet Jeremiah, alluding to the promises of God's law contained in the twenty-sixth of Leviticus and the twenty-eighth of Deuteronomy, says: "They shall come and rejoice in Zion, and shall have plenteousness of goods which the Lord shall give them, namely, in wheat, wine, oil, young sheep and calves; and their soul shall be as a well watered garden; for they shall no more be sorrowful. Then shall the maid rejoice in the dance, Yes, both young and old folks: for I will turn their sorrow into gladness, and will comfort them, and make them merry. I will make drunken the hearts of the priests with fat, and my people shall be filled with my goodness, says the Lord." Moreover in the fourth chapter of the third book of Kings we read: "And under Solomon they increased, and were many in number, as the sand of the sea, eating and drinking, and making merry."

Prayer: Thank you Father, for joy and mirth. They are greatly appreciated. Today help me be joyful and mirthful. In Christ's name, Amen.

November 10

A gain, in the eighth chapter of the same book we find: "And Solomon made a solemn feast, and all Israel with him, a very great congregation, which came together out from among all the people, even from the entering in of Hamath to the river of Egypt, before the Lord seven days and seven days, that is, fourteen days in all. Afterward he sent away the people, and they thanked the king, and went to their tents very joyfully, and with glad hearts, because of all the goodness that the Lord had done for David his servant, and for Israel his people." Like to this is that which we read in the eighth chapter of Nehemiah, in these words: "And Ezra, with the Levites, said to all the people which was sad and sorrowful, This day is holy to the Lord your God: be not you sorry, and weep you not; but go your way to eat the fat, and drink the sweet, and send part to them that have not, etc." And the Lord, verily, doth not require us men to be without all sense and feeling of those pleasures which he of his grace has given us to enjoy; neither would he have us to be altogether benumbed, like blocks and stocks and senseless stones: for he himself has graffed in us all the sense and feeling of good and evil, of sweet and sour.

Prayer: Merciful Lord thank you again for the many joys of life you bestow. They are marvelous beyond words and each day they pour down by their thousands. In Jesus's name, Amen.

November 11

A nd the same our God and Maker has, of his eternal goodness and wisdom, ordained a certain natural excellency in his creatures, and has adorned them, and made them so delectable, that we may delight in and desire them; Yes, and that more is, our God has planted in them a nourishing force and virtue to cherish us men, and to keep our bodies in fair and good liking. For David says: "And (he makes grow out of the earth) wine that makes glad the heart of man, and oil to make him have a cheerful countenance, and bread to strengthen man's heart. The trees of the Lord are full of sap, wherein the birds make their nests, and sing, etc." Moreover, it is reported that Jacob, the patriarch, did drink to drunkenness; and of Joseph and his brethren the scripture says: "And in drinking with him they were made drunken with wine." Now no man will take this drunkenness of theirs for that excessive bibbing, which the holy scripture doth everywhere condemn; but for a certain sweet and pleasant measure in drinking, wherewith being once satisfied they were made the merrier. For that mad kind of drunkenness bereaves the senses, and is so far from causing men to be jocund and merry, that, clean contrariwise, it makes them wayward, uncivil, out of order, beastly, swinelike.

Prayer: Keep us all from excess. Amen.

November 12

Alike phrase of speech useth Haggai the prophet, where he says: "Consider your own ways in your hearts; you sow much, but you bring little in; you eat, but you have not enough; you drink, but not to drunkenness:" that is, not to sweet and pleasant sufficiency, that, being filled and jocund therewith, you need desire no more, but for that plenty give thanks to the Lord, your good benefactor, for bestowing it on you. This do I somewhat more largely declare, because of the Anabaptists, and certain senseless Stoics, and other new sprung up hypocrites, the Carthusian monks, who, as they go about to make men mere blocks, so do they, with most tragical outcries, condemn utterly all allowable pleasure and lawful delights. They, to colour and commend their odd opinion to the ears of men, abuse many places of the sacred scriptures: "Woe (say they) to you which now are full, and do laugh now; for the time will come, when you shall hunger and weep:" when as indeed this and such like sayings were uttered of God against the wicked, and such as do unthankfully abuse the benefits and creatures of their good God.

Prayer: Help me receive with joyful moderation all that you provide and help me to remember from whence they come, today. Amen.

November 13

And therefore, for a conclusion of that which I have hitherto said, I add this; that godly men must still take careful heed, that they let not loose the reins to lust, and so exceed the golden mean. For mean and measure in these allowed pleasures also is liked and looked for, as well as in other things. For we must not only do good to them that are familiar with us, but to them also whom we did never see before, in keeping hospitality for way faring strangers, so far as our substance will stretch to maintain it. For if otherwise your wealth be slender, as that it will do no more but maintain thine own house and family, no parcel of God's law doth bind or bid you to distribute to other men the wealth which you yourself dost need as much or more than they. It is sufficient for you to provide that they of thine own household be not a burden to other men's backs.

Prayer: Lord, keep me from being a burden! To anyone! About anything!! But also help me to bear the burdens of others, to lighten and ease their load and provide with respite those who struggle under heavy loads. In Jesus's name, Amen.

November 14

So then the man, whose wealth is small, is not compelled to spend that little which he has in doing honor or showing courtesy to other men. Let those who are indifferently stored, and richer men who have wealth at will, be courteous and liberal to entertain strangers with frank hospitality. Let their minds be set to use liberality to their own praise and honesty, and not given to greediness and dishonest sparing of every odd halfpenny. For some you shalt find, who, though they be indifferent well stored with wealth and possessions, are then notwithstanding so wholly given over to the gathering of more, that neither for their own honesty's sake, nor for any show of courtesy, they will once bestow a trinket upon any man whatsoever, be he their own countryman, or a stranger unknown.

Prayer: Father we're grateful that you provide guidance for every aspect of our lives. Even for the most basic things. Amen.

November 15

These kinds of fellows are always chambered, and keep themselves close in secret counting-houses; their bags are their pillows whereon they sleep and dream of their ruddocks; they are not seen to stir abroad, lest peradventure occasion should be offered them to give entertainment, or to show some civility to aliens and strangers. The scripture doth give a far better report of the most holy and famous patriarchs, our grand predecessors. Lot sat in the gates of Sodom to wait for strangers and wayfaring men, to the end he might take them home to his house, and give them entertainment so well as he could. And if it fell out that he met with a stranger, he did not desire him home to his house for fashion's sake only, that is, with feint or feigned words; but he used in earnest all the means he could to compel him perforce to take up his inn, and lodge with him that night. Of our father Abraham you read in Genesis, that in the very heat of the day, as he sat in the door of his tent, he espied three men that were travelers, whom at the first sight, although he knew them not, he entertained very lovingly, and bade them welcome heartily.

Prayer: Oh Lord, forbid me laziness! Today! In your Son's name, Amen.

November 16

For he stands not to look when they should come and request to refresh themselves with him; but starteth up, and meeteth them before they come to the door of his tent, where he himself preventeth them in speaking first to them; and, when he had courteously after his country-manner with obeisance saluted them, he biddeth them very lovingly home to his house, and says: "I beseech you, my Lord, if I may find favor in your sight, pass not away, I pray you, from your servant." Lo, here he calls a traveler, and a stranger too, by the name of Lord. And although he were in the land, where he dwelt, a man of high authority and very great name, then notwithstanding he did, as it were, forget himself and say: "Pass not, I pray you, away from your servant." He calls himself a servant of strangers.

Prayer: Father teach me to be hospitable. Help me to welcome all who would come to my home and help me to be welcoming when I'm not at home. This is your will for us and we are obliged by love to do it. Amen.

November 17

Neither did Abraham use these words to make a show only of bounteous liberality: but when he had by entreaty requested them to stay, and by their grant obtained his desire, he bestirreth his stumps to accomplish in deeds the thing that he had promised; he makes haste to Sara, which was in the tent, and says: "Make ready at once three measures of fine meal, knead it, and make cakes." The scripture then addeth further this clause: "And Abraham, running to his beasts, caught a calf tender and good, and gave it to a young man, which hasted, and made it ready at once. And he took butter and milk, and the calf which he had prepared, and set it before them, and stood himself with them;" that is, did himself serve them, as they ate under the tree. This is wonderful verily, and to be thought on deeply.

Prayer: Lord thank you for those who in our lives teach us to be welcoming. Let us heed their message and teaching and become ourselves to others also an example of hospitality. In Jesus's name, Amen.

November 18

T hose goods were well and worthily bestowed upon so bountiful, liberal, and courteous a man as Abraham was, which knew how to use his wealth so honestly and with so commendable courtesy. Neither was he alone in all his house so frank and liberal; as his wife and family were readily given and very willing to put that holy exercise in desire and practice.

Prayer: As Thanksgiving nears, dear Lord, let me spend this time counting all my blessings upon myself and my family.   Let me be here in your throne room and ask nothing for myself but instead simply express my gratitude to you. Thank you, Father, 10,000 times thank you.

November 19

All things therefore were ready with a trice. In making preparation, also, no diligence was wanting; choice was made of all things; for riffraff and refuse-gear was not served to these strangers, but the best and likeliest of all that was found. The good man himself taketh pains like a servant. He himself bringeth in his country fare, which far doth excel all costly cakes and princelike dishes; and sets his guests to meat with butter and milk, and serveth the last course with veal, well fed, and housewife-like dressed. Neither was he content with this courtesy and entertainment, but humbled himself further then, and waited at the table, while his guests were at meat. The table, lo, was served by him, which had those great and ample promises made him by God; which is the father of all the faithful, which is the root and grandsire of Christ our Lord, which was the friend of God and confederate to puissant kings, being himself the most honorable prince in all the land, as he that had in war overcome and vanquished four of the mightiest kings of all the East, and brought them back again to slavery and bondage, delivering his people whom they had taken captive.

Prayer: As Thanksgiving nears, dear Lord, let me spend this time counting all my blessings upon myself and my family. Let me be here in your throne room and ask nothing for myself but instead simply express my gratitude to you. Thank you, Father, 10,000 times thank you.

November 20

This excellent and worthy man, I say, may well be a pattern for all wealthy men to follow, in bestowing honor, courtesy, and hospitality upon strangers and men unknown. For, lastly, beside his rare and seldom seen hospitality, he showed moreover this point of courtesy, that, when they rose from meat, he bare them company some part of the way. Let our wealthy cheapskates, therefore, at the last be ashamed of, and leave their stingy lives and insatiable covetousness. What pleasure, I pray you, have they of their riches? to whom do they good? whom do they honor with their close-kept coin? Or what honor or honesty doth their money procure or get them, while they live among men? Why do not the wiser sort of wealthy men rather leave this crew of miserable wretches, and hearken to the apostle's words, who says, "Remember to keep hospitality; for by that means many have lodged angels unwittingly and unawares?" And verily, he speaketh there of Lot and Abraham. Neither is it to be doubted, but that we entertain the very angels of God, and Christ himself, as often as we show courtesy and hospitality to good and godly mortal men.

Prayer: As Thanksgiving nears, dear Lord, let me spend this time counting all my blessings upon myself and my family. Let me be here in your throne room and ask nothing for myself but instead simply express my gratitude to you. Thank you, Father, 10,000 times thank you.

November 21

L astly, let the goods of wealthy men serve, not to the entertainment of men of credit only, but to the relief also of poor and needy creatures. For that wholesome saying of Paul must be beaten into their heads; "Charge them that are rich that they do good, that they be rich in good works, that they be ready to give, glad to distribute, laying up in store for themselves a good foundation against the time to come, that they may lay hold upon eternal life." With this doctrine of the apostle doth the prophet Isaiah very well agree, where he says touching Tyre: "Their occupying also and their wares shall be holy to the Lord: their gains shall not be laid up nor kept in store; but it shall be theirs that dwell before the Lord, that they may eat enough, and have clothing sufficient." Lo, here Isaiah teacheth us the means to lay up treasure that ever shall endure. Moreover, in the sixth chapter of Matthew the very same is repeated that was spoken of before. Let every one also call to his memory the other wholesome sentences of the Lord his God, to stir him up to the giving of alms. In Deuteronomy Moses says: "Beware that you harden not thine heart, nor shut to thine hand from your needy brother: but open thine hand liberally to him. You shalt give him, and let it not grieve thine heart to give to him: because that for this thing the Lord your God shall enrich and bless you in all your works, and in all you puttest thine hand to.

Prayer: As Thanksgiving nears, dear Lord, let me spend this time counting all my blessings upon myself and my family. Let me be here in your throne room and ask nothing for myself but instead simply express my gratitude to you. Thank you, Father, 10,000 times thank you.

November 22

The world shall never be without poor; and therefore I command you, saying, Open thine hand liberally to your brother that is poor and needy in the land." In the Psalms we find: "A good man is merciful, and lendeth; and guideth his words with discretion. He disperseth abroad, and giveth to the poor: his righteousness remaineth for ever; his horn shall be exalted with honor." Solomon also says: "Let mercy, or well-doing, or faithfulness never part from you: bind them about your neck, and write them in the tables of thine heart; so shalt you find favor and good estimation in the sight of God and men." Again, "Honor the Lord with your substance, and of the firstlings of all thine increase give to the poor: so shall your barns be filled with plenteousness, and your presses shall flow over with sweet wine." And again, "Whosoever stoppeth his ear at the cry of the poor, he shall cry himself, and not be heard." With these in all points do the sayings of the apostles and evangelists plainly agree. "Give to every one that asks of you." Again: "Verily, I say to you, inasmuch as you have showed mercy to the least of these my brethren, you have showed it to me."

Prayer: As Thanksgiving nears, dear Lord, let me spend this time counting all my blessings upon myself and my family. Let me be here in your throne room and ask nothing for myself but instead simply express my gratitude to you. Thank you, Father, 10,000 times thank you.

November 23

Which sentence surely is worthy to be noted, and deeply printed in the hearts of all Christians. For if the Lord Jesus reputeth that to be bestowed on himself, which you bestowest on the poor; then undoubtedly he thinketh himself neglected and despised of you, so often as you neglectest or despisest the needy. This is undoubtedly true and most surely certain: for the Lord and Judge of all people assureth us by promise, that at the end of the world, in that last judgment, he will give sentence in this manner and order: "Come, you blessed of my Father, possess the kingdom, etc. For I was hungry, and you gave me meat; I was thirsty, and you gave me drink:" and so forward, as is to be seen in the twenty-fifth chapter of St Matthew's Gospel. Hereto also belongeth the words of St John the apostle, where he says: "Whoso has this world's good, and sees his brother have need, and shutteth up his compassion from him, how dwelleth the love of God in him?" And from hence, undoubtedly, did first arise the common voice of them of old, which were wont to say: "If you seest a needy body die with hunger, and dost not help him, while you mayest, you hast killed him, and given consent to his death." Let him therefore, which has store of earthly goods, know for a surety, and in his heart be throughly persuaded, that he is bound especially to do good to the needy.

Prayer: As Thanksgiving nears, dear Lord, let me spend this time counting all my blessings upon myself and my family. Let me be here in your throne room and ask nothing for myself but instead simply express my gratitude to you. Thank you, Father, 10,000 times thank you.

November 24

Moreover let him that is wealthy do good to all men, so near as he can. For the Lord says: "Give to everyone that asks of you." And Tobit giveth his son this lesson, saying: "Turn not your face from any poor man." But if you canst not, through lack of ability, do good to all men, then succor them chiefly whom you perceivest to be godly-disposed.

Prayer: Father, help me to be as gracious to others as you have been to me. In Christs name, Amen.

November 25

Now our duty is to aid, and stand them in stead, with counsel, comfort, help, money, meat, drink, lodging, raiment, commendations, and with all things else wherein we perceive that they lack our helping hand: touching which I spake somewhat in the tenth sermon of the first Decade. We must also succor them readily, with a willing heart and a cheerful I mind: "for God requires a cheerful giver." And in helping them let us do liberally: for Tobit says, "Be merciful after your power; If you have much, give plenteously; if you have little, do your diligence gladly to give of that little. For in so doing the Lord shall bless both you and thine." Thus much, my brethren, have I hitherto said touching the lawful use of earthly goods. God grant that every one of you may print these sayings in his heart, and put in practice this holy work. Let us pray to the Lord that he will vouchsafe so to direct us in his ways, that for the getting of those transitory goods we lose not the everlasting treasure of his heavenly kingdom.

Prayer: Oh dear Lord, teach me always to be merciful. I am so prone to be otherwise. As a result, I alienate myself from you and others. Change my heart and my mind and show me a better way to be. Merciful. In Christ's name, Amen.

November 26

I shall not do amiss, I think, my reverend brethren, if to the treatise which I have already made of earthly riches, and of the use and abuse of the same, I do here also add a discourse of the divers calamities, wherewith man, so long as he liveth in this frail flesh, is continually vexed and daily afflicted. For since that many men do either lose their temporal goods, or else can by no means get them, which are the causes why they be oppressed with penury and neediness; it cannot be but profitable and very necessary too for every good man to know out of the word of God the very reason and ground of his consolation in his miseries; lest, being swallowed up of too great sorrow, and entangled in utter desperation, he give himself over to be Satan's bond-slave. Now this treatise serveth for the whole life of man. For I mean not to speak of any one calamity alone, as of poverty, or penury, but generally of all the miseries that happen to man. Verily, since man is born to grief and misery, as birds to flying and fishes to swimming; his life can never possibly be either sweet or quiet, unless he know the manner and reason of his calamity.

Prayer: When difficulties arise, Father, keep my mind and heart fixed on Jesus, my refuge and fortress. Otherwise, my cares will overwhelm me and I will sink as Peter did. In His name, Amen.

November 27

And if so be he know the reason thereof, religiously taken and derived out of the word of God; then his life cannot choose but be sweet and quiet, howsoever otherwise it seem to be most bitter and intolerable. The mind of man, verily, is sorely afflicted and grievously tormented with lamentable miseries; but the same, on the other side, is sweetly eased and mightily upholden by the true knowledge of those miseries, and holy consolations, derived and taken out of the word of God. First of all, it is requisite to lay before our eyes and reckon up the several kinds and especial sorts of mortal men's calamities. The evils verily are innumerable, which daily fall upon our necks; but those which do most usually happen are the plague or pestilence, sundry and infinite diseases, death itself, and the fear of death, whose terror to some is far more grievous than death can be.

Prayer: Father, problems are sure to arise. When they do, I ask only the patience to endure them without complaining and mercy towards those involved. In Jesus's name, Amen.

November 28

To these be added the death and destruction of most notable men, or such of whom we make most account; robberies, oppressions, endless ill chances, poverty, beggary, lack of friends, infamy, banishment, persecution, imprisonment, enforced torments, and exquisite punishments of sundry sorts and terrible to think on, unseasonable and tempestuous weather, barrenness, dearth, frost, hail, deluges, earthquakes, the sinking of cities, the spoiling of fields, the burning of houses, the ruin of buildings, hatred, factions, privy grudges, treasons, rebellions, wars, slaughters, captivity, cruelty of enemies, and tyranny; also the lack of children; or troubles, cares, and hellish lives by the matching of unmeet mates in wedlock, by children naughtily disposed, maliciously bent, disobedient and unthankful to father and mother; and lastly, care and continual grief in sundry sorts for sundry things, which never cease to vex our minds.

Prayer: Help me, Lord, to stop worrying so much about what may happen. It normally isn't the problems I encounter, but the problems I imagine which are most harmful. Give me the sense to know that you are Lord of all. In Christ's name, Amen.

November 29

Yes, the saints are through all their life time afflicted and vexed, when as contrarily the wicked abound with all kinds of joy and delightful pleasures: whereupon it cometh, that great temptations and complaints arise in the minds of the godly. The wicked do gather by their happy state and pleasant life, that God doth like their religion, and accept their manner of dealing, whereby they are confirmed and grounded in their errors. And on the other side the godly, by reason of the miseries which they have long suffered, do revolt from godliness, and turn to the ungodly, because they think that the state of the wicked is far better than theirs. Now it is good to know, and severally to learn, all this out of the scriptures. That the godly are and have been afflicted, as well as the wicked, since the beginning of the world, it is manifest to be seen in the example of Abel and Cain: for, as the one was pitifully slain of the other for his sincere worshipping of God, so was the other for the murder made a vagabond, not daring for fear to abide in any place to take his rest in. Jacob, surnamed Israel, is read to have been vexed with many calamities. The same is reported also of the Egyptians, while they persecuted the Israelites.

Prayer: Lord, let the wicked repent and let the difficulties they face draw to their attention the brevity of their lives and their need to turn to you for salvation. Use trials to improve your saints as well. Amen.

November 30

S aul was vexed, and David afflicted. The Lord our Savior, with his disciples, bare the cross of grief and trouble: again, on the other side, the Jews, who cruelly persecuted Christ and his disciples, were horribly destroyed, and that worthily too, for their villainous injury. Unspeakable are the evils which the church of Christ did suffer in those ten most bloody persecutions before the reign of Constantine the great: but Orosius, the notable, diligent, and faithful historiographer, makes mention, that due and deserved punishments were out of hand laid upon the necks of those persecuting tyrants; of whom I will speak somewhat in place convenient. And by the testimonies both of God and man, and also by manifold experience, we see it proved, that as well the godly as ungodly are touched with miseries. Yes truly, the best and holiest men for the most part are troubled and afflicted, when the wicked and worser sort are free from calamities, leading their lives in ease and pleasures. And while the good do suffer persecution and injuries, the wicked rejoice thereat For the Lord in the gospel says to his disciples: "Verily, verily, I say to you, you shall weep and lament, the world shall be glad; but you shall be sorrowful."

Prayer: I realize, Father, that it only seems as though some people 'get away' with their sins. I know they don't. Nor will I. Keep me ever aware more of my own shortcomings than the shortcomings of others. Amen.

December 1

But now, what kind of temptations those be, which arise in the hearts of the godly through their tribulations; and what those men, which are not altogether godless nor the enemies of God, do gather of the felicity wherein the wicked are, the scripture in many places teacheth us, and especially in that wonderful discourse of Job and his friends. The prophet Habakkuk complaineth, and says: "O Lord, how long shall I cry, and you not hear? how long shall I cry out to you for the violence that I suffer, and you not help? why am I compelled to see iniquity, spoiling, and unrighteousness against me? why dost you regard them that despise you, and holdest your tongue while the wicked treadeth down the man that is more righteous than himself? The wicked doth circumvent the righteous; and therefore wrong judgment proceedeth." In Malachi the hypocrites do cry: "It is but vain to serve God: and what profit is it that we have kept his commandments, and that we have walked humbly before the face of the Lord? Now therefore we call the proud and arrogant blessed and happy: for the workers of wickedness live happily and are set up; and they tempt God, go on in their wickedness, and are delivered."

Prayer: The advent of your Son's presence in our midst is coming soon. Come, Lord Jesus. Come. Amen

December 2

The holy prophet Asaph containeth all this most fully and significantly in the Psalm, where he says: "My feet were almost gone, my treadings had well nigh slipped: for I was grieved at the wicked, when I did see the ungodly in such prosperity. For they are in no peril of death; they are, I say, troubled with no diseases, whereby they are drawn, as it were, to death, but are lusty and strong. They come into no misfortune like other men; but are free from the evils wherewith other folk are plagued: and this is the cause that they are so holden with pride, and wrapped in violence as in a garment. Their eyes swell with fatness, and they do even what they lust. They stretch forth their mouth to heaven, and their tongue goeth through the world: Yes, and they dare to say, Tush, how should God perceive it? Lo, these are the ungodly, these prosper in the world, and these have riches in possession. Then, said I, have I cleansed my heart in vain, and washed mine hands in innocency: and I bear punishment every day. And while I thought thus to myself, I had almost departed from the generation of God's children."

Prayer: Lord of life, give light to us so as to illuminate your Son's nearness. Help us set aside our pride and flee to him as sensible people would. Send your Son into our hearts. Amen.

December 3

Now since this is so, it followeth consequently to beat out the causes of these calamities: for in so doing we shall be the better able to judge rightly of the miseries both of the godly and wicked sort of people. The causes of calamities are many, and of many sorts: but the general and especial cause is known to be sin. For by disobedience sin entered into the world, and death by sin; and so, consequently, diseases, and all evils in the world. They are very light-headed and vain fellows, that refer these causes to I cannot tell what blind constellations, and movings of planets. For we by our evil lusts and corrupt affections do heap up day by day one evil on another's neck. And at our elbows stands the Devil, who roundeth us in the ears, and eggeth us forwards; and, as helps to spur us on, there are a crew of naughty packs, that never cease to train us in. And daily there do rise up divers instruments of tribulation, wherewith the most wise and just God doth suffer us men to be exercised and tormented.

Prayer: It was our sin that brought your Son here, Lord. Not to strike us down but to lift us up and redeem us. But when he comes again, he will come as judge. Oh Lord, without your forgiveness, none of us could endure that coming. In His name, Amen.

December 4

But the same causes of affliction are not always found to be in the holy worshippers of God, as are in the wicked despisers of his name. The saints are often afflicted, that by their trouble the glory of God may be known to the world. For when the disciples of Christ did see the blind man in the gospel, which was blind from his mother's womb, they said to the Lord: "Master, who sinned, this man, or his parents, that he was born blind? Jesus answered, Neither did this man sin, nor his parents; but that the works of God might be made manifest in him." Likewise, when the Lord heard say that Lazarus was sick, "This disease (says he) is not to death, but to the glory of God, that by it the Son of God may be glorified." And then, if we touch this matter to the quick, there can none in the world be found without sin; so that, if the Lord will mark our iniquities, he shall always find somewhat to be punished in us: as it is at large declared in the book of Job.

Prayer: Lord, thank you for the purification your Son's sacrifice makes possible. As I live each day, but especially this day, teach me what that purification should look like so that I might examine myself and adjust my life in accordance with your will. In Christ's Name, Amen.

December 5

Furthermore, the Lord doth suffer his spouse, the church, which he loveth full dearly, to be troubled and afflicted to this end and purpose; that he may openly declare, that the elect are defended, preserved, and delivered by the power and aid of God, and not by the policy or help of man. For Paul says: "We have this treasure in earthen vessels, that the excellency of the power may be God's, and not of us: while we are troubled on every side, but not made sorrowful; we are in poverty, but not in extreme poverty; we suffer persecution, but are not forsaken therein; we are cast down, but we perish not; we always bear about in the body the dying of the Lord Jesus, that the life of Jesus might also be made manifest in our body. For we which live are always delivered to death for Jesus' sake, that the life also of Jesus might be made manifest in our mortal flesh." Also the same apostle says: "Virtue is made perfect in infirmity."

Prayer: Thank you for your body on this earth, Lord. Thank you for your Church. Thank you for the privilege of participating in it. Amen.

December 6

Again, as the afflictions of the holy martyrs and faithful saints of Christ are testimonies of the doctrine of faith, as our Savior in the gospel says, "They shall deliver you up to councils, and in their synagogues they shall scourge you; Yes, you shall be brought before kings and rulers for my sake, that this might be for a witness to them and the people:" even so, in like manner, are the saints, overladen with miseries, made examples for us to learn by how to overcome and despise the world, and to aspire to heavenly things. Finally, the Lord doth try those that be his by laying the cross upon their necks, and purgeth them like gold in the fire: he cutteth from us many occasions of evil, that he may bring us to the bearing of greater and more plentiful fruit. The wisdom of the Lord doth therein follow the manner of goldsmiths, who put their gold into the fire to purge, and not to mar it: and he imitateth also good husbandmen, who, when their corn is somewhat too rank, do mow it down; and prune their trees, not to destroy, but to make them bear more abundant fruit.

Prayer: Lord of life, as we walk with you bless us to walk with each other in harmony. In that way, we can be light to the world as you intend. In Christ's name, Amen.

December 7

And this flesh of ours, verily, in peace and quietness is luskish, lazy, drowsy, and slow to good and honest exercises; it is content, and seeks no further than earthly things; it is wholly given to pleasures; it doth utterly forget God and godly things: now therefore it is not expedient only, but also very necessary, to have this dull and sluggish lump stirred up and exercised with troubles, afflictions, and sharp persecutions. The saints herein are like to iron, which by use is somewhat worn and diminished, but by lying still unoccupied is eaten more with rust and canker. Most truly therefore said St Peter: "Dearly beloved, think it not strange, that you are tried with fire, which thing is to try you, as though some strange thing happened to you: but rejoice rather, in that you are partakers of the afflictions of Christ; that, when his glory is revealed, you may be merry and glad."

Prayer: Help us overcome the flesh and live by the Spirit more each day, as your Son's coming draws daily nearer. In His name, Amen.

December 8

For Paul to Timothy says: "Remember that Jesus Christ of the seed of David was raised from the dead according to my gospel; for which I am afflicted, as an evil doer, even to bonds: and then I suffer all things for the elect's sakes, that they might also obtain the salvation which is in Christ Jesus with eternal glory. It is a faithful saying: For if we be dead with him, we shall also live with him: if we be patient, we shall reign with him: if we deny him, he shall also deny us." For in his epistle to the Romans he says: "Those which he knew before he did also predestinate, that they should be like-fashioned to the shape of his Son, that he might be the first-begotten among many brethren. Moreover, whom he did predestinate, them also he called; and whom he called, them also he justified; and whom he justified, them also shall he glorify." Again, in the same epistle he says: "We rejoice also in tribulations; knowing that tribulation worketh patience; patience proof; proof hope: and hope makes not ashamed, etc." This do the private examples of the saints, and public examples of the whole church, very plainly declare.

Prayer: Thank you for choosing me, and making me your own. I don't know why, or how you choose those you do, but I trust your wisdom and your right. In Christ's name, Amen.

December 9

Abraham, Isaac, and Jacob, had never known that God's helping hand had been so faithful and always present with them; they had never been grounded in so sure hope, nor showed such especial fruit of their excellent patience; if they had not been exercised with many perils, and, as it were, oppressed with infinite calamities. Whereupon it cometh, that David cried: "It is good for me, Lord, that you hast troubled me." The church of Israel was oppressed in Egypt; but to the end that it might with the more glory be delivered, and pass into the land of promise. The Jewish church was afflicted by them of Babylon and the Assyrians, so that their temple was overthrown, and the saints carried captive with the worst of the people. But the godly sort in their very captivity do feel the wonderful help of God, and by that means are made the better by their afflictions; so that the name of the Lord was known among the Assyrians, the Chaldeans, the Medes and Persians, to his great glory and renown, as it is at large declared in the histories of Daniel, Esther, and Ezra.

Prayer: Father in heaven, without question if your help were absent, nothing would survive or even exist. This is more wonderful and praiseworthy than human words can express. Amen

December 10

Here also is to be noted, that certain punishments are appointed of the Lord as plagues for certain sins; so that most commonly a man is plagued by the very same things wherein he sinned against the Lord. David offended God with murder and adultery; and therefore is he punished with the shame of his own house, with whoredom, incest, and detestable murder of his own children; and lastly, driven out and banished his kingdom. It was pride and arrogance, wherein Nebuchadnezzar sinned; and therefore, being distract of his wits and turned into a beastly madness, he led his life for a certain time with beasts of the field. But as Nebuchadnezzer was, when God thought good, restored to his kingdom; so David did in time convenient feel the mercy of the Lord in settling him in his seat again. For this saying of the Lord is firmly ratified forever, not only to David, but to everyone that believeth, which is in these words set down in the scriptures: "If his children forsake my law, and keep not my commandments, I will visit their sins with rods, and their iniquities with scourges: then will I not utterly take my goodness from him; I will not break my covenant, neither will I change the thing that is once gone out of my mouth."

Prayer: Teach us to remember that our sins are deadly and have as a consequence death itself. Thank you, indeed, that Christ has borne that penalty for us. We await his coming with grateful hearts. Amen.

December 11

Therefore it is to our profit that the Lord afflicteth us; as he himself testifies in the revelation of Christ, uttered by John the apostle and evangelist, saying: "Them which I love I rebuke and chasten." And Solomon, long before that, did say: "My son, refuse not the chastening of the Lord, neither faint when you art corrected of him. For whom the Lord loveth, him he chasteneth; and then delighteth in him, as a father in his son." Now, touching the persecutions and terrible plagues laid upon the neck of the whole church of God, or several martyrs of the same; as they were, for the most part, breathed out of worldly tyrants against the saints for their open confession and testimonies of their faith, and truth of the gospel, so most commonly the causes of those broils were the sins and offences of the saints, which the justice of God did visit in his holy ones, no doubt to the good and salvation of the faithful.

Prayer: Thank you again for sending Christ to bear my guilt and sin away. I'm so grateful. I have no idea what life would be without your gift, and I don't want to know. In His name, Amen.

December 12

For of that bloody persecution under the emperors Diocletian and Maximinian, which caused many thousands, Yes, many millions, of martyrs to come to their endings, we read this following in the history of Eusebius of Caesarea, who learned it not by hear-say, but was himself an eye-witness of the same: "When as by too much liberty and wantonness the manners of the church were utterly marred, and the discipline thereof corrupted; while among ourselves we envy one another, and diminish one another's estimation; while among ourselves we snatch at and accuse ourselves, moving deadly war among ourselves; while dissimulation sitteth in the face, deceit lurketh in the heart, and falsehood is uttered in words, so that one evil is heaped still on another's neck; the Lord beginneth by little and little, and with the bridle to check the mouth of his tripping church, and, reserving the congregations touched, he beginneth first to suffer them to feel persecution which served as soldiers in the camps of the Gentiles.

Prayer: When I am wrong, correct me Father, and don't allow me to attempt to run and hide from your discipline. Instead help me to understand that in and through it you wish to teach me something that will make me more like Christ. In His name, Amen.

December 13

B ut when as by that means the people could not be made to remember themselves, insomuch that they ceased not to persist in their wickedness, and that the very guides of the people and chief of the church, unmindful of God's commandment, were set on fire among themselves with strife, envy, hatred, and pride, so that they might think they rather exercised tyranny than the office of ministers, because they had forgotten Christian sincerity and pureness of living; then at length the houses of prayer and churches of the living God were thrown to the ground, and the holy scriptures set on fire in the broad and open streets." And then here I make difference betwixt sin and sin. For the saints sin, but then they abstain commonly from heinous crimes; although now and then too they fall into them, as it is evident by the example of David: but then, for the most part, they fly from theft, murder, whoredom, and other grievous sins like to these. And while the saints are afflicted by tyrants, it is not for the neglecting of justice and true religion; but for the contemning of superstition, and steadfast sticking to Christ and his gospel.

Prayer: Oh Father, above all things I must steadfastly stick with Christ.   But I cannot do it alone.   Send your Spirit every moment to help. Amen.

December 14

T he Lord therefore doth forgive, and in the blood of Christ wash away, the sins of the holy martyrs, reputing them to suffer death not for the sins which they have committed, but for the zeal and love of true religion. He also punisheth the tyrants for the death of his martyrs; because, in putting them to death, they follow their own tyrannous affection, and not the just judgment of the living God. The Lord's mind, verily, was by tyrants to chasten his people Israel: but the tyrants (as Isaiah in his tenth chapter witnesseth) did not take it to be so; but rather, following their own affections, they passed all measure in afflicting them, and never sought after justice and equity: they therefore are punished of the Lord for killing his innocent and guiltless servants. For the thing which the Lord did persecute in his people, (their sins, I mean, and offences,) that do the tyrants neither punish nor persecute: but the thing that pleased God, (the love, I mean, of true religion, and the utter detesting of idolatry,) that they are mad upon, and persecute it with sword and fire and unspeakable torments. To this therefore doth that saying of St Peter belong: "See that none of you be punished as a murderer, or as a thief, or as an evil-doer, or as a busy-body in other men's matters: but if any man suffer as a Christian man, let him not be ashamed, but rather glorify God on this behalf."

Prayer: Maker, Redeemer, Sustainer.   Lord of all in Trinity, Father, Son and Spirit. We praise and honor you for making, saving, and keeping us. Prepare us each day for the return of the Son. This may be that very day. Aid me in and for readiness. Amen.

December 15

Then, for all this, I would not that heinous offenders should any whit despair. They have the example of the thief that was crucified with Christ; that let them follow: let them, I say, confess their faults, believe in Christ, commit themselves wholly to his grace and mercy, and lastly, suffer patiently the pain of their punishment; and, in so doing, there is no doubt but they shall be received of Christ into Paradise, and live there forever, as the thief doth with Christ. And although the godly be slain among transgressors, then is he no more defiled by suffering with them than Christ our Lord was, being hanged among thieves. For though the godly and ungodly be wrapped and coupled together in one kind of punishment, then are they severed by their unlike ending; while the wicked, after this bodily death, is carried to hell, there to burn without intermission; and the godly taken immediately into heaven, to live with Christ his Lord, to whom he committed and commended himself.

Prayer: Father, for these next 10 days I will simply, one last time this year, sit quietly in your presence. And wait. And wait as long as I have life, for the coming of your Son. Amen.

December 16

Touching this matter, and the causes of the afflictions of the holy men of God because good men do suffer the same and like punishment that the evil sort do, it is to be marked, that there is not therefore no difference betwixt them, because there is no diversity in the thing that they suffer. For as in one and the same fire gold doth shine, and chaff doth smoke; and under one flail the husk is broken, and the corn purged; and as the scummy froth is not mixed with the oil, although one weight of the same press doth crush both out at once: even so one and the self-same misery, falling upon the good and the bad, doth try, fine, and melt the good; and on the other side condemn, waste, and consume the evil sort Whereupon it cometh to pass, that in one and the same affliction the evil do detest and blaspheme the Lord, when contrarily the good do pray to and praise his name for that he laments upon them. So much matter makes it in afflictions to mark not what, but with what mind, every man doth suffer.

Prayer: Silent waiting for Christ.

December 17

For stir up dirt and sweet ointments alike, and you shall have the one stink filthily, and the other cast forth a sweet-smelling savour. Therefore in that hurly-burly, and irruption made by the barbarous people, what did the Christians suffer which was not rather to their profit, while they did faithfully consider those troubles? especially because they, humbly considering the sins for which God, being wroth, did fill the world with so many and great calamities, although they be far from committing heinous, grievous, and outrageous offences, do then nevertheless not repute themselves so clear of all faults, as that they judge not themselves worthy to suffer temporal calamity for the crimes they commit every hour and moment.

Prayer: Silent waiting for Christ.

December 18

For oftentimes many things are wickedly dissembled, while wicked doers are not taught, corrected, chided, and admonished of their evil behaviors, either because we think the pain too much to tell them their faults; or while we are afraid to have the heavy looks of them with whom we live; or else avoid their displeasure, lest peradventure they should hinder or hurt us in temporal matters, when as either our greediness desires to have somewhat more, or our infirmity feareth to lose the things which it has already in hold and possession: so that, although the life of the wicked displease the good, for which cause they fall not into the same damnation, which is after this life prepared for the evil; then, since they do therefore bear with, and forbear, their damnable sins, because they fear them in lighter and smaller trifles, they are justly scourged with them in this temporal life, albeit they be not punished with them eternally. While they be punished by God with the wicked, they do justly feel the bitterness of this life, for the love of whose sweetness they would not be bitter in telling the wicked of their offences. This therefore seemeth to me to be no small cause why the good are whipped with the evil, when it pleaseth God to punish the naughty manners of men with the affliction of temporal pains.

Prayer: Silent waiting for Christ.

December 19

For they are scourged together, not for because they lead an evil life together, but because they love this temporal life together. I do not say alike, but together; when the better sort ought to despise it, that the evil, being rebuked and corrected, might obtain the eternal life; to the getting whereof if they would not be our fellows and partners, they should be carried and lovingly drawn, even while they be our enemies; because, so long as they live, it is always uncertain whether their minds shall be changed to be better or no. Wherefore they have not the like but a far greater cause to admonish men of their faults, to whom the Lord says by the mouth of the prophet: 'He verily shall die in his sin, but his blood will I require at the hand of the watchman.'

Prayer: Silent waiting for Christ.

December 20

For to this end are the watchmen, that is, the guides of the people, ordained in the churches, that they should not forbear to rebuke sin and wickedness. And then, for all this, that man is not altogether excusable of this fault, which, although he be no guide or overseer of the people, doth, notwithstanding, know many things worthy of oversight, and then wink at them in those with whom he liveth and is conversant, because he will give them none offence, for fear lest he lose those things, which in this world he useth as he ought not, or is delighted in so as he should not." And so forth. For all this have I hitherto rehearsed out of St Augustine.

Prayer: Silent waiting for Christ.

December 21

The last and hindermost cause of the calamities which oppress the holy saints of God is, because the Lord, in afflicting his friends, doth thereby give a most evident testimony of his just judgment, which shall fall upon his enemies for their contemning of his name and majesty. For St Peter says: "The time is that judgment must begin at the house of God: if it first begin at us, what shall the end be of those which believe not the gospel of God? And if the righteous scarcely be saved, where shall the ungodly and sinner appear?" And like to this is that notable sentence of the Lord's, which he spake, when he went to the place of execution, saying: "If they do this in a moist tree, what shall be done in the dry?" If the saints, by whom are meant the fruitful trees bringing forth most precious fruits of good works, are, by the sufferance of God, in this world so miserably tormented and wrongfully vexed; what shall we say, I pray you, of the wicked, which are so far from virtue and good works? They shall, undoubtedly, be plagued with unspeakable pains and punishments.

Prayer: Silent waiting for Christ.

December 22

For touching the causes of those calamities wherewith the wicked are tormented; they can be none other than the heinous crimes which they commit from day to day; and are therefore punished by God's just judgment, to the end that all men may perceive, that God hates wicked men and wickedness alike. So we read that Pharaoh was afflicted. Saul fell upon his own sword, and was slain in the mount Gilboa, with many thousand Israelites, because he had sinned against the Lord, which purposed to destroy him for an example of his judgment, and a terror to them that should follow after. Antiochus Epiphanes, Herod the Great, Herod Agrippa, and Galerius Maximianus, the emperor, were taken horribly with grievous diseases, and died of the same. The reason was, because they sinned against God and his servants; on whom he determined to take a vengeance, and to make them proofs of his just judgment; so to be examples for tyrants to perceive what plagues remain for those which seek the blood of the godly and faithful.

Prayer: Silent waiting for Christ.

December 23

A nd although our good God doth ordain all things for the best to his creatures, and sendeth in a manner all calamities and miseries to draw us from wickedness; then because hypocrites and wicked people despise the counsels and admonitions of God, and neither will acknowledge God when he striketh, nor turn to him when he calls them, all things do turn to their destruction (even as to them which love the Lord all things work to the best), and therefore do they perish in their calamities: for in this world they feel the wrath of the almighty God in most horrible punishments; and in the world to come, when once they are parted out of this life, do for ever bear far greater and bitterer pains than any tongue can tell.

Prayer: Silent waiting for Christ.

December 24

But if it happen that the wicked and ungodly sort do not in this life feel any plague or grievous affliction, then shall they be punished so much the sorer in the world to come. There is no man that knoweth not the evangelical parable of the rich unmerciful glutton, who, when as in this life he lived as he lusted, in passing delights, was notwithstanding in hell tormented with unquenchable thirst, and parched with fire which never ceased burning. The felicity therefore of the wicked in this life is nothing else but extreme misery. For St James the Apostle says: "You have lived in pleasure upon earth, and been wanton; you have nourished your hearts, as in a day of slaughter;" which, I say, will turn to you, as to well-fed beasts, that are fatted up to be slain to make meat of.

Prayer: Silent waiting for Christ.

December 25

For Jeremiah goeth a little more plainly to work, and says: "O Lord, you art more righteous than that I should dispute with you: then notwithstanding I will talk with you. How happeneth it that the way of the ungodly doth prosper so well, and that it goeth so well with them which without shame offend in wickedness? You hast planted them, they take root, they grow, and bring forth fruit." And immediately after: "But draw you them out, O Lord, like a sheep to be slain, and ordain or appoint them against the day of slaughter." With this also doth that agree, which the prophet Asaph, after he had roundly and largely reckoned up the felicity of the wicked, addeth, saying: "You, verily, hast set them in slippery places; you shalt cast them down headlong, and utterly destroy them. O with how sudden calamities are they oppressed; they are perished and swallowed up of terrors! Even as a dream that vanisheth so soon as one awaketh; you, Lord, shalt make their image contemptible in the city." For David also before him did cry, saying: "Then a little, and the ungodly shall be nowhere; and when you lookest in his place, he shall not appear. I have seen the ungodly in great power, and flourishing like a green bay-tree: and I went by, and, lo, he was gone; I sought him, but he could not be found."

Prayer: Lord Jesus, welcome! You are the resolution of our problems and the solution for our sin. You make life make sense and you protect us even in the hour of death. Oh Lord, stay with us always. Be with us always. Abide with us always. In your name, Amen.

December 26

In like manner also doth Malachi the prophet witness, that there is great difference, in the day of judgment, betwixt the worshipper and despiser of God, and betwixt the just and unjust dealer: "For the day of the Lord shall come, in which the proud, and those that work wickedness, shall be burnt as stubble with fire from heaven, so that there shall remain to them neither root nor branch." They that are wise, therefore, will never hereafter be offended at the felicity of the wicked: they will never desire and long to be made partakers of their unhappy prosperity: they will not grudge at all to bear the misery of the cross, which they do daily hear to be laid by God upon his saints, to the end they may be tried and fined from the dross of the flesh and this unclean world. Thus far have I sufficiently reasoned of the causes of calamities.

Prayer: Dear Father as we await That Day, keep us in Christ and in his love. Hinder us from wandering, and if need be cripple us to keep us from running to our destruction. In Christ's name, Amen.

December 27

Let us now see, my reverend brethren, how, and in what order, the godly and sincere worshipper of God doth behave himself in all calamities and worldly afflictions. His courage quaileth not, but kicketh rather all desperation aside, because he understands, that he must manfully in faith bear all sorts of evils. Therefore doth he arm himself with hope, patience, and prayer. There are, verily, among men some which, so soon as they feel any affliction, do presently cry, as the common voice is, That it had been best if they never had been born, or else destroyed as soon as they were born. A very wicked saying is this, and not worthy to be heard in a Christian man's mouth. But far more wicked are they which stick not to destroy themselves, rather than by living they would be compelled to suffer any longer some small calamity, or abide the taunts of the open world. And then on the other side again men must reject the unsavoury opinion of the Stoics, touching their *indolentia*, or lack of grief: touching which I will recite to you, dearly beloved.

Prayer: Father in heaven, allow me to endure all kinds of evils with patience and fortitude, staying in the center of your will and abiding always in Christ, for whose sake I pray, Amen.

December 28

"We are too unthankful towards our God, unless we do willingly and cheerfully suffer calamities at his hand. And then such cheerfulness is not required of us, as should take away all sense and feeling of grief and bitterness: otherwise there should be no patience in the saints' suffering of the cross of Christ, unless they were both pinched by the heart with grief, and vexed in body with outward troubles. If in poverty there were no sharpness, if in diseases no pain, if in infamy no sting, and in death no horror, what fortitude or temperancy were it to make small account of and set little by them? But since every one of them doth naturally nip the minds of us all with a certain bitterness engrafted in them, the valiant stomach of a faithful man doth therein show itself, if he, being pricked with the feeling of this bitterness, howsoever he is grievously pained therewith, doth notwithstanding by valiant resisting and continual struggling worthily vanquish and quite overcome it. Therein doth patience make proof of itself, if, when a man is sharply pricked, it doth notwithstanding so bridle itself with the fear of God, that it never breaketh forth to immoderate unruliness. Therein doth cheerfulness clearly appear, if a man, once wounded with sorrow and sadness, doth quietly stay himself upon the spiritual consolation of his God and creator.

Prayer: Oh Father, the year draws to a close and every day I see around me the horrors of those who live without you and without any hope, or faith, or love. How could they have any of those good things seeing how they care nothing for you. Awaken them, for their sakes. Amen.

December 29

This conflict, which the faithful sustain against the natural feeling of sorrow and grief, while they study to exercise patience and temperance, the apostle Paul has finely described in words as followeth: 'We are troubled on every side, but not made sorrowful: we are in poverty, but not in extreme poverty: we suffer persecution, but are not forsaken therein: we are cast down, but we perish not.' You seest here, that to bear the cross patiently is not to be altogether senseless and utterly bereft of all kind of feeling: as the Stoics of old did foolishly describe the valiant man to be such an one, as, laying aside the nature of man, should be affected alike in adversity and prosperity, in sorrowful matters and joyful things; Yes, and such an one as should be moved with nothing whatsoever. And what did they, I pray you, with this exceeding great patience? Forsooth, they painted the image of patience, which neither ever was, nor possibly can be, found among men. Yes, while they went about to have patience over exquisite and too precise, they took away the force thereof out of the life of man. At this day also there are among us Christians certain new upstart Stoics, which think it a fault not only to sigh and weep, but also to be sad and sorrowful for any matter.

Prayer: In the coming year help me above all else to be new in Christ daily. In Jesus's name, Amen.

December 30

A nd these paradoxes, verily, do for the most part proceed from idle fellows, which, exercising themselves rather in contemplation than in working, can do nothing else but daily breed such novelties and paradoxes. But we Christians have nothing to do with this iron-like philosophy, since our Lord and master has not in words only, but with his own example also, utterly condemned it. For he groaned at and wept over both his own and other men's calamities, and taught his disciples to do the like. 'The world (says he) shall rejoice, but you shall be sorrowful, you shall weep.' And lest any man should make that weeping to be their fault, he declares openly, that they are happy which do mourn. And no marvel: for if all tears be disliked, what should we judge of the Lord himself, out of whose body bloody tears did fall? If all fear be noted to proceed of unbelief, what shall we think of that horror, wherewith we read that the Lord himself was stricken? If we dislike all sorrow and sadness, how shall we like of that where the Lord confesses that his soul is heavy to the death?

Prayer: Lord even our sorrow and sadness can be used by you to minister and teach. Help us to resist the temptation to shrink from everything we imagine to be trying or difficult. Help us abstain from being afraid of every blowing leaf. In Christ's name, Amen.

December 31

" " Thus much did I mind to say, to the intent that I might revoke godly minds from desperation; lest peradventure they do therefore out of hand forsake to seek after patience, because they cannot utterly shake off the natural motions of grief and heaviness: which cannot choose but happen to them which of patience do make a kind of senselessness, and of a valiant and constant man a senseless block, or a stone without passions. For the scripture doth praise the saints for their patience, while they are so afflicted with the sharpness of calamities as that thereby their stomachs are not broken, nor their courage is utterly quailed; while they are so stung with the prick of bitterness as that they are filled with spiritual joy; while they are so oppressed with heaviness of mind as that then they be cheerful in God's consolation. And then is that repugnancy still in their hearts, because the natural sense doth fly from and abhor the thing that it feels contrary to itself; when as, on the other side, the motions of godliness doth even through these difficulties, by striving, seek a way to the obedience of God.

Prayer: Gracious King, another year has ended and a new begins tomorrow. Thank you for this year and all your gifts and kindnesses and in the new year oh Lord please do help me to be more like Jesus, a better servant, a better member of my family, a better member of the church, a better citizen, and a better Christian. Without you I can do nothing. But in Christ I can do all things which you call me to do. Make it so, Father. In Christ's name, Amen.

ISBN: 978-1-329-56029-1

Printed in Great Britain
by Amazon